POVERTY
american style

POVERTY
american style

edited by

HERMAN P. MILLER

U.S. Bureau of the Census

Generously Donated to

The Frederick Douglass Institute

By Professor Jesse Moore

Fall 2000

Wadsworth Publishing Company, Inc.

Belmont, California

Fourth printing: August 1968

L. C. Cat. Card No.: 66–19108
Printed in the United States of America

For Elaine

Preface

For most people poverty is a word without specific meaning. The Gallup Poll suggests that people at different income levels do not define it in the same way. Many men who make $10,000 or more a year think of the poor as those with less than $5,000 a year; many who make substantially less than $5,000 do not think of themselves as poor at all. This word poverty, which is used so loosely, is in reality a very complex concept that can be defined, measured, and analyzed in many different ways. Like a chameleon, it takes on the coloration of the milieu in which it is used. It has one meaning in India and another in the United States. The meaning of poverty in America today is quite different from its meaning at the turn of the century.

One of the objectives of this book is to explore the meaning of the concept of poverty—to show how it has changed with time and how, even today, it is viewed differently by economists, sociologists, psychologists, and others who study it professionally.

Above all, the aim of this book is to show the diversity of opinion that underlies all of the major issues that are involved in the analysis of poverty. For example, current estimates of the number of poor in the United States, made by respected authorities, vary by as much as 100 percent.

The diversity of opinion is greatest, of course, in the field of public policy. The anti-poverty tools of the New Deal—social security for the aged, aid to dependent children, unemployment compensation, and minimum wage legislation—were useful for their time and still have relevance; but they do not do the job completely. America is developing new tools such as area redevelopment, manpower training, and the Economic Opportunity Act with its stress on education and rehabilitation. On the horizon are proposals like the negative income tax and the guaranteed annual income.

The attack on poverty in America, which is currently in progress, has widened and deepened the thinking about social problems. It has created an intellectual excitement and turmoil that has been virtually absent from the American scene since the depression of the thirties. Some of this excitement, it is hoped, will be reflected in the selections that have been made for this book.

This book was conceived and largely completed during my year as a Regents Lecturer at the University of California at Los Angeles. I am grateful to Professor Werner Z. Hirsch for providing me with a "home" at the Institute of Government and Public Affairs, where I spent 365 memorable days reading, writing, and thinking about poverty. Thanks are also due to the UCLA faculty members and graduate students who participated in a seminar on poverty sponsored by the Institute and who forced me to structure my thinking about this most important subject.

The contributions of Sar Levitan to this volume go far beyond the two excellent articles I have selected from his work. He helped organize the volume, suggested several of the articles that have been reproduced, and critically reviewed the entire manuscript.

Morton Marcus of UCLA performed all of those functions which are most tedious to an author but which often make the difference between a careful job and a sloppy one. He assisted in the editing, prepared the manuscript for the printer, obtained permissions for publication, and read the proofs. For his help, I am most grateful.

Contents

1
Introduction

The Rediscovery of Poverty in America

Today America girds itself for another round in its intermittent bout with poverty. This is not a new battle. It has been waged since the founding of the Republic, and, by and large, it has been waged successfully. However, despite the generally high levels of living that prevail, America now finds that millions of its citizens are not sharing fully in the abundance that has been created. The purpose of the War on Poverty is to correct this situation; the purpose of this book is to elucidate some of the problems that will be encountered in the struggle: What is poverty and who are the poor? How many poor are there and is the number increasing or decreasing over time? Can we ever eliminate poverty? There are different and contradicting answers to each of these questions.

All who have studied the problem of poverty in America acknowledge that it is complex. Depending upon the researchers' backgrounds, however, different things are stressed. Economists, for example, tend to emphasize economic growth and income maintenance. Some of them believe that since the poor lack money, we should give them more and get on with the more basic problem of increasing economic growth. This view leads to a search for overall income-maintenance schemes like the negative income tax or the guaranteed annual income. Psychologists and social workers, on the other hand, see poverty in psychological terms. They tend to emphasize opportunity rather than income. From this perspective, the key to the problem is to change behavior and provide exits from poverty—to provide opportunities for the children of the poor to move to higher levels. This focus stresses health, education, training, housing, and the elimination of restrictive barriers.

Both viewpoints are, of course, valid; any meaningful anti-poverty program must combine income maintenance with improved government services for the poor. A further requirement is a healthy economy. If government services, particularly education, are improved but meaningful avenues for employment are not simultaneously provided, the nation may simply be adding to its woes.

To appreciate the success of America's bout with poverty, one need look only at the long way America has come in its short history. Today, most American families are well provided with the good things in life. Their incomes are at an all-time high. They have decent homes, good schools, some security in old age; and, generally, they live in an abundance that was undreamed of until recently and that still seems unreal in many parts of the world.

But it was not always so. Only a short time ago in the span of history, settlers came to these shores with very little. They cleared a continent, battled the hostile forces of man and nature, settled the land, and hacked a new society out of the wilderness. The fruits of their efforts are now taken for granted, but they were purchased at a price. It took courage for families to uproot themselves from the comforts of the Atlantic shores and fan out into a hostile land. It took foresight to defer the immediate gratification of wants and to put the surpluses that accrued from agriculture and commerce into the construction of a network of roads, canals, and railroads that facilitated the development of the country. It took faith in democratic ideals to open our shores to Europe's unwanted millions, to make good farmland available to them at a low price, and to entrust to them the creation of local schools in which to educate their children.

These acts of courage and faith reflect the national characteristics —industriousness combined with frugality, a respect for learning, a willingness to take chances, and a mobile social system—which, with other factors, promoted our phenomenal economic growth.

The American Strategy against Poverty

Poverty was first recognized as a social problem in the United States about 100 years ago. It existed before that time, to be sure; but it was regarded as an individual rather than a social problem. In the pre-

Civil War period, the prevalent American attitude was that a man's misfortunes were his own affair and that society could or should do little about them. If things did not go well in the East, young men were exhorted to go West. It was a big, rich, unsettled country; and if a man could not find his niche, he had no one to blame but himself. This view could develop and be sustained only in a predominantly rural society with an abundance of unoccupied good land.

Industrialization after the Civil War brought in its wake many social evils: poor housing, inadequate schools, bad working conditions, low wages, and unemployment. The effort to combat these ills led to many major social reforms, including public-health and -housing regulations, abolition of child labor, regulation of hours of work and working conditions, and workmen's compensation. Social reform was the keynote in the fight against poverty at the turn of the century.

Still fresh in many minds is the attack on poverty under Franklin D. Roosevelt during the thirties. At that time, under the impetus of a worldwide depression, the now familiar anti-poverty tools were forged— social security, old-age assistance, aid to dependent children, unemployment compensation, and the rest. These programs were enacted to relieve the distress of the poor by providing them with income maintenance and social security and to improve the economic system by providing the poor with purchasing power.

The major emphasis in the fight against poverty today is, in the words of President Kennedy, "rehabilitation and not relief." Today it is felt that the poor themselves must be changed if they are to be brought into the mainstream of American life. In order to achieve this goal, the Economic Opportunity Act of 1964 was passed. Most of the money is being spent on education and training programs.

Although this is not the only program designed to combat poverty in the United States, there is, nevertheless, some justification for regarding the Act as the start of a massive effort to rehabilitate people who are defeated and unmotivated and generally regarded as beyond redemption. These people are being approached on a large scale for the first time in our history.

The Reasons behind the New Attack on Poverty

The reasons for the War on Poverty are many; it would be unwise and incorrect to simplify too much. The high rate of unemployment for nearly a decade is undoubtedly a major factor behind the new anti-poverty program, as is the threat of continued or perhaps even increased unemployment due to automation. The contributions of a latter-day muckraker like Michael Harrington and a sensitive and sensible President, who first proposed the war on poverty in the fall of 1963, are also important and should not be overlooked. There are other factors too, but I am inclined to agree with Nathan Glazer that racial tension "is undoubtedly the chief reason why poverty has become a major issue in this country."

A casual glance at the statistics on poverty will show that in 1963 about 2.0 million of the 7.2 million poor families were nonwhite. On the basis of this figure, one might conclude that nonwhites constitute only a small fraction (about one fourth) of the poor. This conclusion, however, is a distortion of two significant factors in the situation.

1. The total number of poor families included 1.5 million aged persons, who today represent a passive element among the poor. During the depression, the aged were very active as a pressure group for social reform. The movement that organized around Dr. Francis Townsend, who advocated a liberal guaranteed income for the aged, is perhaps the most striking example of the activity of the aged poor. Although some important pressure groups still exist among the aged, these groups appear to be much less forceful and effective today than they were thirty years ago. If those over 65 years old are removed from the total of 7.2 million poor families, nonwhites constitute one third of the poor.

2. Even this percentage understates the importance of the Negro as a component of the poor because it includes many persons who are only temporarily poor, and they are more likely to be white than nonwhite. If only those families that have had substandard incomes for two successive years are counted as poor, nonwhites represent 40 per cent of the total.

These figures highlight the role of the Negro in shaping the new anti-poverty program, with its emphasis on education, training, and rehabilitation rather than handouts. During the 1930s, Negroes were largely tucked away in the rural South, where they worked mainly as subsistence farmers or sharecroppers. Although their need then was as great as, and perhaps even greater than, that of other segments of the population, they were not instrumental in developing the programs against poverty that were enacted at that time. Today it is primarily the Negro leadership that is focusing attention on the poor. Negroes have been particularly hard hit by the rapid economic changes in recent years. Unemployment rates for Negroes, particularly Negro youth, have been painfully high for nearly a decade. For some years, the nation suffered under the delusion that the next turn in the business cycle or a remedial tax cut might clear things up; but the dislocations for this segment of the population clearly require more direct measures.

The riots in several major northern cities in recent years suggest that a large dissident element among Negro youth does not need to be told by governmental statistics that they are being by-passed by society, as were their fathers and grandfathers before them. They are aware of job vacancies as delivery boys, bus boys, handymen, and other menial occupations, but are not inclined to flock to them. There is one major difference between these boys and their forebears: Negro youth today will not stand idly by. In all regions of the country, a revolution is in progress—a revolution that demands civil rights, dignity, and meaningful employment.

President Johnson recognized that this revolution may in large measure be responsible for the War on Poverty when he said: "... the real hero of this struggle is the American Negro. His actions and protests—his courage to risk safety and even life—have awakened the conscience of the nation. His demonstrations have been designed to call attention to injustice, to provoke change and stir reform.... And who among us can say that we would have made the same progress were it not for his persistent bravery, and his faith in American democracy?" Regardless of what one may think of the President as a social historian, the fact cannot be ignored that the chief policy-maker in this country views the problem in this way.

The rural poor, the aged poor, and even the hillbillies in Appalachia and the Ozarks could not arouse the nation to their urgent needs. They continued to suffer year after year in quiet desperation while their children were poorly educated, while they lived in hovels, and while they suffered awesome indignities of body, mind, and spirit. Action came only recently. It followed a prolonged period of marches, sit-ins, and other forms of protest by the Negro community. The war on poverty and these protests are indisputably related.

The Outlook for the Future

Many have dreamed about ultimate victory in the fight against poverty. At the turn of the century, David Lloyd George requested funds from the British parliament to wage "warfare against poverty." He firmly believed that within his own lifetime he would see "a great step towards that good time when poverty ... will be as remote to the people of this country as the wolves which once infested its forests." In 1928, Herbert Hoover also saw victory in sight: "We shall soon with the help of God be in sight of the day when poverty will be banished in this nation."

Despite the hopes of such able and farsighted men as Lloyd George and Herbert Hoover, poverty still remains. It is a different kind of poverty from the one these statesmen had in mind; but, even by the standards of 1900, poverty remains a problem in America. Now, once again, there is talk about ultimate victory. Can this be just a pipe dream? In what ways are the present prospects for success better than those of the past? At least three major differences can be detected between the present and 50 years ago:

1. In the early 1900's, most Americans were poor even by the low standards of the time; and by today's standards, all but a very small part of the population at the turn of the century would be considered poverty stricken. Conditions had improved by the prosperous twenties; but, even then, over half of the nation's families had incomes below the poverty line as it is defined today. With victory so far away, the confidence of these men about the outcome is difficult to understand.

2. Productivity has been growing rapidly in recent years. There is good reason to believe that this trend will continue and that the national income will be far higher than it has been in the past. Part of the increase will undoubtedly be devoted to the eradication of poverty. The prospects for growth are far greater than the average citizen realizes. Here is how the matter has been summed up by the Council of Economic Advisers: "If average productivity gains until the year 2000 no more than match those of the last seventeen years, output per man-hour will be three times as great as today. If working hours and labor-force participation rates were to remain unchanged, average family income would approximate $18,000 in today's prices." With this kind of leverage, the allocation of a small additional fraction of the national income to the eradication of poverty becomes a real possibility.

3. The United States appears to have mastered that old bugaboo of capitalism—cataclysmic depressions. Over a quarter of a century has passed since there has been a major depression in the United States. The government is committed to eliminating booms and busts, and it has been largely successful in its effort. We have reason to hope, therefore, that great depressions, like bubonic plagues, are things of the past. This freedom from fear of want for society as a whole will permit us to devote our creative energies to the elimination of want for the poorest segments of society.

Part one
Perspectives

2
Historical Perspectives

I don't want to see poverty abolished;
too much good has come of it!
—Robert Frost

How properly to alleviate the troubles
of the poor is one of the greatest troubles of the rich. But one thing agreed
upon by all professional philanthro-
pists is that you must never hand over
any cash to your subject.
—O. Henry

Write a sermon on blessed poverty.
Who have done all the good in the
world? Poor men. Poverty is a good
hated by all men.
—Ralph Waldo Emerson

All of history might be viewed as one incessant struggle against
the niggardliness of nature. In one small segment of our planet the battle
has gone well for man. Economic conditions in the United States may
leave much to be desired, but there has been gradual improvement; and
the prosperity has been widely shared. For most of mankind, however,
each rising sun casts anew the black shadow of hunger and despair. It is
the same shadow that has been cast for thousands of years, and the end
is nowhere in sight. Life hangs by a thread: a drop of rain, a piece of
bread. Pope Paul VI, who has seen much poverty in Europe, wept at what
he saw in Bombay—a poignant reminder that poverty is relative.

The relativity of poverty is a theme that repeats and repeats in the articles that follow. The excerpts from Stampp are intended to provide a backdrop for current discussions about Negro poverty. Americans forget that only a little over 100 years have passed since Frederick Douglass slaved on a Maryland farm "almost in a state of nudity." Douglass' plight diminishes neither the shabby treatment received by the Negro today nor the continuing need for action in the improvement of their lot. It does, however, provide a benchmark for measuring progress.

Little that is new is being said about poverty today. Robert Hunter's conclusions, based on his study of poverty at the turn of the century, could have been written last week. They are biting, clear, and filled with an insight that could be obtained only by someone who has lived with the poor. Hunter recognized, as few do today, the distinction between pauperism and poverty; he attacked the "utility of poverty"—that archaic notion which some economists still preached in his time; and he foresaw the way in which our state system would create geographic inequities in the elimination of poverty. Nearly all of his prescriptions for the amelioration of poverty have become law.

There are probably not many people in the United States today who believe that there is any utility in poverty. Some may still recommend poverty for the artist on the ground that great art can come only from suffering. Few, however, would apply this harsh standard to the general population. Yet, not too long ago, there were many who believed that poverty (for others) was not only good but necessary. An eighteenth-century expression of this quaint viewpoint is represented by the excerpt from Bernard Mandeville's *Fable of the Bees*. Reference to a more recent expression of this same idea by a friend of the poor (Charles Booth) may be found in the article by Hunter.

Economists have long speculated about the causes of poverty and its cure, but not until the industrial revolution was well under way was the eventual elimination of poverty entertained as a serious possibility. Malthus theorized about poverty but saw no solution because of the tendency, in his view, for surpluses to be absorbed by an increase in population. The basic fallacy of the Malthusian theory is that it is inapplicable to industrial societies in which output per capita systematically grows more rapidly than population.

The Marxian theory was equally dismal and wrong. Barring a change in the capitalistic system, economic growth, according to Marx, could lead only to greater profits for capital and greater misery for the mass of mankind. Henry George, the most eminent American economist of the nineteenth century, was also pessimistic.

By the end of the century, the eventual eradication of poverty began to be considered a real possibility. When Alfred Marshall, the leading economist of his day, expressed, in 1895, his belief "that poverty and ignorance may gradually be extinguished," he based it on the empirical fact that there had been "steady progress of the working classes during the present century."

George Bernard Shaw was one of the most eloquent of all spokesmen for the poor. To him, the first duty of every man was to avoid being poor, and the highest priority of social legislation was the elimination of poverty. He viewed poverty as "a public nuisance as well as a private misfortune." The Shavian notion that the poor would behave better if they had more money is widely accepted today, although it is being questioned in some quarters (see the article by Haggstrom in Chapter 3).

Although some aspects of poverty are universal, poverty in America has a very special flavor and meaning. The causes and cures of poverty in an affluent society are aptly presented in an excerpt from Galbraith's book *The Affluent Society*.

Robert Hunter
Poverty in America circa 1900

... We are perhaps too prone to think of those in poverty as effortless beings, who make no fight for themselves and wait in misery until some one comes to assist them. Such an opinion is without any foundation. It is based upon knowledge gained by acquaintance with the pauper and vagrant, and is in no wise applicable to the workers in poverty. It is small wonder that workers who are underfed, underclothed, and poorly housed, are sometimes won from their hard and almost hopeless toil by sensual pleasures. Nor is it surprising that they are driven to despair by the brutal power of the economic forces which dominate their lives. Without the security which comes only with the ownership of property, without a home from which they may not be evicted, without any assurance of regular employment, without tools with which they may employ themselves they are pathetically dependent upon their physical efficiency,— their health and strength, and upon the activity of machinery, owned by others, and worked or left idle as the owners consider it wise or profitable. In their weak and unorganized condition, they are unlike the skilled workers, made powerful by their unions and by their methods of collective bargaining; they are fighting alone, each one against another....

Having been drawn, about twelve years ago, to some interest in

From *Poverty* (New York: The Macmillan Company, 1904), pp. 318–340. Robert Hunter (1874–1942) was an American sociologist and social worker.

the problems of poverty, there happened to me the common experience of all those of like interests. The poor in the broader sense of that word were busily at work and trying rather to conceal than to make evidence of their poverty; while the beggars, vagrants, idlers, and dependents of all sorts were more or less always pressing forward their necessities. It was natural, therefore, for me to confuse the problem of poverty with that of pauperism and to take up with some enthusiasm the ideas which are a part of the propaganda of many useful charitable organizations. To the charitable workers these problems of vagrancy and pauperism seem possible of solution. Many reforms—among which wise giving, friendly visiting, work-rooms, work-tests, model lodging-houses, rent-collecting, etc., are a few—were, in the early nineties, making rapid headway. They were, at that time, ranked first in importance in the category of organized movements for diminishing the evils of pauperism. Many committees were at work promoting these reforms, and in different cities I was able to help in their efforts. The result of their work was not discouraging, but in every instance they came hard up against one almost insurmountable obstacle. The pauper and the vagrant were not dissatisfied; they clamored for alms, but they did not wish to alter their way of living. Even those who possessed the capacity for industrial usefulness and who might have become self-supporting did not wish to go back again into the factories, mills, or mines. In fact, so far as one could see, they were as unwilling as the others to alter their ways of living. However miserable their lot seemed to those of us on the Committees, to them it seemed to be, on the whole, acceptable enough to bring a certain sort of content. However malarious and poisonous and undrained, they loved their valley of idleness and quiet; they hated the hill upon which they were constrained to toil; they shrank from its disappointments, its bruises, its weariness and bitterness, while its meanness and ugliness of life were but slightly less mean and ugly than their own. The children, bred into the ways of pauperism, nearly always took up the vices of their parents. They were pleasure-loving, and whatever was toilsome seemed abhorrent to them. The girls took the easier path; it appeared unquestionably more desirable to their childish standards, and for a time at least it gave them more of everything, for which most human beings seem to hunger,—finery, leisure, and a kind of pleasure. The men and boys liked vagrancy, and those who were not attracted to these ways settled down into a satisfied, imperturbable pauperism. They lived in God only knows what misery. They ate when there were things to eat; they starved when there was lack of food. But, on the whole, although they swore and beat each other and got drunk, they were more contented than any other class I have happened to know. It took a long time to understand them. Our Committees were busy from morning until night in giving them opportunities to take up the fight again, and to become independent of relief. They always took what we gave them; they always promised to try; but as soon as we expected them to fulfil any promises, they gave up in despair, and either wept or looked ashamed, and took to misery and drink again,—almost, so it seemed to me at times, with a sense of relief. I am reminded now of a vagrant whom I knew well and for many years believed to be sincerely trying to become "a man," as we used to say. He has turned up wherever I have happened to be—in Chicago or New York. He has always looked me up, and together we have conspired to overcome his vagrant instincts. We have always failed, and after a few weeks' work Jerry disappears, and I know what has become of him. At last, in his case as in many others, I have become convinced that he is more satisfied and content with the life of a vagrant than with the miserable lot of an unskilled, underpaid workman.

But as long as one works with, or observes only, the dependent classes, the true, or at least what seems to me the true, explanation of this apparent satisfaction of vagrants and paupers remains in the dark. It was not until I had lived for several years among the toilers in a great industrial community that the reason for the content of the dependent classes became clear to me. In this community of workers several thousand human beings were struggling fiercely against want. Day after day, year after year, they toiled with marvellous persistency and perseverance. Obnoxious as the simile is, they worked from dawn until nightfall, or from sunset until dawn, like galley slaves under the sting of want and under the whip of hunger. On cold, rainy mornings, at the dusk of dawn, I have been awakened, two hours before my rising time, by the monotonous clatter of hobnailed boots on the plank sidewalks, as the procession to the factory passed under my window. Heavy, brooding men, tired, anxious women, thinly dressed, unkempt little girls, and frail, joyless little lads passed along, half awake, not one uttering a word as they hurried to the great factory. From all directions thousands were entering the various gates,— children of every nation of Europe. Hundreds of others—obviously a hungrier, poorer lot than those entering the gates; some were most ragged and almost shoeless, but all with eager faces—waited in front of a closed gate until finally a great red-bearded man came out and selected twenty-three of the strongest, best-looking of the men. For these the gates were opened, and the others, with downcast eyes, marched off to seek employment elsewhere or to sit at home, or in a saloon, or in a lodging-house, until the following morning, when they came wistfully again to some factory gate. In this community, the saddest in which I have ever lived, fully fifty thousand men, women, and children were all the time either in poverty or on the verge of poverty. It would not be possible to describe how they worked and starved and ached to rise out of it. They broke their health down; the men acquired in this particular trade a painful and disabling rheumatism, and consumption was very common. The girls and boys followed in the paths of their parents. The wages were so low that the men alone often could not support their families, and mothers with babies toiled in order to add to the income. They gave up all thought of joyful living, probably in the hope that by tremendous exertion they could overcome their poverty; but they gained while at work only enough to keep their bodies alive. Theirs was a sort of treadmill existence with no prospect of anything else in life but more treadmill. When they were not given work in the mill, they starved; and when they grew desperate, they came to my office and asked for charity. Here was a mass of men whose ways of living were violently opposed to those of the vagrant or the pauper. They were distorting themselves in the struggle to be independent of charity and to overcome poverty. That they hated charity must be taken without question. The testimony of scores of men is proof of it, even if, indeed, their very lives were not. But despite all their efforts they lived in houses but little, if any, better than those of the paupers; they were almost as poorly dressed; they were hardly better fed. . . .

It is easier to understand the reason for the abhorrence which the pauper and the vagrant and the prostitute have for that terrible struggle with poverty, and only less easy is it to understand their apparent willingness to live on rubbish or alms. Furthermore, it is clear that the poverty which undermines the workers is the great and constantly active cause of the fixed states of degeneracy represented by the pauper, the vagrant, the inebriate, etc. In other words, when the working people, by reason of whatever misery poverty brings, once fall into the abyss, they so hate the life of their former struggles and disappointments and sorrows that almost no one, however well-intentioned or kindly, can induce them to take it up again. In the abyss they become merely breeders of children, who persist in the degeneration into which their fathers have fallen; and, like the tribe of Ishmael or the family of the Jukes, they have neither the willingness nor the capacity to respond to the efforts of those who would help, or force, them back again into the struggle.

However merciful and kind and valuable the works of the charitable and the efforts of those who would raise up again the pauper and the vagrant, they are not remedial. In so far as the work of the charitable is devoted to reclamation and not to prevention, it is a failure. Not that any one could wish that less were done in the direction of reclamation. The fact only is important that effort is less powerful there than in overcoming the forces which undermine the workers and those who are struggling against insurmountable difficulties. It is an almost hopeless task to regenerate the degenerate, especially when, if the latter are to succeed, they must be made to take up again the battle with those very destructive forces which are all the time undermining stronger, more capable, and more self-reliant men than they. The all-necessary work to be done is not so much to reclaim a class which social forces are ever active in producing, as it is to battle with the social or economic forces which are continuously producing recruits to that class. The forces producing the miseries of pauperism and vagrancy are many, but none are so important as those conditions of work and of living which are so unjust and degrading that men are driven by them into degeneracy. When the uncertainties, hardships, trials, sorrows, and miseries of a self-supporting existence become so painful that good, strong, self-reliant men and women are forced into pauperism, then there is but little use in trying to force the paupers and the vagrants back into the struggle.

It is not necessary to debate the relative importance of individual or social forces, or of heredity or environment, upon the extent of poverty, in order to prove that social forces are constantly and everywhere active in bringing poverty to a great mass of people. Leaving all such questions out of the discussion, we can nevertheless be certain that obstacles can be too great for even the strongest of men to overcome. And this is almost precisely what happens to the masses in poverty. As a class they have the longest hours of work, they have the lowest pay—often not even living wages; they have competition of the severest kind to face—unskilled workers from every land come to seek their employment; they are oppressed by sweating methods, their employment is irregular; their tenements are the most insanitary, and their rents relatively the highest that any class pay; the prices for food and fuel are exorbitant, because they must buy in small quantities; when they find it necessary to go into debt they are fleeced by loan sharks; they are most often ill; they bear the burden of more deaths than any other class; and being without savings, they are in actual distress as soon as they are unable to work, or as soon as they are unemployed as a result of economic or other causes. Furthermore, the children are prevented from having fair opportunities to master the difficulties which ruined their fathers. Their health is imperilled and not seldom destroyed by insanitary homes; they are injured morally and otherwise by a *necessary* street life; their food is in many cases so poor that it will not feed the brain, and they are consequently unable to learn; they are early pressed to do a man's labor and are often ruined physically and blighted in other ways by this early and unnatural toil. With all of these and many other obstacles and disadvantages working their ruin, only the strongest and most fortunate are able to put forth the struggle necessary to master their fate. For the others, their life's course lies up an almost baffling precipice.

About a half-century ago there were so many persons in London becoming paupers, vagrants, mendicants, etc., that a group of people organized together to make the way of the pauper, vagrant, and mendicant so thorny and difficult that the workers, toiling up the precipice, would hold the abyss beneath them in even greater aversion than it was thought they were in the habit of doing, and that the able-bodied dependents in the abyss would be forced to turn from their way and seek again the path of self-support. This may, in certain places and at certain times, be necessary; but would it not seem a more wholesome, not to say kindlier, policy to see that the obstacles—the unnecessary obstacles, now preventing the rise of those workers in poverty—be removed?

This, however, is not by any means easy of accomplishment. The first difficulty lies in the complex nature of the problem itself. It is inextricably woven in with all other social and economic problems. If what Charles Booth says is true (and many economists agree with him), that our "modern system of industry will not work without some unemployed margin, some reserve of labor"; if it is necessary, as another economist has said, that "for long periods of time large stagnant pools of adult effective labor power must lie rotting in the bodies of their owners, unable to become productive of any form of wealth, because they cannot get access to the material of production"; and if at the same time "facing them in equal idleness are unemployed or under-employed masses of land and capital, mills, mines, etc., which, taken in conjunction with this labor power, are theoretically competent to produce wealth for the satisfaction of human wants,"—if these things are essential to our modern system of production, then the poverty of this large mass of workers must continue unrelieved until the system itself is reorganized. As a matter of fact, it would be useless to deny or ignore the fact that much of our poverty is directly due to a whole series of economic disorders which seem actually to make waste of human life necessary. And, in so far as poverty is a result of such deeply seated and fundamental economic disorders, due either to the method by which industry is organized or to the present ownership of the means and materials of production, it will, in all probability, find a solution only through struggles between the workers and the capitalists. No one who watches the trend of the times can doubt that these struggles, both in the industrial and in the political field, are growing more and more serious. Furthermore, in so far as poverty is a result of individual weaknesses, not themselves due to social causes, it can be dealt with only by moral and personal forces. But complex as the problem is, and varied as the remedies must be, we may be sure that poverty is, to a considerable extent, due to social causes which are clearly to be seen and which are possible of remedy.

Besides the complexity of the problem, there is still another, perhaps an even greater, obstacle firmly set in the path of constructive reform. And this is a political difficulty; namely, the anarchic principle of

state rights which divides this country into two score and more small legislative areas. National problems of the character herein dealt with cannot
therefore be treated in a national way, as they are in most countries abroad.
Legislation concerning child labor, tuberculosis, tenements, factories, dangerous trades, sanitation, etc., must be of a variety of kinds, often warring
with each other, throwing industrial advantages now to this state and now
to that. The child-labor laws which have been won in the Northern states
by years of vigorous agitation give an advantage to the parasitic industries
of the South. It is even likely that the textile industry may move to the
South partly at least in order to have the privilege of employing little
children. Manufacturers threaten the state legislatures (more often, to be
sure, than they carry out the threat) that they will move into another state
if any laws protecting the workmen are passed. There is perhaps a certain
business justification for such protests, for, unquestionably, by reason of
our legislative anarchy, a parasitic industry in one state may thrive while
an industry in another state, shorn of its parasitic privileges by legislation,
may remain at a standstill, if it does not actually lose its trade. For this
reason social and industrial legislation is usually more difficult to obtain
in America than in any other great industrial country. Our political machinery itself, therefore, seriously retards and perhaps renders impossible
any national standard of education, of sanitation, of working or of living
conditions, etc. It is probable that there can be no national solution of
some of these more remedial of the problems of poverty.

Another obstacle stands in the way of justice. The selfish interests
of capitalists and land-owners too often either prevent good legislation or
vitiate, by their influence, its enforcement. One can understand the determined opposition of men to socialistic measures seriously changing or
violating the so-called rights of property; but it is not so easy to understand opposition to measures which, while affecting property interests, do
not destroy any rights which may be exercised without injury to another.
When property rights become property wrongs by injuring others, especially when they cause the physical degeneration and the human misery
represented in poverty, they may for a time, but will surely not always,
stand in the way of remedial action. The sense of justice may for a time
be so warped and distorted as to value property more than human life,
but only for a time. The real cause of our present errors of judgment in
this matter lies in the corruption of our political institutions. The business
and propertied interests have bought the bosses of our political machinery,
and at present our laws are made and enforced in the interest of the
owners. When the shame of our cities is notorious; when state and national
governments are in the hands of corrupt politicians, owned by corporate
interests; when "the laws which should preserve and enforce all rights
are made and enforced by dollars;" when "it is possible . . . with dollars to

'steer' the selection of the candidates of both the great parties for the highest office *in our Republic*, ... so that the people, as a matter of fact, must elect one of the 'steered' candidates;" when "it is possible to repeat the operation in the selection of candidates for the executive and legislative conduct and control of every state and municipality in the United States, and with a sufficient number of dollars to 'steer' the doings of the law-makers and law-enforcers of the national, state, and municipal governments of the people, and a sufficient proportion of the court decisions to make absolute any power created by such direction;" when the country is being daily betrayed by the "enemies of the republic,"—it seems utopian to appeal to these powers to do justice to their workers. This may seem a dark view to take of our political institutions, but, considering the great mass of evidence accumulated in the last few years, it is surely warranted. So far as the problem of poverty is concerned, we can perhaps hope for little in the way of justice or reform during the next few years. For, by the help of this corruption, reform is fought at three stages: in the legislature, in the courts, and at the time of its enforcement.

... There are probably in fairly prosperous years no less than 10,000,000 persons in poverty; that is to say, underfed, underclothed, and poorly housed. Of these about 4,000,000 persons are public paupers. Over 2,000,000 working-men are unemployed from four to six months in the year. About 500,000 male immigrants arrive yearly and seek work in the very districts where unemployment is greatest. Nearly half of the families in the country are propertyless. Over 1,700,000 little children are forced to become wage-earners when they should still be in school. About 5,000,-000 women find it necessary to work and about 2,000,000 are employed in factories, mills, etc. Probably no less than 1,000,000 workers are injured or killed each year while doing their work, and about 10,000,000 of the persons now living will, if the present ratio is kept up, die of the preventable disease, tuberculosis. We know that many workmen are overworked and underpaid. We know in a general way that unnecessary disease is far too prevalent. We know some of the insanitary evils of tenements and factories; we know of the neglect of the street child, the aged, the infirm, the crippled. Furthermore, we are beginning to realize the monstrous injustice of compelling those who are unemployed, who are injured in industry, who have acquired diseases due to their occupation, or who have been made widows or orphans by industrial accidents, to become paupers in order that they may be housed, fed, and clothed. Something is known concerning these problems of poverty, and some of them at least are possible of remedy.

To deal with these specific problems, I have elsewhere mentioned some reforms which seem to me preventive in their nature. They contemplate mainly such legislative action as may enforce upon the entire country certain minimum standards of working and of living conditions. They would make all tenements and factories sanitary; they would regulate the hours of work, especially for women and children; they would regulate and thoroughly supervise dangerous trades; they would institute all necessary measures to stamp out unnecessary disease and to prevent unnecessary death; they would prohibit entirely child labor; they would institute all necessary educational and recreational institutions to replace the social and educational losses of the home and the domestic workshop; they would perfect, as far as possible, legislation and institutions to make industry pay the necessary and legitimate cost of producing and maintaining efficient laborers; they would institute, on the lines of foreign experience, measures to compensate labor for enforced seasons of idleness, due to sickness, old age, lack of work, or other causes beyond the control of the workman; they would prevent parasitism on the part of either the consumer or the producer and charge up the full costs of labor in production to the beneficiary, instead of compelling the worker at certain times to enforce his demand for maintenance through the tax rate and by becoming a pauper; they would restrict the power of employer and of ship-owner to stimulate for purely selfish ends an excessive immigration, and in this way to beat down wages and to increase unemployment.

Reforms such as these are not ones which will destroy incentive, but rather they will increase incentive by more nearly equalizing opportunity. They will make propertied interests less predatory, and sensuality, by contrast with misery, less attractive to the poor. . . . the process of Justice is to lift stony barriers, against which the noblest beat their brains out, and from which the ignoble (but who shall say not more sensible?) turn away in despair. Let it be this, rather than a barren relief system, administered by those who must stand by, watching the struggle, lifting no hand to aid the toilers, but ever succoring those who flee and those who are bruised and beaten.

Kenneth M. Stampp
Negro Poverty under Slavery

... everywhere in the South a depressingly large number of slaves lived on ... dismal fare throughout the year. On countless farms and plantations the laborers never tasted fresh meat, milk, eggs, or fruits, and rarely tasted vegetables. "All that is allowed," recalled a former slave on a cotton plantation, "is corn and bacon, which is given out at the corncrib and smoke-house every Sunday morning. Each one receives, as his weekly allowance, three and a half pounds of bacon, and corn enough to make a peck of meal." No slave on this estate, he added bitterly, was "ever likely to suffer from the gout, superinduced by excessive high living."

An experienced Louisiana physician claimed that the diet of slaves on the majority of plantations was "mostly salt pork, corn bread, and molasses—rarely ... fresh meat and vegetables." An Alabamian reported that planters in his region had the "erroneous impression ... that Pork—and the fatter the better—is the only proper substance of animal food for Negroes." A Virginian affirmed that "corn meal, with little or no meat, and no vegetable diet is extremely hard fare. I believe that there are extremely few masters who starve their slaves to actual suffering, ... [but] I have no doubt that the slow motion, and thin expression of countenance, of many slaves, are owing to a want of a sufficiency of nourishing food." ...

The problem of slave sustenance involved not only the need for an ample and balanced diet but also the need for a practical system of food preparation. Usually the master held each family of slaves responsible for cooking their own food and paid little attention to how well they did it. He required them to carry their noon meals to the fields in the morning and to wait for their evening meals until they returned to their cabins at night. In some cases he expected the slaves to grind their own corn and gather their own firewood, a great burden after a long day of toil. He did not always provide cooking utensils. Without these, cooking was a simple process, as a former slave recalled: "When the corn is ground, and fire is made, the bacon is ... thrown upon the coals to broil. ... The corn meal is mixed with a little water, placed in the fire, and baked. When it is 'done brown,' the ashes are scraped off, and being placed upon a chip,

From *The Peculiar Institution* by Kenneth M. Stampp, pp. 284–295. © Copyright 1956 by Kenneth M. Stampp. Reprinted by permission of Alfred A. Knopf, Inc.

Kenneth M. Stampp is Morrison Professor of History, University of California, Berkeley, and author of *The Era of Reconstruction, 1865–1877* (Knopf, 1965).

which answers for a table, the tenant of the slave hut is ready to sit down upon the ground to supper.". . .

The children on Hammond's plantation received two shirts, "made very long," each fall and spring; but like most slave children they received no shoes. As a child in Maryland, Frederick Douglass "was kept almost in a state of nudity; no shoes, no stockings, no jacket, no trousers; nothing but coarse sack-cloth or tow-linen, made into a sort of shirt, reaching down to my knees. This I wore night and day, changing it once a week." Douglass wore the usual costume of slave children throughout the South. A visitor pictured the children on a South Carolina plantation as "ragged, dirty, shoeless urchins"—and this was an accurate picture of most of them everywhere. . . .

The common run of slave cabins were cramped, crudely built, scantily furnished, unpainted, and dirty. A resident of Liberty County, Georgia, presented a picture of slave housing which he thought would be "recognized by the well-informed as a fair average" for the entire South. These "average" dwellings were covered with crudely cut, loose-fitting clapboards. They were not lined within, "so that only the thickness of a single board kept out the winter's air and cold." They were warmed by a clay chimney; the windows were unglazed.

That an appalling amount of slave housing was of a quality far below this "average," well-informed Southerners frequently admitted. Poor housing was at least as common as insufficient clothing, and southern doctors lectured incessantly to slaveholders about their shortsightedness. "One of the most prolific sources of disease among negroes," wrote an Alabama physician, "is the condition of their houses. . . . Small, low, tight and filthy; their houses can be but laboratories of disease." According to a Mississippian, "Planters do not always reflect that there is more sickness, and consequently greater loss of life, from the decaying logs of negro houses, open floors, leaky roofs, and crowded rooms, than all other causes combined." Occasionally a slaveholder learned the truth of this complaint from his own experience. A Louisianian finally concluded that most of the sickness among his slaves was "owing to working all day without rest and then sleeping in crowded dirty apartments." He resolved to cover the dirt floors with plank.

On South Carolina and Georgia rice and cotton plantations visitors found houses "in the most decayed and deplorable condition." Some of them were not more than twelve feet square, "built of logs, with no windows—no opening at all, except the doorway, with a chimney of sticks and mud." The three slave cabins on a small plantation in northern Mississippi were "small, dilapidated and dingy; the walls were not chinked, and there were no windows—which, indeed, would have been a superfluous luxury, for there were spaces of several inches between the logs, through which there was unobstructed vision. . . . Everything within the cabins was colored black by smoke." On a Maryland farm a former slave remembered houses that were "but log huts—the tops partly open—ground floor—rain would come through."

Everywhere houses such as these were plentiful. The dwellings of the great mass of southern slaves were drab and cheerless, leaky in wet weather, drafty in cold. Like their food and clothing, their housing usually did not much exceed the minimum requirements for survival.

Henry George
The House of Have and the House of Want

. . . It is true that wealth has been greatly increased, and that the average of comfort, leisure, and refinement has been raised; but these gains are not general. In them the lowest class do not share. I do not mean that the condition of the lowest class has nowhere nor in anything been improved; but that there is nowhere any improvement which can be credited to increased productive power. I mean that the tendency of what we call material progress is in nowise to improve the condition of the lowest class in the essentials of healthy, happy human life. Nay, more, that it is to still further depress the condition of the lowest class. The new forces, elevating in their nature though they be, do not act upon the social fabric from underneath, as was for a long time hoped and believed, but strike it at a point intermediate between top and bottom. It is as though an immense wedge were being forced, not underneath society, but through society. Those who are above the point of separation are elevated, but those who are below are crushed down.

This depressing effect is not generally realized, for it is not apparent where there has long existed a class just able to live. Where the lowest class barely lives, as has been the case for a long time in many parts of Europe, it is impossible for it to get any lower, for the next lowest step is out of existence, and no tendency to further depression can readily show itself. But in the progress of new settlements to the conditions of older

From *Progress and Poverty* (New York: D. Appleton and Co., 1880), pp. 8–9. Reprinted by permission of Appleton-Century-Crofts.

Henry George (1839–1897) was a newspaper editor in California who developed and advocated a system of taxation based upon the value of land exclusive of improvements. His policies remain influential today.

communities it may clearly be seen that material progress does not merely fail to relieve poverty—it actually produces it. In the United States it is clear that squalor and misery, and the vices and crimes that spring from them, everywhere increase as the village grows to the city, and the march of development brings the advantages of the improved methods of production and exchange. It is in the older and richer sections of the Union that pauperism and distress among the working classes are becoming most painfully apparent. If there is less deep poverty in San Francisco than in New York, is it not because San Francisco is yet behind New York in all that both cities are striving for? When San Francisco reaches the point where New York now is, who can doubt that there will also be ragged and barefooted children on her streets?

This association of poverty with progress is the great enigma of our times. It is the central fact from which spring industrial, social, and political difficulties that perplex the world, and with which statesmanship and philanthropy and education grapple in vain. From it come the clouds that overhang the future of the most progressive and self-reliant nations. It is the riddle which the Sphinx of Fate puts to our civilization, and which not to answer is to be destroyed. So long as all the increased wealth which modern progress brings goes but to build up great fortunes, to increase luxury and make sharper the contrast between the House of Have and the House of Want, progress is not real and cannot be permanent. The reaction must come. The tower leans from its foundations, and every new story but hastens the final catastrophe. To educate men who must be condemned to poverty, is but to make them restive; to base on a state of most glaring social inequality political institutions under which men are theoretically equal, is to stand a pyramid on its apex.

Bernard Mandeville
Is Poverty Necessary? Yes

... No Man would be poor and fatigue himself for a Livelihood if he could help it: The absolute necessity all stand in for Victuals and

From *The Fable of the Bees*, with commentary by F. B. Kaye (Oxford: The Clarendon Press, 1924), pp. 287–288 and 311–312. Originally published in 1714. Reprinted by permission of Oxford University Press.

Bernard Mandeville (1670–1733) was born in Holland but lived in London, where his satirical wit and doggerel verse achieved considerable influence.

Drink, and in cold Climates for Clothes and Lodging, makes them submit to any thing that can be bore with. If no body did Want no body would work; but the greatest Hardships are look'd upon as solid Pleasures, when they keep a Man from Starving.

. . . in a free Nation where Slaves are not allow'd of, the surest Wealth consists in a Multitude of laborious Poor; for besides that they are the never-failing Nursery of Fleets and Armies, without them there could be no Enjoyment, and no Product of any Country could be valuable. To make the Society happy and People easy under the meanest Circumstances, it is requisite that great Numbers of them should be Ignorant as well as Poor. Knowledge both enlarges and multiplies our Desires, and the fewer things a Man wishes for, the more easily his Necessities may be supply'd.

The Welfare and Felicity therefore of every State and Kingdom, require that the Knowledge of the Working Poor should be confin'd within the Verge of their Occupations, and never extended (as to things visible) beyond what relates to their Calling. The more a Shepherd, a Plowman or any other Peasant knows of the World, and the things that are Foreign to his Labour or Employment, the less fit he'll be to go through the Fatigues and Hardships of it with Chearfulness and Content.

Reading, Writing and Arithmetick, are very necessary to those, whose Business require such Qualifications, but where People's livelihood has no dependence on these Arts, they are very pernicious to the Poor, who are forc'd to get their Daily Bread by their Daily Labour. Few Children make any Progress at School, but at the same time they are capable of being employ'd in some Business or other, so that every Hour those of poor People spend at their Book is so much time lost to the Society. Going to School in comparison to Working is Idleness, and the longer Boys continue in this easy sort of Life, the more unfit they'll be when grown up for downright Labour, both as to Strength and Inclination. Men who are to remain and end their Days in a Laborious, Tiresome and Painful Station of Life, the sooner they are put upon it at first, the more patiently they'll submit to it for ever after.

. . . Abundance of hard and dirty Labour is to be done, and coarse Living is to be complied with: Where shall we find a better Nursery for these Necessities than the Children of the Poor? none certainly are nearer to it or fitter for it. Besides that the things I called Hardships, neither seem nor are such to those who have been brought up to 'em, and know no better. There is not a more contented People among us, than those who work the hardest and are the least acquainted with the Pomp and Delicacies of the World.

These are Truths that are undeniable; yet I know few People will be pleased to have them divulged; what makes them odious is an unreasonable Vein of Petty Reverence for the Poor, that runs through most Multitudes, and more particularly in this Nation, and arises from a mixture of Pity, Folly and Superstitution. It is from a lively Sense of this Compound that Men cannot endure to hear or see any thing said or acted against the Poor; without considering, how Just the one, or Insolent the other. So a Beggar must not be beat tho' he strikes you first. Journeymen Tailors go to Law with their Masters and are obstinate in a wrong Cause, yet they must be pitied; and murmuring Weavers must be relieved, and have fifty silly things done to humour them, tho' in the midst of their Poverty they insult their Betters, and on all Occasions appear to be more prone to make Holy-days and Riots than they are to Working or Sobriety.

Alfred Marshall
Is Poverty Necessary? No

... the conditions which surround extreme poverty, especially in densely crowded places, tend to deaden the higher faculties. Those who have been called the Residuum of our large towns have little opportunity for friendship; they know nothing of the decencies and the quiet, and very little even of the unity of family life; and religion often fails to reach them. No doubt their physical, mental, and moral ill-health is partly due to other causes than poverty, but this is the chief cause.

And in addition to the Residuum there are vast numbers of people both in town and country who are brought up with insufficient food, clothing, and house-room, whose education is broken off early in order that they may go to work for wages, who thenceforth are engaged during long hours in exhausting toil with imperfectly nourished bodies, and have therefore no chance of developing their higher mental faculties. Their life is not necessarily unhealthy or unhappy. Rejoicing in their affections towards God and man, and perhaps even possessing some natural refinement of feeling, they may lead lives that are far less incomplete than those of many who have more material wealth. But, for all that, their poverty is

From *Principles of Economics*, 3rd ed. (London: Macmillan & Company, 1895), pp. 2-4. Reprinted by permission of The Macmillan Company, New York, and Macmillan & Co., Ltd., London.

Alfred Marshall (1842–1924) was a professor of economics at Cambridge who organized economic theory and gave cohesion to the neoclassical school of economic thought.

a great and almost unmixed evil to them. Even when they are well, their weariness often amounts to pain, while their pleasures are few; and when sickness comes, the suffering caused by poverty increases tenfold. And though a contented spirit may go far towards reconciling them to these evils there are others to which it ought not to reconcile them. Overworked and undertaught, weary and careworn, without quiet and without leisure, they have no chance of making the best of their mental faculties.

Although then some of the evils which commonly go with poverty are not its necessary consequences; yet, broadly speaking, "the destruction of the poor is their poverty," and the study of the causes of poverty is the study of the causes of the degradation of a large part of mankind.

Slavery was regarded by Aristotle as an ordinance of nature, and so probably was it by the slaves themselves in olden time. The dignity of man was proclaimed by the Christian religion: it has been asserted with increasing vehemence during the last hundred years: but it is only through the spread of education during quite recent times that we are beginning at last to feel the full import of the phrase. Now at last we are setting ourselves seriously to inquire whether it is necessary that there should be any so-called "lower classes" at all: that is, whether there need be large numbers of people doomed from their birth to hard work in order to provide for others the requisites of a refined and cultured life; while they themselves are prevented by their poverty and toil from having any share or part in that life.

The hope that poverty and ignorance may gradually be extinguished, derives indeed much support from the steady progress of the working classes during the present century. The steam-engine has relieved them of much exhausting and degrading toil; wages have risen; education has been improved and become more general; the railway and the printing-press have enabled members of the same trade in different parts of the country to communicate easily with one another, and to undertake and carry out broad and far-seeing lines of policy; while the growing demand for intelligent work has caused the artisan classes to increase so rapidly that they now outnumber those whose labour is entirely unskilled. A great part of the artisans have ceased to belong to the "lower classes" in the sense in which the term was originally used; and some of them already lead a more refined and noble life than did the majority of the upper classes even a century ago.

This progress has done more than anything else to give practical interest to the question whether it is really impossible that all should start in the world with a fair chance of leading a cultured life, free from the pains of poverty and the stagnating influences of excessive mechanical toil;

and this question is being pressed to the front by the growing earnestness of the age.

The question cannot be fully answered by economic science; for the answer depends partly on the moral and political capabilities of human nature; and on these matters the economist has no special means of information; he must do as others do, and guess as best he can. But the answer depends in a great measure upon facts and inferences, which are within the province of economics; and this it is which gives to economic studies their chief and their highest interest.

George Bernard Shaw
Poverty Infects

Such poverty as we have today in all our great cities degrades the poor, and infects with its degradation the whole neighborhood in which they live. And whatever can degrade a neighborhood can degrade a country and a continent and finally the whole civilized world, which is only a large neighborhood. Its bad effects cannot be escaped by the rich. When poverty produces outbreaks of virulent infectious disease, as it always does sooner or later, the rich catch the disease and see their children die of it. When it produces crime and violence the rich go in fear of both, and are put to a good deal of expense to protect their persons and property. When it produces bad manners and bad language the children of the rich pick them up no matter how carefully they are secluded; and such seclusion as they get does them more harm than good. If poor and pretty young women find, as they do, that they can make more money by vice than by honest work, they will poison the blood of rich young men who, when they marry, will infect their wives and children, and cause them all sorts of bodily troubles, sometimes ending in disfigurement and blindness and death, and always doing them more or less mischief. The old notion that people can "keep themselves to themselves" and not be touched by what is happening to their neighbors, or even to the people

From *The Intelligent Woman's Guide to Socialism and Capitalism* (Garden City: Garden City Publishing Co., Inc., 1928), pp. 42–45. Reprinted by permission of The Public Trustee and The Society of Authors, London.

George Bernard Shaw (1856–1950) was a Nobel Prize-winning playwright, a critic, journalist and leading Fabian Socialist.

who live a hundred miles off, is a most dangerous mistake. The saying that we are members one of another is not a mere pious formula to be repeated in church without any meaning: it is a literal truth; for though the rich end of the town can avoid living with the poor end, it cannot avoid dying with it when the plague comes. People will be able to keep themselves to themselves as much as they please when they have made an end of poverty; but until then they will not be able to shut out the sights and sounds and smells of poverty from their daily walks, nor to feel sure from day to day that its most violent and fatal evils will not reach them through their strongest police guards.

Besides, as long as poverty remains possible we shall never be sure that it will not overtake ourselves. If we dig a pit for others we may fall into it: if we leave a precipice unfenced our children may fall over it when they are playing. We see the most innocent and respectable families falling into the unfenced pit of poverty every day; and how do we know that it will not be our turn next?

It is perhaps the greatest folly of which a nation can be guilty to attempt to use poverty as a sort of punishment for offences that it does not send people to prison for. It is easy to say of a lazy man "Oh, let him be poor: it serves him right for being lazy: it will teach him a lesson." In saying so we are ourselves too lazy to think a little before we lay down the law. We cannot afford to have poor people anyhow, whether they be lazy or busy, drunken or sober, virtuous or vicious, thrifty or careless, wise or foolish. If they deserve to suffer let them be made to suffer in some other way; for mere poverty will not hurt them half as much as it will hurt their innocent neighbors. It is a public nuisance as well as a private misfortune. Its toleration is a national crime.

We must therefore take it as an indispensable condition of a sound distribution of wealth that everyone must have a share sufficient to keep her or him from poverty. This is not altogether new. Ever since the days of Queen Elizabeth it has been the law of England that nobody must be abandoned to destitution. If anyone, however undeserving, applies for relief to the Guardians of the Poor as a destitute person, the Guardians must feed and clothe and house that person. They may do it reluctantly and unkindly; they may attach to the relief the most unpleasant and degrading conditions they can think of; they may set the pauper to hateful useless work if he is able-bodied, and have him sent to prison if he refuses to do it; the shelter they give him may be that of a horrible general workhouse in which the old and the young, the sound and the diseased, the innocent girl and lad and the hardened prostitute and tramp are herded together promiscuously to contaminate one another; they can attach a social stigma to the relief by taking away the pauper's vote (if he has one), and making him incapable of filling certain public offices or being elected to certain public authorities; they may, in short, drive the deserving and respectable poor to endure any extremity rather than ask for relief; but they must relieve the destitute willy nilly if they do ask for it. To that extent the law of England is at its root a Communistic law. All the harshnesses and wickednesses with which it is carried out are gross mistakes, because instead of saving the country from the degradation of poverty they actually make poverty more degrading than it need be; but still, the principle is there. Queen Elizabeth said that nobody must die of starvation and exposure. We, after the terrible experience we have had of the effects of poverty on the whole nation, rich or poor, must go further and say that nobody must be poor. As we divide-up our wealth day by day the first charge on it must be enough for everybody to be fairly respectable and well-to-do. If they do anything or leave anything undone that gives ground for saying that they do not deserve it, let them be restrained from doing it or compelled to do it in whatever way we restrain or compel evildoers of any other sort; but do not let them, as poor people, make everyone else suffer for their shortcomings.

John Kenneth Galbraith
The Disgrace of Poverty midst Affluence

. . . poverty does survive. There is no firm definition of this phenomenon and again, save as a tactic for countering the intellectual obstructionist, no precise definition is needed. In part it is a physical matter; those afflicted have such limited and insufficient food, such poor clothing, such crowded, cold and dirty shelter that life is painful as well as comparatively brief. But just as it is far too tempting to say that, in matters of living standards, everything is relative, so it is wrong to rest everything on absolutes. People are poverty-stricken when their income, even if adequate for survival, falls markedly behind that of the community. Then they cannot have what the larger community regards as the minimum necessary for decency; and they cannot wholly escape, therefore, the

From *The Affluent Society* (Boston: Houghton Mifflin Co., 1958), pp. 323–333. Copyright © 1958 by John Kenneth Galbraith. Reprinted by permission of the author and the publisher.

John Kenneth Galbraith is Paul M. Warburg Professor of Economics, Harvard University, and former American ambassador to India. His widely read works include *Economic Development* (Houghton Mifflin, 1964).

judgment of the larger community that they are indecent. They are degraded for, in the literal sense, they live outside the grades or categories which the community regards as acceptable. In the mid-fifties, by acceptable estimate, one family in thirteen in the United States had a cash income from all sources of less than a thousand dollars. In addition a very large number of individuals, not members of families, were in this income class. To some extent family life is itself a luxury of an adequate income. The hard core of the very poor was declining but not with great rapidity.

. . . One can think of modern poverty as falling into two broad categories. First there is what may be called *case* poverty. This one encounters in every community, rural or urban, however prosperous that community or the times. Case poverty is the poor farm family with the junk-filled yard and the dirty children playing in the bare dirt. Or it is the grey-black hovel beside the railroad tracks. Or it is the basement dwelling in the alley.

Case poverty is commonly and properly related to some characteristic of the individuals so afflicted. Nearly everyone else has mastered his environment; this proves that it is not intractable. But some quality peculiar to the individual or family involved—mental deficiency, bad health, inability to adapt to the discipline of modern economic life, excessive procreation, alcohol, insufficient education, or perhaps a combination of several of these handicaps—have kept these individuals from participating in the general well-being.

Second, there is what may be called *insular* poverty—that which manifests itself as an "island" of poverty. In the island everyone or nearly everyone is poor. Here, evidently, it is not so easy to explain matters by individual inadequacy. We may mark individuals down as intrinsically deficient; it is not proper or even wise so to characterize an entire community. For some reason the people of the island have been frustrated by their environment.

This is not the place to explore in detail the causes of insular poverty. They are complex and many of the commonly assigned causes are either excessively simple or wrong. The resource endowment or the fertility of the land, the commonplace explanations, have little to do with it. Connecticut, a state of high incomes, has few resources and a remarkably stony soil. West Virginia is richly endowed. Connecticut has long been rich and West Virginia poor. . . .

The most certain thing about modern poverty is that it is not efficiently remedied by a general and tolerably well-distributed advance in income. Case poverty is not remedied because the specific individual inadequacy precludes employment and participation in the general advance. Insular poverty is not directly alleviated because the advance does not necessarily remove the specific frustrations of environment to which the people of these islands are subject. . . .

These circumstances have caused a profoundly interesting although little recognized change in what may be termed the political economy of poverty. With the transition of the very poor from a majority to a comparative minority position, they ceased to be automatically an object of interest to the politician. Political identification with those of the lowest estate has anciently brought the reproaches of the well-to-do, but it has had the compensating advantage of alignment with a large majority. Now any politician who speaks for the very poor is speaking for a small and also inarticulate minority. As a result the modern liberal politician aligns himself not with the poverty-ridden members of the community but with the far more numerous people who enjoy the far more affluent income of (say) the modern trade union member. Ambrose Bierce, in *The Devil's Dictionary,* called poverty "a file provided for the teeth of the rats of reform." It is so no longer. Reform now concerns itself with people who are relatively well-to-do—whether the comparison be with their own past or with those who are really at the bottom of the income ladder.

The poverty-stricken are further forgotten because it is assumed that with increasing output poverty must disappear. Increased output eliminated the general poverty of all who worked. Accordingly it must, sooner or later, eliminate the special poverty that still remains. As we have just seen, this is not to be expected or, in any case, it will be an infinitely time-consuming and unreliable remedy. Yet just as the arithmetic of modern politics makes it tempting to overlook the very poor, so the supposition that increasing output will remedy their case has made it easy to do so too.

To put the matter another way, the concern for inequality had vitality only so long as the many suffered privation while a few had much. It did not survive as a burning issue in a time when the many had much even though others had much more. It is our misfortune that when inequality declined as an issue, the slate was not left clean. A residual and in some ways rather more hopeless problem remained.

An affluent society, that is also both compassionate and rational, would, no doubt, secure to all who needed it the minimum income essential for decency and comfort. The corrupting effect on the human spirit of a small amount of unearned revenue has unquestionably been exaggerated as, indeed, have the character-building values of hunger and privation. To secure to each family a minimum standard, as a normal function of the society, would help insure that the misfortunes of parents, deserved or otherwise, were not visited on their children. It would help insure that poverty was not self-perpetuating. Most of the reaction, which no doubt would be almost universally adverse, is based on obsolete attitudes. When poverty was a majority phenomenon, such action could not be afforded. A poor society . . . had to enforce the rule that the person who did not work could not eat. And possibly it was justified in the added cruelty of applying the rule to those who could not work or whose efficiency was far below par. An affluent society has no similar excuse for such rigor. It can use the forthright remedy of providing for those in want . . .

Nonetheless any such forthright remedy for poverty is beyond reasonable hope. Also, as in the limiting case of the alcoholic or the mental incompetent, it involves difficulties. To spend income requires a minimum of character and intelligence even as to produce it. By far the best hope for the elimination, or in any case the minimization, of poverty lies in less direct but, conceivably, almost equally effective means.

The first and strategic step in an attack on poverty is to see that it is no longer self-perpetuating. This means insuring that the investment in children from families presently afflicted be as little below normal as possible. If the children of poor families have first-rate schools and school attendance is properly enforced; if the children, though badly fed at home, are well nourished at school; if the community has sound health services, and the physical well-being of the children is vigilantly watched; if there is opportunity for advanced education for those who qualify regardless of means; and if, especially in the case of urban communities, law and order are well enforced and recreation is adequate—then there is a very good chance that the children of the very poor will come to maturity without grave disadvantage. In the case of insular poverty this remedy requires that the services of the community be assisted from outside. Poverty is self-perpetuating because the poorest communities are poorest in the services which would eliminate it. To eliminate poverty efficiently we should invest more than proportionately in the children of the poor community. It is there that high-quality schools, strong health services, special provision for nutrition and recreation are most needed to compensate for the very low investment which families are able to make in their own offspring.

The effect of education and related investment in individuals is to enable them either to contend more effectively with their environment, or to escape it and take up life elsewhere on more or less equal terms with others. The role of education as an antidote to the homing instinct which crowds people into the areas of inadequate opportunity and frustration is also clear. However, in the strategy of the attack on insular poverty a place remains for an attack on the frustrations of the environment itself. This is particularly clear in the case of the slum. Slum clearance and expansion of low and middle-income housing removes a comprehensive set of frustrations and greatly widens opportunity. There is a roughly parallel opportunity in the rural slum. By identifying a land use which is consistent with a satisfactory standard of living, and by assisting with the necessary reorganization of land and capital, public authority can help individuals to surmount frustrations to which they are now subject. The process promises to be expensive and also time-consuming. But the question is less one of feasibility than of will.

Nor is case poverty in the contemporary generation wholly intransigent. Much can be done to treat those characteristics which cause people to reject or be rejected by the modern industrial society. Educational deficiencies can be overcome. Mental deficiencies can be treated. Physical handicaps can be remedied. The limiting factor is not knowledge of what can be done. Overwhelmingly it is our failure to invest in people.

. . . The myopic preoccupation with production and material investment has diverted our attention from the more urgent questions of how we are employing our resources and, in particular, from the greater need and opportunity for investing in persons.

Here is a paradox. When we begin to consider the needs of those who are now excluded from the economic system by accident, inadequacy, or misfortune—we find that the normal remedy is to make them or their children productive citizens. This means that they add to the total output of goods. We see once again that even by its *own terms* the present preoccupation with material as opposed to human investment is inefficient. . . .

But increased output of goods is not the main point. Even to the most intellectually reluctant reader it will now be evident that enhanced productive efficiency is not the *motif*. . . . The very fact that increased output offers itself as a by-product of the effort to eliminate poverty is one of the reasons. No one would be called upon to write at such length on a problem so easily solved as that of increasing production. The main point lies elsewhere. Poverty—grim, degrading, and ineluctable—is not remarkable in India. For few the fate is otherwise. But in the United States the survival of poverty is remarkable. We ignore it because we share with all societies at all times the capacity for not seeing what we do not wish to see. Anciently this has enabled the nobleman to enjoy his dinner while remaining oblivious to the beggars around his door. In our own day it enables us to travel in comfort through south Chicago and the South. But while our failure to notice can be explained, it cannot be excused. "Poverty," Pitt exclaimed, "is no disgrace but it is damned annoying." In the contemporary United States it is not annoying but it is a disgrace.

Rose D. Friedman
Things Are Getting Better All the Time

In the eighteenth and early nineteenth centuries, getting enough to eat—that is, enough calories to eliminate hunger—was the major problem of the populace in almost the entire world, with the possible exception of Great Britain and North America. A family that had enough bread was considered in easy circumstances. It did not occur to students of living standards of that day that the working classes might have essential needs over and above subsistence. The level of living per capita and per day of a working-class family "varied between a maximum of about two and a half to three pounds of wheat during the best years and an extremely low minimum which, as late as the eighteenth century, often fell below a single pound of bread a day." The subsistence minimum, an income that allowed the purchase of three pounds of wheat per capita per day—the equivalent of 3,500 calories—"did not represent a realizable possibility but *an ideal* whose attainment would solve every social problem." In the eighteenth century, this minimum was attained in France in only one out of four years.

As economic conditions improved, sociologists modified the concept of minimum subsistence by calculating the physiological minimum more and more generously. They paid increasing attention to type of nutrition as well as number of calories. In addition, the minimum began to include some expenditure for things other than food, such as lighting, heat, and clothing.

Half the people of the world today still get less than 2,250 calories per day, and live on a diet primarily of cereal in the form of millet, wheat, or rice. Another 20 percent get less than 2,750 calories per person per day. For this vast multitude, getting enough to eat is still the major problem. Only the well-to-do three-tenths of the human race today get more than 2,750 calories as well as a varied diet which provides the calories that not only satisfy hunger but also maintain a healthy body. Considerably fewer than three-tenths of the human race have a level of living at which expenditures on food absorb less than half the budget. The inhabitants of the United States are among these fortunate few.

From *Poverty: Definition and Perspective* (Washington: American Enterprise Institute for Public Policy Research, 1965), pp. 5–12. Copyright © 1965 by American Enterprise Institute for Public Policy Research. Reprinted by permission of the publisher.

Rose D. Friedman has been on the staff of the National Resources Committee, the Federal Deposit Insurance Corporation, and the Bureau of Home Economics. She is currently engaged in research in the economics of consumption.

It is admitted by all that the average level of living in the United States today is among the highest in the world, and that it has risen greatly over the past century. But, some complain, many Americans have been left behind and have not shared in this rising level of living. Are they right? In every society and at all times there are wide variations among people in the standard of living. These wide variations exist today in the United States. But does that mean that a segment of the population has been excluded from the benefits of a rising standard of living? Has progress brought gains primarily to those at the top of the heap? Or to those at the bottom as well? Or primarily to those at the bottom?

Let us look at what has been happening to the level of living of the people at the lower end of the income distribution, the relatively poor. First, some general observations, and then some statistical evidence.

Technological change and industrial progress have wrought many changes in the basket of goods available to American consumers. In many respects, however, this progress has been far more important to the persons at the bottom of the income pyramid than to those at the top. To take just a few examples. Radio and television have brought news and entertainment into the homes of people at all income levels. But surely, at least as an entertainment medium, these innovations have meant far more to the poor than to the rich—as did the phonograph and the movies when they were developed. Concerts, theaters, dances, and lectures were always available to the rich—either through public performances, or in a still earlier era, by live performances in the home. For the masses, first the phonograph, then the movies, and now TV and radio provide opportunities for cultural enrichment that were once almost the exclusive privilege of the well-to-do. And the masses have availed themselves of the opportunity with abandon, as the ubiquitous TV aerial vividly documents. According to David Caplovitz in *The Poor Pay More*, "95 percent of the families—all but 25 of the 464 interviewed—own at least one television set. Sixty-three percent have a phonograph—about half owning one separate from their TV set, and another 12 percent owning a television-phonograph console. . . . The 95 percent of set-owners among these families which include a substantial proportion in the lower-income range of the working-class, is about the same as that found among samples of working-class families in the country at large, these including many skilled workers and home owners. . . . As much as any statistics, these figures reflect the style of life of these young families. There is an accent on entertainment brought into the home by modern technology."

On a more practical level, electricity, running water, central heating, indoor toilets, telephones, automobiles, all of which we take for granted today, have changed the pattern of living available to the majority of American consumers even in the past 35 years. Says Herman

Miller, in *Rich Man—Poor Man:* "Today electricity in the home is taken for granted as a more or less inalienable right of every American. Practically every home—on the farm as well as in the city—is electrified. Even on southern farms, ninety-eight out of every hundred homes have electricity. In 1930, nine out of every ten farm homes were without this 'necessity.' And the country was much more rural then than now."

The poor in rural areas have benefited especially from technological improvements. For them, even more than for the poor in metropolitan centers, access to communication by means of telephone, to urban centers by means of the automobile, and to entertainment and education by means of radio and television have meant a great improvement in the social level of living.

Inside plumbing and central heating that are today part of the specifications for an "adequate level of living were unavailable to all but the very rich in this country less than a century ago—and are unavailable to most people in the world today. Again, these improvements brought a far greater change to the life of the masses than of the classes. Servants could always provide the rich with the conveniences that water systems and central heating have for the first time now made available to the masses—and the same economic progress that has made these available to the masses has made servants scarcer for the classes.

These are all general and non-quantitative indicators of the changes that have occurred in the standard of life of the ordinary family. What of the quantitative evidence?

First, nutrition, the basic need of humanity: how far we have moved from the situation of earlier centuries or from the situation that prevails in most of the world today can be seen by the almost complete neglect of calorie requirements in judging the adequacy of the diets in this country. In terms of simple calorie requirements, the problem for the American people today is too many, not too few calories. In evaluating the diets reported by families in the Household Food Consumption Survey, 1955, of the U.S. Department of Agriculture, one report states, "Calorie averages, in particular, were high. Even if a generous deduction were made for waste in the kitchen and at the table, the food consumed probably still would provide more calories than actually needed. The prevalence of overweight in the population is an indication of over-eating."

As the quantity and quality of food available in the more advanced countries increased, attention shifted from getting enough to eat to eating the right food, from number of calories to the importance of other nutrients. As we shall see later there are no definitive standards of nutritive adequacy and the tentatively accepted standards are revised periodically as new knowledge becomes available. Nonetheless we can get some idea of the changes that have taken place in the nutritive adequacy of the diet of the American people by using the standard currently accepted. Table 1 gives the relevant evidence for the one-third of city dwellers with the lowest incomes.

As of 1936, the average diet of the lowest third yielded less than the currently (1964) recommended allowances for six of the eight nutrients for which the National Research Council specifies amounts. From 1936 to 1955, consumption increased at least 50 percent for all but one of the eight nutrients. And by 1955, the average amount consumed by the poorest third exceeded the National Research Council's allowances for seven of the eight nutrients. (The allowances specified in Table 1 are for men aged 18–35; the group with the highest allowances in general.) More detailed evidence indicates that even for the one exception, Niacin, the amount consumed exceeded the allowance for all groups except men 18–35 and boys 12–18.

One report from the Household Food Consumption Survey, 1955, summarizes the improvement in nutrition as follows: "Diets in the United States have improved markedly since the 1930's. In 1936 when a large-scale household food consumption survey was made, a third of the diets were classed as "poor." When we apply the same standards to diets of the households surveyed in 1955, only a little over a tenth (13 percent) may be considered 'poor.' "

As to how the poor fared relative to the rich, this same report says, "Diets of families in the lowest income third showed much greater improvement between 1936 and 1942 and between 1942 and 1948 than did diets of families in the upper income third. Between 1948 and 1955 all of the income groups shared fairly equally in the moderate changes."

Table 1. Change in Nutritive Value of City Diets of the Lowest Income Third from 1936 to 1955

Nutrient	NRC recommended allowances per adult male 1964 [1]	Nutritive value of city diets of lowest income third per person per day [2] 1936	1955	% increase 1936–55
Energy value—cal.	2900	2580	2910	13
Protein gr.	70	66	94	42
Calcium gr.	.8	.64	1.00	56
Iron (milligr.)	10	10.2	16.4	61
Vit. A. value I.U.	5000	5520	8700	58
Thiamine	1.2	.79	1.42	80
Riboflavin	1.7	1.20	2.04	70
Niacin	19.0	9.4	17.4	85
Ascorbic Acid	70.0	58.0	94.0	62

[1] National Research Council, Food and Nutrition Board, *Recommended Dietary Allowances*, sixth revised edition, 1964.
[2] U.S. Department of Agriculture, *Dietary Evaluation of Food Used in Households in the United States*, Household Food Consumption Survey, 1955, Report #16, Table 19, p. 30.

If a healthy body is the first need, a healthy mind is the second. Schooling is another example of the far greater significance to the masses than to the classes of the improvement that has occurred in the standard of living of the American people. Less than a century ago (1870), only 57 percent of all children between 5 and 17 years of age attended school. By the turn of the century, this had risen to 76 percent, by 1920, to 82 percent, and by 1960 to 89 percent. It was this low in 1960 only because children were starting school at 6 years of age instead of at 5. Nearly 97 percent of all children between 7 and 17 years of age were in school in 1960. Even more dramatic are the figures on schooling at a higher level. In 1870, only 2 percent of the relevant age group graduated from high school. This tripled to 6 percent by 1900, tripled again to 17 percent by 1920, and again to 50 percent by 1940. It had reached 62 percent by 1956. Enrollment in institutions of higher education—junior colleges, colleges, and universities—was less than 2 percent of the relevant age group in 1870, and more than 30 percent in 1960. There is still scope for improvement, but much the greater part of this particular road has already been traveled.

To go from the specifics of food and schooling to the level of living as a whole, we can use income per family as a rough index of level of living —though as we shall see later it has many defects as a precise measure. As Table 2 shows, just 35 years ago, more than half of the people in this country would have been labeled "poor" by the poverty line of $3,000 income so popular today; 20 years ago, 30 percent; today, 21 percent—and these statements are based on statistics that allow fully for changes in the price level. In 1929, a year of great prosperity, about 11 million American families and individuals had incomes below $2,000 compared with 7 million in 1962. Despite a 63 percent rise in the total number of families and individuals from 1929 to 1962, the number with incomes below $2,000 actually fell by 36 percent.

By almost any yardstick, there surely has been a major reduction in the number of families with low income in this country over the past three decades. It simply is not true that any large segment of the American people has been left behind and has failed to share in the country's economic progress. If the trend in growth of real income of the past 35 years were to continue, the fraction of the population below the currently popular poverty line of $3,000 per family would become negligible before the end of the century. Of course, if the growth in real income continues, one of its manifestations will be a rise in what is regarded as the standard of poverty so that the poor will continue to be with us. All groups will continue to share in economic progress and the people then labeled poor will have a higher standard of living than many labeled not poor today. How much poverty there is now or will be then depends on the yardstick used to define poverty.

Table 2. Distribution of Consumer Units by Real Income Level

Family personal income (in 1962 dollars) (before income tax)	1929 No. (millions)	%	1947 No. (millions)	%	1962 No. (millions)	%
Under $2,000	11.2	31	7.2	16	7.1	12
2,000– 3.000	7.2	20	6.3	14	5.3	9
3,000– 4,000	6.9	19	6.3	14	5.9	10
4,000– 6,000	5.6	15	11.7	26	12.2	21
6,000– 8,000	2.4	7	6.0	14	10.8	18
8,000–10,000	1.1	3	3.1	7	6.7	11
10,000 and over	1.9	5	4.1	9	10.9	19
Total	36.1	100	44.7	100	58.6	100

Source: Jeanette M. Fitzwilliams, "Size Distribution of Income in 1962," *Survey of Current Business*, April 1963, Table 3; Herman P. Miller, *Rich Man—Poor Man;* (New York: Thomas Y. Crowell Co., 1964), p. 29. This table includes single individuals, i.e., family units of 1, as well as larger family units and therefore overstates the number of families at the lower income levels, since single individuals in general have lower incomes than family units. On the other hand, the income concept used is total income including, in addition to money income, imputed income from an owned home and food produced at home. For this reason, the number of consumer units is smaller at the lower levels than in the statistics used in the Economic Report of the Council of Economic Advisers. Only money income is used in [the Economic Report].

3
Perspectives from
Four Disciplines

Poverty has a formidable ally in our own ignorance of what we must do to root out poverty. When one stands "eyeball to eyeball" with poverty, preparing for mortal struggle, he will admit, if he is candid, that he does not know exactly what is best to do or how to do it.

There is a surprising dearth of hard knowledge about the root causes and dynamics of poverty. . . . Our prescriptions for the cure of poverty are unsure and lacking in consensus.
                                    —Michael S. March

The study of poverty does not fit neatly into any of the major disciplines. Economists, sociologists, and psychologists are all concerned with the causes and consequences of poverty. Rarely, however, do they approach the problem with the same set of questions or the same theoretical framework. As a result, there are great variations in the way in which poverty is defined and analyzed, and in the remedial measures that are prescribed. The selections in this chapter contrast the conceptual framework of poverty used by eminent social scientists from different disciplines.

Economists think of poverty in economic terms, which is the way it is defined and measured in the federal statistics that are used to evaluate the anti-poverty program. A family is considered poor by most economists if it does not have sufficient goods and resources to maintain a minimum standard of living at a given time and place. This conception of the problem has led economists like Milton Friedman to prescribe measures for subsidizing poverty rather than eliminating its causes. Kenneth Boulding, in the article presented here, suggests that it might be cheaper in the long run to subsidize poverty-prone cultures in our society than to try to eliminate them.

Sociologists generally have a broader conception of poverty than the one described above. They include "style of life" as well as income in determining whether a family or group of families is counted among the poor. Remedial action for the "culture of poverty," described by Oscar Lewis, calls for a set of policies far different from the income-maintenance programs prescribed by some economists.

Psychologists approach poverty from a behavioral point of view. They are interested primarily in the relationship between poverty and such deviant behavior as crime, delinquency, and illegitimacy. Haggstrom takes the position that the poor behave the way they do not only because of a lack of income but also because of a sense of powerlessness. According to his framework, a meaningful anti-poverty program requires the involvement and active participation of the poor in the solution of their social and economic problems. Higher incomes alone will not change the behavioral problems that led to poverty in the first place.

The current widespread discussions about poverty have resulted in a greater understanding of the limitations of the traditional approaches to the problem. Symptomatic of the current feeling in many fields is the statement by Theodore W. Schultz, former president of the American Economic Association. "... poverty for want of a theory is lost in economics notwithstanding all of the statistics that show the size and distribution of personal income and the age, sex, and family composition of people with low income.... A vast catalogue of the attributes of poor people is at hand. But, for all that, there is no integrated body of economic knowledge and no agenda of economic hypotheses to get at important economic questions about poverty." This dissatisfaction with the state of professional knowledge about poverty has been expressed by numerous other social scientists and by political leaders as well. It has led to greater sophistication in thinking about social problems and a greater willingness to spend money for the collection of data and the evaluation of programs.

Kenneth E. Boulding
Economist

Poverty is not a condition of the individual person but is always a condition of a society or of a subculture within a society.

I am prepared to defend this statement strongly in the case of what I would call "chronic" poverty. I am less prepared to defend the statement in the case of "accidental" poverty—poverty which is the result of some peculiar turn of fortune. An individual may lose his health or his capital by unfortunate accidents or unsuccessful ventures. If chronic poverty results, however, it reflects the fact that the individual has passed from one subculture of his society to another and a poorer one. The poor relation in the rich family is in a different position from the poor man who has no rich relations. Their psychology is different, and their whole style of life and consumption is likely to be different.

Within wide limits, poverty is a state of mind more than it is a state of income. While I am prepared to concede individual cases, therefore, I shall adhere to my main thesis that poverty is a product of social systems. Some cultures and subcultures breed poverty as surely as a waterfront breeds rats. Other societies and subcultures pursue unremittingly the long, hard climb out of poverty.

One of the most striking phenomena in the world today is not the contrast between the rich and the poor within a country but the extraordinary contrast between rich and poor countries. In the eighteenth century, it is doubtful whether the per capita income of the richest country was more than five times that of the poorest. In the twentieth century, the per capita income of the richest country is at least forty times that of the poorest, and this difference may increase before it diminishes; for the rich countries are getting richer faster than the poor countries, and the gulf widens between them all the time. It is this gulf which constitutes the main problem of poverty today. Persons regarded by a rich society as very poor would be regarded as relatively rich in a poor society. We see this illustrated in the fact that to the American, the migrant laborer is the poorest of the poor and constitutes in his mind a serious social problem. To the Mexican villager, joining the ranks of our migrant workers is seen as a road to riches

From "Reflections on Poverty," *The Social Welfare Forum: 1961* (New York: Columbia University Press, 1961), pp. 45–58. Copyright © 1961, National Conference on Social Welfare, Columbus, Ohio. Reprinted by permission of the publisher.

Kenneth E. Boulding is Professor of Economics, University of Michigan, and the author of numerous influential works including *The Skills of the Economist* (Howard Allen, Inc., 1958).

and as a way to lift the grinding burden of the poverty under which he labors. And yet Mexico is one of the richer of the poor countries. To hundreds of millions of Asians and Africans, the standard of life of the Mexican laborer would seem almost luxurious.

It is well for us to remember that this extraordinary gulf which now stretches between the rich and the poor in space is really a gulf in time. Three or four hundred years ago, the European peasant led a life as poor and probably as miserable as the Indian peasant does now. The discrepancy between the rich countries and the poor countries has arisen not primarily because of exploitation—it is not that the poor countries have produced a lot and the rich have taken it away from them; it is rather that the rich have participated in a process of economic growth which has as yet barely touched the poor countries. Relative rates of economic growth, therefore, are the key to this whole problem. Slight differences in the rate of economic growth can carry two countries to very different conditions in a relatively short time. Thus, if income in one country grows by 2 percent and in another by 3 percent and they start from the same level, in only a little over seventy years or a single lifetime the income of the faster growing country is twice that of the slower growing. If two countries start from the same per capita income and one grows at a modest 2 percent while the other stagnates, in only 200 years the growing country will have an income fifty times that of the stagnant one. Much of the world's history in the last 200 years is explicable in terms of this simple arithmetic. . . .

The foundation of all economic development is an increase in the productivity of labor in food production. In precivilized society one person can produce only enough food for himself and his family. Under these circumstances, there is no opportunity for specialization and no opportunity for the growth of cities. This is apt to be characteristic of food-gathering societies. With the invention of agriculture and domestication of crops and animals, the food producer began to produce more than he and his family could eat. As soon as some authority got around to taking the suplus away from him, civilization began. Urban civilization (that which goes on in the *civis*), in its classical phase was based on agriculture and exploitation, that is, on politics. The farmer grows more than he needs to feed himself; the surplus is taken from him and feeds armies, artisans, priests, and kings. The agricultural surplus is transmuted into art and literature, Parthenons and cathedrals.

Now we are passing into what is called "postcivilization," which is as radically different from civilization as civilization is different from pre-civilization. The transition to postcivilization is characterized by a steady and fairly rapid increase in the productivity of labor, not only in agriculture but also in manufacturing. This process has carried us in agriculture to the point where now 5 percent of the population of an advanced country could easily feed the whole. Classical civilization required about 80 percent of the population to feed the whole, so meager was the food surplus on which it was supported. In the production of innumerable commodities of convenience and necessity and even of luxury, the same process has been going on. In a rich society, virtually every man may now have conveniences and luxuries which previously were the privilege of the very few; he enjoys a variety and quantity of consumer goods which would have seemed fabulous riches even to the kings of ancient times.

This has come about through the organization of human knowledge which we call science. It is the organized growth of knowledge which produces the growth of productivity and the abolition of poverty. As long as knowledge was confined to the skill of the craftsman, it grew very slowly; for it died out in every generation and had to be renewed in the apprentice. The sheer cost of the maintenance of the knowledge supply prevented much increase of it. The growth of science meant that specialized resources were devoted to the advancement of knowledge and of technology. The development of schools, universities, libraries, and the consequent specialization in knowledge and in know-how, meant that organized human societies could acquire, transmit, and increase knowledge in a quantity almost of a different order of magnitude from that of even classical civilization.

Even organized knowledge, however, is not equally productive when applied to different occupations and different commodities. The productivity of labor in agriculture has perhaps increased ten or twenty times since the Middle Ages, and on this all of our industrial development depends. In the same period, however, the productivity of much industrial labor has increased hundreds of times and with automation may now increase thousands of times. In the same period, however, the productivity of labor in many services has barely increased at all or may even have declined. Thus, it takes about the same time to give a man a haircut as it did 500 years ago. There has been little improvement in the productivity of labor in teaching since the time of Aristotle. One suspects that in many fields of administration and organizing activity, productivity has actually declined. All this means that in the course of economic development, there are radical changes in the structure of relative prices. The prices of those goods and services in which productivity has not risen, rise relatively to those of goods and services the productivity of which has risen. The barber is better off than he was a hundred years ago not because his productivity has increased, but because his terms of trade have improved. He can buy a great deal more with an hour's barbering than he could previously. He is only able to do this, however, because in other occupations productivity has increased. Generally speaking, in those occupations in which the productivity increases most, the terms of trade show the least improvement.

Now let us look at the pockets of poverty that can exist within a rich society. One of the main concerns of the profession of social work is with these pockets of poverty. Within American society, for instance, we have the migrant, the elderly, the sharecropper, the slum dweller, the aged poor, minority groups, ministers of religion, and graduate students. The latter two are objectively poor, but in the sense that they do not usually regard themselves as members of the poverty cultures, they are not subjectively poor. All the other categories in this list represent poverty subcultures within the general framework of American society. Some of these subcultures perpetuate themselves from generation to generation and remain intractable islands of poverty and stagnation in a rapidly advancing society. . . . These may be subcultures, for instance, in which a relatively small proportion of the total labor force is actually engaged in productive work. This may be because of involuntary unemployment in an urban environment, or perhaps the subculture is that to which the porch-sitting, coon-hunting hillbilly belongs.

An interesting problem arises here as to the extent to which poverty is voluntary; that is, is accepted as a way of life, in the sense that activity devoted to getting richer is open to the individual or his culture but is deliberately, or perhaps unconsciously, rejected. Thoreau at Walden Pond would not have figured much in the national income statistics, and he demonstrated, as one unfriendly critic said, that if a man wanted to live like a woodchuck, he could do it very inexpensively. On the other hand, it is doubtful that Thoreau regarded himself as poor in any sense of the word whatever. The eager social worker who might want to lift him from his abject poverty would probably have been given a chilly reception. Similarly, one suspects that a certain amount of the poverty of the hillbilly or of the subsistence farmer, and even perhaps of the urban slum dweller and of the bum, involves the rejection of the psychological cost of getting rich and a rejection of the whole middle-class way of life rather than the inability to find opportunities.

This is something we need to know more about. On the whole, I am against making a man rich against his will. A truly voluntary poverty can be a noble way of life inspired by a high ethic and can be both a contribution and a challenge to a world that is overly concerned with getting rich. On the other hand, I am deeply suspicious of sentimentalizing about poverty; most poverty, I suspect, is involuntary, and there is nothing pleasant or ennobling about it. I have known even voluntary poverty undertaken for the highest motives to be crippling to the human spirit.

. . . we have identified one source of poverty—the low proportion of the population or of the total human activity in the labor force. Another important source, of course, is low productivity of labor once it is applied, in production either for domestic purposes or for export. This is overwhelmingly true in agricultural poverty. The poor farmer, on the whole, is the man with the poor farm. His income is low because he does not produce anything much. Nevertheless, as we have noted, there are instances where unfavorable terms of trade are important as a source of poverty. Agriculture, on the whole, tends to suffer from this situation, especially in an advancing society. It is an ironic paradox of agriculture that the more progressive it is technologically, the worse its terms of trade are likely to be. This is because a technically progressive agriculture is always declining as a proportion of the total economic activity. The only way to effect a relative transfer of population from a relatively declining industry into the relatively advancing industries is by making the declining industry relatively unprofitable. In the past 200 years we have had to squeeze people out of agriculture not only relatively, but absolutely. This has been achieved mainly because agricultural incomes have been considerably lower than their industrial counterparts. However, in that part of agriculture in which productivity is high, the poor terms of trade do not matter so much. The worst pockets of poverty are likely to be found in those segments of an occupation in which productivity has not risen, but in which because of the rise in productivity in other segments of the occupation, the terms of trade have become less favorable. The poverty of the marginal and submarginal farmer is a good case in point.

Poverty among urban populations is a more complex matter. In urban areas also we may have pockets of low productivity. This may be because the high productivity of an industrial society is not altogether costless for the individual. To get high wages, a man must submit to a discipline which may be distasteful to him. In any society, there seem to be niches for what might be called the "poor aristocrat." Oddly enough, it is the truly proletarian subcultures in our society which seem to develop this phenomenon. These pass easily into the criminal and the purely exploitative subcultures which survive mainly on [transfer payments] and which produce very little. One of the great questions for social workers is that if we institutionalize [transfer payments], for instance through Aid to Dependent Children, does this act perpetuate the subculture which benefits from the institutionalization? When the dependent children who have been aided ask for aid for *their* dependent children, there is perhaps a certain cause for alarm. Even this, though, may be a cause for congratulation that ours is a society rich enough to support the aristocratic poor who toil not, neither do they spin, but are arrayed in a considerable amount of castoff glory and who sometimes seem like cheerful grasshoppers amid the rather depressed ants who work for them.

Narrowing our unit still further, we now come to the family. One of the questions which I am sure every social worker asks is whether there is a poverty culture self-perpetuated through the poor family. The problem family raises problem children who in turn produce problem families and more problem children. A thriving and productive society can easily find embedded in itself, self-perpetuating parasitic groups. We need more longitudinal studies of these self-perpetuating subcultures to see how important they are and how stable they are. It may be that we can easily afford these groups and it may be more costly to prevent them than to cope with them. On the other hand, society seems to spend a good deal of effort through schools, police, and social work, churches and various social agencies, in trying to abolish these self-perpetuating subcultures—and with remarkably little success. It may be, indeed, that there are certain symbiotic relationships here. Just as the police and the criminals form a cozy little encapsulated symbiotic subsystem so busy about its own affairs that it does not much bother the rest of society, so the social workers and the members of the poverty subcultures may form a symbiotic subsystem, each element of which supports the other. As every student of ecology knows, systems of mixed competitiveness and complementarity (predation) are apt to be highly stable. I hardly dare suggest that the poor are the prey of the social worker, but it is true that the more clients, the more social workers and the more social workers, the fewer clients.

. . . Per capita income in the family, obviously, is highly dependent on the number of dependents. Attempts have been made in a good many societies to shower income on the individual rather than on the family itself and so make per capita incomes a little more equal between families by such devices as family allowances and aid to dependent children. This satisfies a certain sense of static justice. On the other hand, as at Speenhamland, it may have deplorable dynamic consequences. The elasticity of supply of children may be large, and an undertaking to support them may produce them.

We now come right down to the individual . . . The real income of an individual and of a society depends upon the amount of labor he devotes to production and on the productivity of that labor and on the terms of trade, that is, the price at which he can sell that labor or his products. It depends also on the gifts, positive and negative, that he receives or makes. The closer we get to the individual the more important the gifts become as an element in income. Between nations, gifts are relatively unimportant in spite of the hullabaloo about foreign aid. For the young and the old who produce nothing, the gift, may be the sole source of income. For those in the labor force in middle life, personal income may be reduced substantially by the gift which they have to make to the old, the young, and the unproductive. Here we see the great function of taxation in the distribution of personal income. Taxation, of course, may be positive or negative. A negative tax is a positive gift. It can be argued that the gift element in the economy is, in Parsons's terms, really part of the "polity" rather than of the economy, which we should perhaps confine to earned income and to exchange.

The situation is confused by the fact that many things which look like gifts are, in fact, deferred exchanges, such as for instance, the support which those in the labor force in the middle years of life give to the old and to the young. One of the things we know for certain about any age group is that it has no future. The young become middle-aged and the middle-aged become old, and the old die. Consequently, the support which the middle-aged give to the young can be regarded as the first part of a deferred exchange, which will be consummated when those who are now young become middle-aged and support those who are now middle-aged who will then be old. Similarly, the support which the middle-aged give to the old can be regarded as the consummation of a bargain entered into a generation ago. This exchange between the generations, however, is a loose and tenuous affair. The family, which organizes it in primitive society, seems to become less and less capable of this task, and hence the political agencies of society are forced into this role. Social security is, of course, an almost exact formalization of this exchange between the generations. The subsidy of education through taxation is a similar formalization of the support of the young by the middle-aged. The problem is greatly complicated in practice by the existence of cycles both in income and in population. The small cohorts, the scarce generations, and those who come to maturity in peace and prosperity owe a debt, which they never pay, to the large cohorts, the unwanted generations, and those who reach maturity in depression or in war. This is a social injustice which not even the best arrangements of social work or social security can help to assuage. Fortunately, it is a problem which solves itself in the long run when we are all dead.

These reflections have some fairly clear implications for social policy in regard to poverty. We may assume, I think, that one of the prime objectives of the social and economic policy of a modern, developed society is that poverty should be diminished at a high rate, with the objective of its virtual elimination within a reasonably short time. Some poverty can be eliminated through gifts or transfer payments from the producers to the nonproducers. No amount of redistribution of income, however, can eliminate poverty when the per capita income is below the poverty line. In poor societies, therefore, the first priority must always be given not to redistribution but to economic growth, even though some redistribution may be necessary in the interest of sustained growth. A pattern of growth, for instance, in which the mass of people does not benefit at all from the increased income, which is concentrated in the hands of a relatively small class, is politically dangerous and is likely to destroy itself. Even as a society gets richer, there is still a residuum of poverty which can only be dealt with by gifts and support. The problem then becomes to set the minimum below which the society will not allow people to fall. A difficulty here is that poverty is not an easily definable level. It is, as we have seen, as much a state of mind as it is a state of income. Especially is this true where the minimum acceptable level of income is far above that of physical subsistence. It is not unreasonable to suppose, however, that as a society gets richer the minimum level of income which it is prepared to support rises.

A purely mechanical redistribution, however, is insufficient to eliminate poverty. We could suppose, for instance, that we had an income tax which became negative below a certain level of income; that is, above a certain level one would pay taxes, while below a certain level one would receive subsidies. By making the marginal subsidy at some point 100 percent, it would be possible mechanically to prevent anybody's income from falling below a certain level. A mere mechanical device of this kind, however, would probably not be sufficient to prevent the development of poverty cultures or mendicant cultures within the society which became wholly dependent upon these transfers.

We have a similar problem in the support of dependent areas. There are some colonial territories in the world which deserve the name of "mendicant societies." They live almost entirely upon the handouts of the metropolitan power and seem incapable of developing an indigenous source of income or rising productivity. Subcultures like this can easily develop even within a rich community. For this reason, therefore, the control of poverty cannot altogether be divorced from the impact of society on the subcultures which exist within it. The institutions of cultural change are many—the church, the school, the mass media. There is little sense in our society, however, of being able to use these consciously in order to eliminate the poverty cultures. We have here, I suspect, an area in which investment by society is not carried anything like as far as would be profitable because of the fact that the form of the investment is difficult to define and its results are difficult to measure. One of the great problems of social research, therefore, is precisely the measurement of the rate of elimination of poverty cultures through the agencies of cultural change. Once we have more accurate information in this regard, the investment ought to be forthcoming.

In this, as in so many other areas of our social life, we are suffering from a serious misdirection of intellectual resources. The problem of poverty like the problem of war is a problem in social systems. We put extremely few resources, however, into studying these systems, and it is not surprising, therefore, if our knowledge of them is scanty and if our efforts to move them are ineffective. In this respect a large part of what may look like a political and economic problem turns out to be an unsolved intellectual problem. Until we put more resources into what is sometimes called the "meta-task" even at the expense of taking resources from the immediate task, we shall continue to waste resources. Too many people are trying to find the best way to do many things which probably should not be done at all. This is what we might call the "fallacy of suboptimization." It runs through our whole society, so it is not surprising to find it turning up in the area of the elimination of poverty.

What, then, are the long-run prospects for poverty?

Will this process of increasing productivity of labor spread to the whole world and go on until poverty is finally abolished and everybody is at least middle-class? This, of course, would be the state of affairs which the Communists call communism and which we call the affluent society, in which each man decides what standard of life he wishes to adopt (to each according to his needs) and in which he then goes out and earns the income to support it (from each according to his ability). We are pretty close to this situation in the United States. It is one of the nice ironies of history that capitalism will probably get to capitalist communism before socialism gets to socialist communism. Capitalist communism is, in fact, a very desirable state of society, and even the Socialists will probably end up in it when they get so rich that they can afford even to be free. The question is, though, can everybody do this?

The answer is "yes" if we can avoid three traps. The three traps are war, population, and exhaustion. A nuclear war, if it did not put an end to man, might easily destroy any chance of perpetual affluence. Unlimited growth of population could do the same thing, more slowly but just as effectively. The ghost of Malthus has been laid many times, but it will not stay down. If science and technology give us death control, they will force us into birth control. We must eventually have a stable population, and in that event, if we are all going to live to be seventy, the birth and death rate must not exceed about 14 per thousand. This means an average of a little over two children per family and no nonsense.

There are many ways to achieve this end, but the end must be achieved. The third trap might be our inability to develop a non-exhaustive high-level technology. Our existing technology is essentially suicidal in so far as it is based upon geological capital which we are rapidly squandering. We cannot build permanent affluence on fossil fuels, not even uranium, and still less upon deposits of ores. Permanent affluence must depend upon fusion as a source of energy, either in the sun or here on earth, and it must depend upon the use of this energy to concentrate the diffuse elements of the sea and the atmosphere. Fortunately, this high-level technology seems to be almost in sight. It is perfectly possible, however, that either nuclear or population explosions may prevent us from ever attaining it. Planet 3 is at a very crucial stage of its history. In 4,000,000,000 years, there has been nothing like this. This bifurcated repository of complex images that we call man will either make it or break it. From a galactic point of view, this may be mere homocentrism on my part, but I am in favor of his making it— and to this task I commend us all!

Oscar Lewis
Anthropologist

In the nineteenth century, when the social sciences were still in their infancy, the job of recording the effects of the process of industrialization and urbanization on personal and family life was left to novelists, playwrights, journalists, and social reformers. Today, a similar process of culture change is going on among the peoples of the less-developed countries but we find no comparable outpouring of a universal literature which would help us to improve our understanding of the process and the people. And yet the need for such an understanding has never been more urgent, now that the less-developed countries have become a major force on the world scene.

In the case of the new African nations that are emerging from a tribal, nonliterate cultural tradition, the paucity of a great native literature on the lower class is not surprising. In Mexico and in other Latin American countries where there has been a middle class, from which most writers come, this class has been very small. Moreover, the hierarchical nature of Mexican society has inhibited any profound communication across class lines. An additional factor in Mexico has been the preoccupation of both writers and anthropologists with their Indian problem, to the neglect of the urban poor.

This situation presents a unique opportunity to the social sciences and particularly to anthropology to step into the gap and develop a literature of its own. Sociologists, who have pioneered in studying urban slums, are now concentrating their attention on suburbia to the relative neglect of the poor. Today, even most novelists are so busy probing the middle-class soul that they have lost touch with the problems of poverty and the realities

From the Introduction to *The Children of Sánchez* (New York: Random House, Inc., 1961), pp. xxiii - xxvii. © Copyright by Oscar Lewis. Reprinted by permission of Random House, Inc., and Martin Secker & Warburg Limited, London.

Oscar Lewis is Professor of Anthropology, University of Illinois, Urbana. This selection is from his second book about the Sánchez family, part of his studies in the Mexican "culture of poverty."

of a changing world. As C. P. Snow has recently stated: "Sometimes I am afraid that people in rich countries . . . have so completely forgotten what it is like to be poor that we can no longer feel or talk with the less lucky. This we must learn to do."

It is the anthropologists, traditionally the spokesmen for primitive people in the remote corners of the world, who are increasingly turning their energies to the great peasant and urban masses of the less-developed countries. These masses are still desperately poor in spite of the social and economic progress of the world in the past century. Over a billion people in seventy-five nations of Asia, Africa, Latin America, and the Near East have an average per capita income of less than $200 a year as compared with over $2,000 a year for the United States. The anthropologist who studies the way of life in these countries has become, in effect, the student and spokesman of what I call the culture of poverty.

To those who think that the poor have no culture, the concept of a culture of poverty may seem like a contradiction in terms. It would also seem to give to poverty a certain dignity and status. This is not my intention. In anthropological usage the term culture implies, essentially, a design for living which is passed down from generation to generation. In applying this concept of culture to the understanding of poverty, I want to draw attention to the fact that poverty in modern nations is not only a state of economic deprivation, of disorganization, or the absence of something. It is also something positive in the sense that it has a structure, a rationale, and defense mechanisms without which the poor could hardly carry on. In short, it is a way of life, remarkably stable and persistent, passed down from generation to generation along family lines. The culture of poverty has its own modalities and distinctive social and psychological consequences for its members. It is a dynamic factor which affects participation in the larger national culture and becomes a subculture of its own.

The culture of poverty, as here defined, does not include primitive peoples whose backwardness is the result of their isolation and undeveloped technology and whose society for the most part is not class stratified. Such peoples have a relatively integrated, satisfying, and self-sufficient culture. Nor is the culture of poverty synonymous with the working class, the proletariat, or the peasantry, all three of which vary a good deal in economic status throughout the world. In the United States, for example, the working class lives like an elite compared to the lower class of the less developed countries. The culture of poverty would apply only to those people who are at the very bottom of the socio-economic scale, the poorest workers, the poorest peasants, plantation laborers, and that large heterogenous mass of small artisans and tradesmen usually referred to as the lumpen proletariat.

The culture or subculture of poverty comes into being in a variety of historical contexts. Most commonly it develops when a stratified social and economic system is breaking down or is being replaced by another, as in the case of the transition from feudalism to capitalism or during the industrial revolution. Sometimes it results from imperial conquest in which the conquered are maintained in a servile status which may continue for many generations. It can also occur in the process of detribalization such as is now going on in Africa where, for example, the tribal migrants to the cities are developing "courtyard cultures" remarkably similar to the Mexico City *vecindades*. We are prone to view such slum conditions as transitional or temporary phases of drastic culture change. But this is not necessarily the case, for the culture of poverty is often a persisting condition even in stable social systems. Certainly in Mexico it has been a more or less permanent phenomenon since the Spanish conquest of 1519, when the process of detribalization and the movement of peasants to the cities began. Only the size, location, and composition of the slums have been in flux. I suspect that similar processes have been going on in many other countries of the world.

It seems to me that the culture of poverty has some universal characteristics which transcend regional, rural-urban, and even national differences. . . .

In Mexico, the culture of poverty includes at least the lower third of the rural and urban population. This population is characterized by a relatively higher death rate, a lower life expectancy, a higher proportion of individuals in the younger age groups, and, because of child labor and working women, a higher proportion of gainfully employed. Some of these indices are higher in the poor *colonias* or sections of Mexico City than in rural Mexico as a whole.

The culture of poverty in Mexico is a provincial and locally oriented culture. Its members are only partially integrated into national institutions and are marginal people even when they live in the heart of a great city. In Mexico City, for example, most of the poor have a very low level of education and literacy, do not belong to labor unions, are not members of a political party, do not participate in the medical care, maternity, and old-age benefits of the national welfare agency known as *Seguro Social,* and make very little use of the city's banks, hospitals, department stores, museums, art galleries and airports.

The economic traits which are most characteristic of the culture of poverty include the constant struggle for survival, unemployment and underemployment, low wages, a miscellany of unskilled occupations, child labor, the absence of savings, a chronic shortage of cash, the absence of food reserves in the home, the pattern of frequent buying of small quantities of food many times a day as the need arises, the pawning of personal goods, borrowing from local money lenders at usurious rates of interest, spontaneous informal credit devices (*tandas*) organized by neighbors, and the use of second-hand clothing and furniture.

Some of the social and psychological characteristics include living in crowded quarters, a lack of privacy, gregariousness, a high incidence of alcoholism, frequent resort to violence in the settlement of quarrels, frequent use of physical violence in the training of children, wife beating, early initiation into sex, free unions or consensual marriages, a relatively high incidence of the abandonment of mothers and children, a trend toward mother-centered families and a much greater knowledge of maternal relatives, the predominance of the nuclear family, a strong predisposition to authoritarianism, and a great emphasis upon family solidarity—an ideal only rarely achieved. Other traits include a strong present time orientation with relatively little ability to defer gratification and plan for the future, a sense of resignation and fatalism based upon the realities of their difficult life situation, a belief in male superiority which reaches its crystallization in *machismo* or the cult of masculinity, a corresponding martyr complex among women, and finally, a high tolerance for psychological pathology of all sorts.

Some of the above traits are not limited to the culture of poverty in Mexico but are also found in the middle and upper classes. However, it is the peculiar patterning of these traits which defines the culture of poverty. For example, in the middle class, *machismo* is expressed in terms of sexual exploits and the Don Juan complex whereas in the lower class it is expressed in terms of heroism and lack of physical fear. Similarly, drinking in the middle class is a social amenity whereas in the lower class getting drunk has different and multiple functions—to forget one's troubles, to prove one's ability to drink, and to build up sufficient confidence to meet difficult life situations.

Many of the traits of the subculture of poverty can be viewed as attempts at local solutions for problems not met by existing institutions and agencies because the people are not eligible for them, cannot afford them, or are suspicious of them. For example, unable to obtain credit from banks, they are thrown upon their own resources and organize informal credit devices without interest. Unable to afford doctors, who are used only in dire emergencies, and suspicious of hospitals "where one goes only to die," they rely upon herbs or other home remedies and upon local curers and midwives. Critical of priests "who are human and therefore sinners like all of us," they rarely go to confession or Mass and rely upon prayer to the images of saints in their own homes and upon pilgrimages to popular shrines.

A critical attitude toward some of the values and institutions of the dominant classes, hatred of the police, mistrust of government and those in high position, and a cynicism which extends even to the church gives the culture of poverty a counter quality and a potential for being used in political movements aimed against the existing social order. Finally, the subculture of poverty also has a residual quality in the sense that its members are attempting to utilize and integrate into a workable way of life the remnants of beliefs and customs of diverse origins.

Nathan Glazer
Sociologist

... Poverty in the richest country in the world is of course only the first paradox with which we are confronted. Economists and reformers have set the income line for poverty at a figure that spells comfort in the countries of northwestern Europe. On the one hand this tempts critics to interpret poverty in this country not as absolute deprivation, but in relative terms. Our poor, we are told would be the upper middle class of India or the respectable working class of Sweden, and thus we deal with a statistical artifact when we speak of poverty in the United States. This argument—which is extreme—is nevertheless given a certain plausibility by the unqualified insistence of some economists and reformers that all the poor, by the standard of the income test, are poor. But then the critic—whether Irving Kristol or Dwight Macdonald—will note that one quarter of the poor, even in the figures of economists and reformers, own cars, and even more of them own their own homes, and writing from the rather special perspective of New York City, where even well-paid critics do not own cars or their own homes, they will find some reason for their skepticism.

We cannot easily resolve the question of why an income that would spell comfort in some countries is actually poverty in America, but there is no question that it is. We know that some eight million people can demonstrate to the satisfaction of hard pressed and often unsympathetic departments of public welfare that they are truly impoverished, and incapable of providing themselves with food or shelter without public funds. We

From "A Sociologist's View of Poverty," a reading in *Poverty in America,* ed. Margaret S. Gordon (San Francisco: Chandler Publishing Co., 1965), pp. 12–26. Copyright © 1965 by Chandler Publishing Company. Reprinted by permission of the publisher.

Nathan Glazer is Professor of Sociology, University of California, Berkeley, and the author of *The Social Basis of American Communism* (Harcourt, Brace, & World, 1961).

know too that the food and shelter they receive under these limited public allotments is not markedly superior to the food and shelter that the poor enjoyed in this and other industrial countries fifty years ago. If the paupers of Edwardian England lived on tea and bread and margarine and scraps of meat, then the poor of our country are doing only a little better. If the poor fifty years ago lived in crowded and crumbling rooms, with inadequate plumbing and heating, then we find the same living conditions for a large part of our poor population today. There have been gains—the automobiles that have bemused some writers on poverty, the television sets that are almost universal, the clothing that is cheaper and better than that of fifty years ago, the public health services. But it is odd to note the extent to which the improvements in the living conditions of the poor, which are undoubtedly reflected in the income level we now draw to mark the line of poverty, have gone to peripheral improvements—television sets replacing the stoop for conversation and the automobile replacing cheap public transportation.

We certainly have to accept some skepticism at the figure of 40,000,000 poor. On the other hand, the eight million on relief are certainly only a part of the problem. Somewhere in between we have a large population that is without the means to maintain a modest standard of living.

The second large paradox we have to deal with is the sudden rise of public concern and political action over this question in the United States in the past few years. The problem itself has not changed in character. Professor Gordon, for example, has shown that there have been no major changes in the relative impact of unemployment on youth and nonwhites in recent years, as is widely believed, while unemployment itself as well as poverty has declined somewhat. The numbers on the public assistance rolls show a remarkable stability. It is true there is a steady increase in the Aid to Families with Dependent Children category, but this is not much greater than the increase in the population under eighteen.

Some British Comparisons

Let me suggest something even more surprising. In England, with all its wide array of welfare institutions—its extensive programs of national health, social insurance, family allowances—the number that becomes dependent on National Assistance—their equivalent of our public welfare—is a little larger than it is here in proportion to population; that is, about 6 per cent of the population of Great Britain to about 4½ per cent here. Obviously one should not make too much of the fact that the figures are so close—they have more old people on national assistance, fewer children, and there are very large differences in the systems of social insurance and social welfare in the two countries. It is nevertheless enlightening for us to ask: why is there no outcry in England over the problem of poverty when, with all the wealth of social insurance schemes, three million people a year are dependent on weekly grants for direst need from the National Assistance Board?

It was revealing to me to leaf through the past six or seven months of an English weekly devoted specifically to problems of social welfare and social change, *New Society*, in search of articles on poverty in England, which these statistics had suggested to me was as much of a problem as poverty in America. The only article I came upon was a report on President Johnson's war on poverty in the United States.

I would ask further: to the extent that this problem is discussed there, why is it that it is seen as one requiring various adjustments in the social security system, perhaps some new approaches in social work for the worst cases, and the like; while here we see the poverty problem as demanding much more than tinkering with benefits and eligibilities? Here radicals, liberals, and even some conservatives call for a social and psychological revolution, requiring us to develop a completely different attitude to the casualties of industrial society, an attitude capable of remaking them rather than providing simply better care.

Let me try to explain the failure of other countries to see some of their problems as problems of poverty. England is still afflicted with a housing shortage and slums; Sweden still has a severe housing shortage; but this is no longer seen primarily as a problem of poverty. It is seen as a problem of allocation of resources. Since housing is in such large measure in these countries a public utility, the question becomes, who gets it, rather than, why don't people have enough money to pay for it? The questions then are questions of small administrative or larger social decisions—do we favor the young married couple over the aged couple or individual, do we provide housing for the divorced woman, or must she move in with her parents, and so on. This is true of other elements of income too. They depend on laws and regulations and their interpretation. Obviously our situation is very different. Our goods—housing or medical care are prominent examples—are to a much larger degree allocated by the free market. And even if the distribution of income is not much more unequal here than there, its differential impact on the standard of living of those at the lower end of the scale must consequently be much larger.

I would suggest then that one of the reasons for the difference of response to the problem of poverty in England as in the other countries of northwestern Europe is that a floor of services has been built, a standard floor for the entire nation, beneath which theoretically no one may fall. This floor is by definition designed to provide adequacy. Somewhat less effectively, there is also a floor of minimum income, as well as minimum services. The mechanisms by which it is provided consist of a variety of elements, such as old age pensions, unemployment insurance, family allowances, national health insurance and the like, and it turns out, as we have seen, that despite the artful construction, people do slip below the floor. And the proportions that slip below in England are statistically not less than those that here find themselves in such desperate straits that they must apply for public aid. Yet because of the existence and acceptance of these national floors, the common reaction to poverty appears to be, repair the floor, adjust the mechanisms so they eliminate the problem of people slipping below. National assistance is thus viewed, at least officially, as an adaptation to some bad fitting planks in the national floor, rather than a sign of failure and inadequacy and moral defect, as it is here. With the passage of time, it takes steady and hard carpentry work in the welfare state to keep the floor in good shape. Inflation makes old age pensions inadequate; charges are reintroduced for some elements of health care and some people cannot afford them; much of the regular social insurance is related to regular work, and those who have not worked regularly do not qualify for it; many people do not know their rights and legal benefits—as many here do not—and some will not take advantage of them.

Our Emphasis on Individualism

But we must explore these differences in reaction to poverty a bit further. Why is it that our system of social insurance and public assistance form a much more jagged and uncertain floor than does that in England? Is it only a matter of the uncompleted revolution of the New Deal? This is one way of looking at it, but why did the revolution remain so partial? Daniel P. Moynihan has pointed out that we in this country find the idea of a high minimum for all much less attractive than the opportunity of high income for some—and that some by now includes very substantial parts of the working class. We do have a lower floor than in Europe, or rather a more irregular floor, with some parts of it—as in New York, Michigan, and Illinois, quite high, and other parts, as in the South, falling deep into the cellar—but we also have higher plateaus, on which very substantial numbers are located.

I would like to explore some concrete manifestations of this important generalization. If we look at the history of the past few years, when we find Democratic administrations in control nationally, we are surprised to discover that there has been relatively little interest in raising the floor, in completing and filling out our patchy system of social insurance and welfare. This lack of interest is almost as evident in liberal opinion as in conservative opinion. Conservatives prefer people to work and support themselves rather than to become dependent on public means, on a high floor. Oddly enough liberals seem to think the same way. There is little pressure for an increase in the very low social security payments, which would rapidly eliminate a good share of the poverty in the United States. There seems to be much more interest in work training programs, of all kinds, among liberals as well as conservatives—even though the liberals will also add that work training without jobs is insufficient. It is interesting to note that, whereas England is far ahead of us in so many spheres, our work training and retraining programs, under MDTA, the Economic Opportunity Act, and other acts, are considerably in advance of what we find in England. Of course, one reason for this is that our unemployment rates in general are higher, our youth unemployment is much higher, our fear of job loss through technological change considerably greater.

And yet one additional explanation is to be found in our greater interest in protecting the plateaus and opening more routes to them rather than raising the floor. Another example of our concern for the plateaus is the labor unions' insistence on a high minimum wage for youths employed on community work projects which are designed to train them. The unions will not accept the idea that the minimum wage—which is oddly enough one of the supports of the plateaus in our peculiar system, because so much work is done at less than the minimum wage—may be given up even briefly for training. It is even less likely that they would accept the idea of a lower mimimum wage for young and presumably less experienced and less responsible workers in general. The auto insurance companies insist on charging the driver under 25 a good deal more, to make up for his irresponsibility, but the unions will not let the employer pay him less, which the same characteristics might justify. And now the labor movement announces it will open a drive for a $2.00 minimum wage, which can only exacerbate the problems of youth unemployment. The problem is an old one. . . .

Obviously the unions have many good arguments against weakening the line that holds the minimum wage for some work. But we are less interested in the specific content of the arguments here than in what we learn from them about the American style of response in such matters. We might sum up the style in a single word, individualism, and I am willing to use that difficult sponge term because I think I can demonstrate that it does characterize our distinctive inability to build a high floor. For example; unions will argue that no exception can be made to the minimum wage because every wage must be a living wage. But do we need a living wage for every *individual* or do we need a living income for every *family?* It is because we think of the individual worker alone rather than the family that we find it easy to accept as a public policy that 16-year-old dropouts without experience should be paid the same wages as heads of families—which is the policy of our youth employment programs. What is this but a surprising excess of individualism? It is because once again we seem incapable of thinking in family terms that in our Youth Conservation Camps, we will make it possible and easy for all the income (and it is substantial) to be given to the youth himself. It is interesting to reflect on the social change implicit in the departure from the practice of the New Deal's CCC camps, where in contrast almost all the money went to the boy's family, and the program was considered valuable primarily for its contribution to family income and for its conservation work, not for its education in work habits. It is even more sobering to consider whether an incentive to work—so as to improve the country and aid one's family at home—was not perhaps more effective in teaching better work habits—though this was not part of the explicit program of the CCC—than the direct effort to teach good work attitudes and work skills on which we are now engaged.

Alvin Schorr, one of our most subtle analysts of social policy, points out how our programs have again and again begun with the individual, and only as an afterthought have been forced to realize that most individuals are still parts of families: "For example, the Social Security Act was enacted in 1935 and family benefits were added in 1939; disabled workers were covered in 1956, and their dependents in 1958. In the aid to dependent children program, federal participation was at first available only for the children in a family home; participation in aid to mothers was added fifteen years later. Fathers in need because of unemployment [were added only in 1962]"—and we might add only after the evidence that the ADC program that excluded fathers was effectively breaking up homes.

Our jagged floor represents our virtues as well as our defects—if, that is, we are to consider, as I do, that a concern for the individual as an individual, freed from the restraints of the family as well as of other traditional organizations and institutions, is in some measure a virtue. One of the reasons why the unions insist on a living wage for young working people without responsibilities and one of the reasons the government is willing to grant it is that we do expect our young people to move out of their homes young, to support themselves in an independent establishment rather than help support their younger brothers and sisters, to marry young. But then we must also be aware that our systems of wage reward and public assistance also erode more rapidly whatever remains of family and kin loyalty. It is this, we must realize, that makes it possible for impoverished countries, far far poorer than our own, to manage with almost no system of public welfare at all.

Our jagged floor also reflects another mixture of virtues and vices —the degree of autonomy possessed by states and communities in this country, an autonomy which permits some to attain high levels of social concern and social practice, others to fall far short of them. We are well aware of the potential and actual faults of this system of local autonomy: the fact, for example, that some states and counties are too poor to carry out their responsibilities to the poor properly, and that others, even though they may have the funds, will not. The degree of this variation from state to state is, from the point of view of the unified and homogeneous nations of Europe, almost fantastic. New York and Illinois provide an average of more than $200 a month for families with dependent children; Mississippi and Alabama an average of less than $50. In the North and West, aid to families with dependent children is given on the assumption that women with young children should not work but should care for them. In large parts of the South, where Negro women with young children and without male supporters have worked since the days of slavery, they still work.

The Racial Problem

I now come to the most distinctive dimension of American life, which gives a unique coloring to our poverty problem and which is undoubtedly the chief reason why poverty has become a major issue in this country. This is the race problem—and I would place this within the larger context of the ethnic and racial composition of the American people. The chief reason why our impoverished population forms a major social problem, and England's does not, is because of who they are. There they are the bottom stratum of almost randomly defined unfortunates, with no common social definition larger than that of casualties of the welfare state. Here the bottom stratum is a group defined by more than bottomness. It is true that the statistics show that only one quarter of the poor, as defined by the $3,000 income line, are Negroes. But this larger estimate of the poor, as I have pointed out, is in part a statistical artifact. The poorest, as defined by the public assistance rolls, are in much larger proportion Negro, Mexican American, and Puerto Rican. In many of our great cities, the majority of those who seek public assistance are Negroes. It is the civil rights revolution that makes poverty a great issue in America, not merely poverty. And in other developed countries, it is the absence of a great social division coinciding roughly with the line of poverty that keeps poverty from becoming a great issue. It is true that those seeking national assistance in England are probably disproportionately colored, perhaps disproportionately Irish immigrants. But these groups are not yet significant forces in English politics.

Nor can we separate the cluster of issues we have summed up under the ideas of individualism and state and local autonomy from the fact of racial division and ethnic complexity. We cannot in this country set the kinds of standards that a more homogeneous country can—and our efforts to do so bring us far more perplexities. Let me again refer to the debates around the Poor Law Commission of 1909 to indicate a contrast. Sidney and Beatrice Webb at that time analyzed the problems of poverty in industrial society in terms that we can scarcely improve upon today. They defined its causes—in age, illness, poor education, unemployment—

very much the way we do today. Their proposed programs were also similar to those which advanced social workers and labor market economists would suggest today. They emphasized the over-all principle of prevention, and they associated with it three other principles—the principle of Universal Provision, or floor-building, the principle of Curative Treatment, or nonpunitive and truly helpful aid, and finally, the principle of Compulsion. At that point, we may notice the difference. Compulsion meant that if parents could not raise their children properly, they would be taken away. If men would not prepare themselves for useful labor, they would be required to do so. The principle of Compulsion reflects the fact that all Englishmen may potentially agree on what is a proper way to live and what measures a government may adopt to require it. And we see the same principle at work in the advanced countries of northwestern Europe today, where those who will not live properly in public housing may be put under the care of social workers who will teach them how to arrange their lives and to raise and discipline their children.

Recently I have read an account—again by Alvin Schorr—of French social workers. The French system of social security places great emphasis on the care and protection of the family. The social workers themselves are trained primarily in two areas—in nursing, and in the various laws and regulations. They work with single families, and are responsible for getting their families the various kinds of aid the law provides. One gets an image of these self-confident and energetic women—they are all women—confident of the quality of their training and the virtues of the law, arranging matters for these families, in a way in which our social workers would never dare—because ours are aware, as Americans must be, of the vast differences in the attitudes of different families, in their structures, in their ways of life. The sophisticated among us may take this into account—but we all know it is an incredibly complex problem to decide just how to take this into account. Are we turning our poor into middle-class Protestants? Do they want to be so turned? Is this the only way to solve their problems? Is there another route? But these are the questions of the sophisticated. Most of our social workers, we must realize, react with distaste to different standards, norms, values, and behaviors, the same distaste that the self-assured French social worker would probably feel when confronted with the incomprehensible foreigner. . . .

We cannot adopt, to the same degree that other nations can, the principles of compulsion and national uniformity, because the standards which we would make uniform do not as a matter of fact evoke the same general degree of acceptance and commitment that they do in other nations, with a narrower ethnic and racial base. In this country, all these groups have met a remarkable degree of official indifference to the pursuit of their own ways, the creation of their own social institutions, their own schools, their own political movements. The standards of the white Protestants, if they become law and practice, are inhumane or inadequate or ineffective for large parts of our population. And yet practice and law must assume something.

Are children to be held responsible for their parents? Are men to be held responsible for their children? Should effort be rewarded? Must men be motivated to work by the threat of poverty? I would argue that however we answer these questions, on one side or the other, they are much easier to answer in Sweden or Germany or England than in the United States simply because of the greater cultural and ethnic uniformity in those countries.

The Problem of Bureaucracies

I would raise finally another dimension which distinguishes us from the other developed nations. I think we must consider seriously the nature of American bureaucracies. Again, one key fact will suggest to us how significant this problem is. One of the most characteristic programs we have seen proposed in the Community Action Programs to fight poverty consists of efforts to increase pressure on government bureaucracies. We are all acquainted with such programs; they organize the impoverished community to press its demands upon the schools, the housing inspection services, the police, and so on. The assumptions behind such programs, developed by sociologists and social workers, are also clear. Government services respond to pressure. They are better in middle-class areas than working-class areas in part because the pressure there is greater. They can be made responsive to the poor and their needs and demands if the poor organize and put pressure on them. I would now like to suggest, again from the perspective of northwestern Europe, how astonishing such programs are. There, it is assumed that if one wishes to improve education, or the organization of the labor market, or police work, one does something political or legislative or administrative which leads to new forms of organization and new and expanded programs. We do this too, of course, but our more sophisticated social workers and sociologists see little gain from such efforts. They suggest that government funds should go to set up organizations that counterattack other major government efforts, that the best way to improve services is by attack from the outside, rather than by reform from the inside. When local government protests that federal money is used to attack it and its services, the federal administrator will have to explain, but that is the only way to get you to do your job.

I am not sure just how successful this new combative approach will be. I think in the end the art of using government funds for what we may call controlled revolution will turn out to be too demanding for both federal administrators and local community action organizers. But leaving aside the effectiveness of this technique, what do we learn from the fact that it is so popular here, and almost unknown, as far as I know, in the welfare states of Europe? We may conclude that our bureaucracies are more difficult to adapt to new needs than those in Europe, and that reformers, progressive administrators, and clients alike despair of making any great impact upon them, and so prefer to set up competing organizations, or to attack them to force them into change. This is true even where much of the power is in the hands of the reformers, the liberal administrators, and the client population—as it is in New York City. We may speculate upon the causes of this presumed rigidity and inadequacy. I would suggest that one of the underlying causes is the ethnic and racial difference that inevitably develops between bureaucracies and client groups in a nation characterized by a history of waves of immigration into our large cities, each of which takes over the jobs of the bureaucracy at different times. The older group, confronting the newer group, is unable to effectively understand and respond to their problems.

On occasion we do become one nation—in wartime, when there is need for everyone's labor, and we perform wonders that even advanced welfare states come to study. But the pressure on us is rarely that great. We do not run a tight ship. We are not short of labor. We must not compete with dangerous competitors for overseas markets to live. And in the absence of such pressures, and in the presence of ethnic and racial diversity, we find it difficult to draw forth from our government servants and social workers the degree of human effort and empathy and compassion that is necessary to really transform and change people. This is why the simple elaboration of bureaucracies with more funds evokes such little enthusiasm from sociologists and social critics. Economists, I believe, must assume that the reallocation of resources to certain services will improve them. While those who administer these services can never admit it, they are not so sure that the provision of more personnel and resources will improve results.

I believe we must take the measure of our strengths and weaknesses more adequately than we have done, and adapt our efforts to them.

Conclusions

I have tried to suggest some of the major questions we must look into as we try to improve our poverty programs, and have argued that we cannot probably do as much through centrally administered state social services as Europe has done. But I think we can do other things better. Much more of our achievement has come from private, group, voluntary, and nonstate effort—whether in the form of private business for profit or voluntary efforts for social ends. We are remarkably efficient—as Eric Hoffer and others have pointed out—in organizing work. The WPA in the Great Depression and the war effort in the Second World War both stand as examples of the rapid employment in efficient work of millions of workers with relatively little investment in special work education, counselling, social services, and the like. Our entrepreneurs are efficient and ingenious in the development of new kinds of services. Private groups of all kinds—religious, political, trade union, charitable—have been ingenious in designing programs to help their own members and others. The returns from such efforts, where they can be counted, are often as surprising as the weakness of official and governmental efforts is depressing.

For example, of all the new types of social programs that have been started in recent years, volunteer tutoring programs show perhaps the highest degree of success in relation to effort. For another example, consider the Freedom Schools and Community Centers that are being planted in the Deep South. I cannot conceive of official governmental efforts that could be anywhere as effective. The really creative part of our consideration of the problem of poverty must be to learn how to stimulate such efforts, how to support them, how to put government funds into them without blighting them. And since the problem of poverty is so largely concentrated in our Negro population, I am convinced that much of the effort and manpower involved in overcoming it must come from the Negro community, even if the funds that power it come from the Federal government. It is axiomatic to me that Negro organizations—whether they educate, train, advise, employ, organize, or what not—can potentially do far, far more with Negro clients than can governmental organizations. It is in the stimulation of individual and group effort—whether motivated by profit, charity, by group pride, or by the desire for individual fulfillment or salvation, that I see the most productive courses we can follow to overcome poverty.

Warren C. Haggstrom
Psychologist

On the average, the poor in the United States have bad reputations. They are regarded as responsible for much physical aggression and destruction of property; their support is alleged to be a heavy burden on the rest of the community; and they are said not even to try very hard to meet community standards of behavior or to be self-supporting. Poverty, it is said, is little enough punishment for people so inferior and so lacking in virtue.

Roughly speaking, these common opinions about the poor have some accuracy. Socially notorious varieties of deviancy and dependency do flourish in areas of poverty to a greater extent than in the remainder of our society. The middle classes, of course, have their own faults, which are sometimes perceptively observed and described by the poor. The relatively prosperous tend to use their verbal facility to conceal aspects of social reality from themselves and tend to use word-magic to make themselves comfortable about being in their generally undeserved positions of affluence, positions in which they manage to obtain the most pay and security for doing easy and interesting kinds of work.

Since the United States is a middle class society, those who emphasize the bad reputations of the poor are regarded as hard-headed realists, while those who stress the phoniness of the middle classes are considered rather extreme and overly suspicious. When a social worker reports that the lower classes tend in the direction of schizophrenia and character disorders, he is viewed as having made a sober report of the existing state of affairs. Or when a social scientist discovers that the poor are unsocialized, childlike, occupy an early category in *his* category system of degrees of socialization, his discovery is treated as an important basis for further scientific work. But suppose that a leader of the poor announces that social workers tend to be "phonies" and "half-queer" as well, or suggests in his own language that social scientists are usually fuzzy-minded and socially irrelevant. This invidious description is not seen as a suitable hypothesis for investigation and research; it is rather said (without benefit of evidence) to be a symptom of the ignorance or of the personal or political needs of the person making the statement.

We cannot, of course, simply shed the presuppositions which at-

From "The Power of the Poor," reprinted with permission of The Free Press of Glencoe from *Mental Health of the Poor* by F. Riessman, *et al.*, eds., pp. 205–221. © 1964 by The Free Press of Glencoe.

Warren C. Haggstrom is Assistant Professor of Social Work, Syracuse University.

tach to our social positions, and those of us who see the poor from above are likely not to have viewed them from the most flattering perspective. But let us, in the following discussion, attempt to be critical and scientific by orienting ourselves to reasons and evidence rather than to common sense conceptual refinements of our current prejudices. We will first analyze a popular contemporary account of the psychology of poverty, and then advance a different orientation as a more precise explanation for available data.

Psychological Characteristics of the Poor

Social scientists have arrived at a rough consensus about the modal personality in neighborhoods of poverty:

(1) The poor tend to have a keen sense of the personal and the concrete; their interest typically is restricted to the self, the family, and the neighborhood. There is a particular stress on the intimate, the sensory, the detailed, the personal. Not struggling to escape their circumstances, the poor often regard their ordinary lives as being of much intrinsic interest. This is related to their primary concern with the problem of survival rather than with the problem of moving up in society, and to the value which they attach to skills needed in coping with deprivation and uncertainty as distinguished from skills required to make progress. It has frequently been reported that persons in areas of poverty appear to be apathetic, to have little motivation, to be unable to cooperate with each other in the solution of problems which they regard as important, and to lack occupational and verbal skills and leadership traits; and are characterized by parochialism, nostalgic romanticism, and prescientific conceptions of the natural and social orders. Instead of having love for one another as fellow human beings, they achieve positive mutual attitudes through seeing themselves as all in the same boat together.

(2) Caught in the present, the poor do not plan very much. They meet their troubles and take their pleasures on a moment-to-moment basis; their schemes are short-term. Their time perspective is foreshortened by their belief that it is futile to think of the future. Thus, when the poor use conventional words to refer to the future, those words tend to be empty of real meaning. They have little sense of the past and they go forward, but not forward to any preconceived place. Their pleasures and rewards are sought in the present; they find it difficult to delay gratification, to postpone satisfaction.

(3) There is much egoism, envy, and hostility toward those who prosper. There is a feeling of being exploited. There are many negative attitudes and few positive ones. The unity of the poor comes about through suspicion of and resentment toward outsiders, through opposition to com-

mon enemies and hostility to powerful groups. Disillusion about the possibility of advancement stems from a victim complex in relation to the powerful. There is a sense of inability to affect what will happen, a lack of conviction that it is within their power to affect their circumstances. The outside world cannot be trusted; it must be defended against. Outsiders and the outside are seen as risky, likely to injure you when you least expect it. Pessimism and fatalism about being able to affect one's own situation stems from a feeling of being victimized by superordinate, capricious, and malevolent natural and social forces. Their lives appear to them to be fixed by the immutable forces of fate, luck, and chance. While well-to-do people tend to attribute causality to inner forces, the poor tend to make external attributes of causality, seeing themselves as subject to external and arbitrary forces and pressures.

The Social Problem of Poverty
and Its Natural Solution

The poor, in short, are commonly seen as apathetic, childlike, not very competent, and hostile-dependent. Other research, emphasized in the past few years, has pointed out the extent to which the poor tend to occupy specific social categories (minority racial and ethnic groups, the elderly, ADC families, and the like), as well as the continuing large proportion of the population who have low incomes even in such an affluent society as the United States. It has been natural to get concerned about a large proportion of the population, the members of which have behavior patterns and psychological characteristics that tend to place them in opposition to or dependence on the remainder of the community.

Poverty has therefore again become a publicly recognized social problem in the United States. The general perception of a social problem leads to a search for its solution. Since a lack of money is the most universal characteristic of poverty, and since a general increase of income for some social groups would automatically abolish poverty, it seems clear to many persons that certain known steps are suitable to end poverty in the United States. Their view is that public policies should be developed and implemented that emphasize provision of jobs, increased access to education that leads to jobs, and higher minimum wage levels and welfare payments. Scientists, according to this view, can contribute by learning how to measure poverty with greater accuracy and by studying its adverse psychological and other consequences, and they should seek to understand how these consequences might be controlled.

In this natural line of reasoning it is assumed rather than demonstrated that the major problem of the poor is poverty, a lack of money. But this assumption is essential to the associated recommendations for scientific work and social policy. It may be well, therefore, to inquire in a more searching fashion whether the problems of the poor primarily result from a lack of money.

There are a number of phenomena which one could hardly anticipate on the basis of such an assumption:

(1) A given level of real income has various consequences depending upon the circumstances in which a person receives the income.

Among the poor, there are many subgroups, the members of which do not display the presumed psychological consequences of poverty. These include most of that portion of the leadership of the poor which is itself poor, those low income families with high educational aspirations for their children, low income members of religious groups such as the Hutterites, university student families with little income, and the like. In the past, of course, members of the lower middle class have survived on real incomes below those received today by comparable public welfare families—and without losing their capacity to struggle in the pursuit of distant ends. Many from the intelligentsia today in such countries as India and Japan have incomes that, in the United States, would place them with the poor. They may differ from educated Americans in personality characteristics, but they do not have the alleged psychology of poverty either.

(2) Increases in income often do not lead to a diminution of the expected psychological consequences of poverty.

For example, the rise in real per capita public welfare expenditures in the United States have not had a demonstrated effect on the psychological functioning of welfare recipients.

(3) Differences in income between otherwise comparable groups of poor do not appear to be accompanied by differences in psychological functioning.

For example, states vary greatly in the size of their payments to comparable welfare recipient families. Comparable families appear to resemble one another in psychological orientation regardless of relatively major differences in their incomes.

(4) When income remains constant, but persons in a neighborhood of poverty become involved in successful social action on important issues, in their own behalf, their psychological orientation does extend over a greater period of time, their feeling of helplessness does lessen, their skills and activities do gradually change.

For example, no one could have predicted on the basis of articles in the relevant scholarly journals that lowly Negroes from areas of poverty would, with some help, begin to organize with such effect that they would carry timid and ultra-conventional members of the Negro middle classes along with them into a militant struggle for freedom. It has also been reported that many "lower class" Negroes who have become part of the Muslim movement have had their lives transformed in the direction of greater order and achievement.

During this past summer I gathered some data concerning The Woodlawn Organization (TWO), a primarily "lower class," predominantly Negro organization which was initiated about two years ago in Chicago with the assistance of Saul Alinsky and the Industrial Areas Foundation. The poor constitute the bulk of active members, and are an important segment of the leadership of this community organization, which has already demonstrated its effectiveness and power. For example, TWO has delivered a majority of the votes from a Negro area to elect a white alderman who takes a strong civil rights position; the unsuccessful opponent was a Negro from the regular political organization. It has been able to secure its own conditions for implementation of an urban renewal development proposed by the University of Chicago for part of the Woodlawn area. TWO has carried out rent strikes and has taken other successful actions against owners of dilapidated slum buildings; it has organized picketing of stores that sell merchandise to people who cannot afford the high interest on installments; it has organized successful city hall demonstrations of more than a thousand persons. Over this period of widespread involvement, the poor appear to have gradually acquired skills of organization, longer range planning, and other qualities contrary to those which reputedly characterize areas of poverty. I observed a similar process occurring in "lower class" white neighborhoods in Northwest Chicago, where the Northwest Community Organization, another Alinsky associated enterprise, has been in existence for less than two years.

(5) When members of some groups lose or give up their wealth, they do not thereby acquire the psychology of poverty.

One has only to consider the vows of poverty taken by members of some religious orders to illustrate this assertion.

Since the psychology of poverty obtains only under specific and describable circumstances, one cannot therefore use poverty as an explanation for these psychological characteristics which often are associated with poverty. . . .

The Self-Help Doctrine and Its
Consequences for Dependent Persons

In rapidly industrializing societies in which there are many opportunities for individual advancement there typically arises some form of the doctrine of self-help. The common core of self-help views can be stated as follows: A person is good to the extent to which he has assumed responsibility for and accomplished the realization of his potentialities for maximum use of his native capacities in a long, sustained, and arduous effort to reach a distant legitimate goal. With enough effort any normal person can attain such goals; no special ability is needed. . . .

According to the doctrine of self-help, *anyone*, given enough time and enough effort, could achieve success. Thus, to be poor could have either of two meanings. On the one hand, poverty was regarded as the original accompaniment of the highest development of character, the struggling poor who were later to become successful were most worthy of respect. On the other hand, poverty indefinitely prolonged might mean a character defect, a lack of will power. Poverty, therefore, was ambiguous; from it alone one could reach no conclusion about virtue. However, an economy with limited opportunities for success plus the belief in equal opportunity for success according to merit made inevitable an assault on the self-esteem of the permanently unsuccessful. . . .

The financially self-responsible person is assumed to be responsible also in other areas of his life. For this reason dependency can concern any area of superordinate-subordinate relationship, and there is always some stigma associated with any dependency relationship, even though there is often pleasure in divesting oneself of the burden of self-responsibility. Even the relationship of citizen to expert can be distasteful since it makes the citizen intellectually dependent on the expert.

The sharpest psychological impact of dependency has occurred where it is officially defined and therefore clearly perceived and sanctioned by the community. However, most dependency is not so explicitly defined; most of the poor are not "on welfare." Even so, the poor are generally perceived, however unclearly, as having failed, and this perception has hardened the community against them. In the latter case, the doctrine of self-help has intensified the feelings for hopelessness among the poor.

The extent of self-support is only one measure of the extent of dependency, a measure stressed only in connection with the doctrine of self-help. More generally, dependency is the placement of one's destiny in other hands. It is therefore especially characteristic of the areas of poverty, but also characterizes many other aspects of society, including the low echelons of large organizations, organization men at any echelon, and so forth. In a general sense dependency is also destructive, but more subtly so. If extent of self-realization is a measure of personality development, then dependency, which erodes self-realization with the loss of self-responsibility, is a measure of personality inadequacy. If the human personality develops as a decision process through self-responsible choices, then the taking away of self-responsible choices through assuming the subordinate position in a dependency relationship necessarily destroys personality.

The Social Situation of the Poor

Most of the poor are heavily dependent on outside forces. In many places, a poor person is much more likely to be subject to police interrogation and search, or to public identification as the object of police activity, than is a member of a middle class family. Urban renewal programs periodically disrupt the neighborhoods of poverty, scattering the families in several directions in accordance with standards which the poor do not understand or support. Schools function impervious to the concerns of the low income families whose children attend, or else schools may seek themselves to "lead" in the areas of poverty in which they are located, that is, they seek to impose school standards and definitions on the neighborhoods. Settlement houses run recreation programs that meet their own traditional criteria, but neighborhood youth often do not understand these criteria, often cannot engage in accustomed and legal modes of behavior and still participate in settlement house activities, often, involuntarily and without understanding, have to disperse friendship groups in order to participate in a recreation program.

Many families, having bought more than they can afford, especially through high-interest installment financing, have no way to know whether or when their furniture will be repossessed or their check garnisheed. Medical and psychiatric care are inadequate, inadequately understood, and uncertainly available, especially to the poor who do not have connections through welfare. The securing of general relief or categorical assistance is a humiliating experience at best for people imbued with self-help ideas, but the deliberate rudeness intended to discourage as many applicants as possible, the complex agency rules which are not so much bases for action as after-the-fact rationales to provide support for decisions already made, and the subjective and unpredictable decisions of social workers representing agencies to the poor, all combine to place the economic foundation of many families at the mercy of completely incomprehensible forces.

The poor who seek employment must find it in a dwindling supply of jobs available to unskilled and semiskilled persons (including domestics), often seasonal or temporary work. In addition, the landlords of the poor are frequently discourteous, seldom inclined to make adequate repairs on their buildings, and likely to blame the tenants for the condition of the ancient and crumbling structures for which high rents are charged.

In other words the poor, by virtue of their situation, tend to be more dependent than other groups on a larger number of powerful persons and organizations, which are often very unclear about the bases for their actions and unpredictable in their decisions, and which further render the poor helpless by condescending or hostile attitudes, explicit verbal communications which state or imply the inferiority of the poor, and callousness or actual harassment. If we divide the powerful persons affecting the poor into two groups, the benevolent in intention on the one hand, and the callous or punitive on the other, we will find that the majority of both type of power figure treat the poor as inferior and reach down to relate to them.

The situation of poverty, then, is the situation of enforced dependency, giving the poor very little scope for *action,* in the sense of behavior under their own control which is central to their needs and values. This scope for action is supposed to be furnished by society to any person in either of two ways. First, confidence, hope, motivation, and skills for action may be provided through childhood socialization and continue as a relatively permanent aspect of the personality. Second, social positions are provided which make it easy for their occupants to act, which make it possible for decisions of their occupants to be implemented in their futures. Middle class socialization and middle class social positions customarily both provide bases for effective action; lower class socialization and lower class social positions usually both fail to make it possible for the poor to act.

Thus, the dependency of the poor is not primarily a neurotic need to occupy dependency positions in social relationships, but rather it results from a deprivation of those minimal social resources, at every period of their lives, which the poor need and therefore must seek. The poor are not victims of the social system in the sense that "organization men" are victims. They are rather, as Michael Harrington has emphasized, the *other* America, outsiders to the major society. In consequence, members of the majority society are usually outsiders to the poor.

The initial dependency and its consequences are reinforced by the hardening of a consensus in the majority community about the nature of the poor, stabilization of the patterns of behavior in areas of poverty, and partial internalization of ideas and patterns of behavior in the children who grow up in both communities. Thus, the positions of poor persons in relationship to superordinate forces are expressions of two communities, a superior and powerful community and an inferior and weaker community; two communities with institutionalized ways of living which prop up the superordinate position of the one in relation to the other.

People isolate and segregate those they fear and pity. The stronger of the two communities has traditionally acted to alleviate the results perceived to be undesirable without changing the relationship of the two communities or ending the division into two communities. Since persons designing and implementing such programs did not consider the consequences of the division for their aims, they were able to maintain an intention to bring the poor into their society. The recommendations have been for improved law enforcement; public welfare; public housing; social settlements; higher horizons educational programs; social work with "hard core" families; urban renewal, clean-up, paint-up, and fix-up programs; block and neighborhood organizations; and the like. All these plans and programs have usually shared two characteristics: (1) they are initiated and supported from outside the neighborhoods of poverty and imposed on the poor; and (2) they fail to make any lasting positive impact on neighborhoods of poverty. That is, although a few persons and families become affluent and leave the neighborhoods, the majority remain poor and continue in an atmosphere of apathy, disorganization, and hostility, toward the programs designed to rescue them. These programs, presupposing the inferiority of the people in the area, perpetuate and exacerbate the inequality. Definitions of the poor are carried by the institutionalized helping hands. Insofar as these agencies have any *social* impact, the definitions embedded in them become self-fulfilling. But, although the powerful external social agencies—powerful in relation to the poor—are not very effective in carrying out their official tasks in areas of poverty, they do enable the stronger community to believe that something is being done about the social problem of poverty, reducing guilt and shame to such an extent that there remains little motivation to develop some effective means to bring the poor into the larger society.

On the basis of this sketch of the dynamics of the situation of the poor, the following classification can be made of the sources of the "psychology of poverty."

(a) In any modern industrial society the overall amount of power of the society tends constantly to increase, although the rate of increase may vary. Although everyone in the society may secure ownership of additional *material* goods as a result of technological progress, the additional *power* tends to be secured only by those persons and social systems with preexistent power. The poor boy with strong internalized drives and skills for success and the large corporation with effective control over technological advances in its field both illustrate the tendency for socially created power to attract to itself additional power. But the poor most often have neither the power created through childhood socialization nor that to be secured through attachment to a strong social system in which they have influence. In some countries, the population is predominantly poor, and this populace may have some power through the political process. But, in the United States the poor are an unorganized or ineffectively organized minority, unable even to exert influence in the political sphere. Thus, increments in power tend to attach to those with power, and the balance of power in a country such as the United States tends naturally to tilt against the poor.

(b) The fact of being powerless, but with needs that must be met, leads the poor to be dependent on the organizations, persons, and institutions which can meet these needs. The situation of dependency and powerlessness through internal personality characteristics as well as through social position leads to apathy, hopelessness, conviction of the inability to act successfully, failure to develop skills, and so on.

(c) As a consequence of the self-help doctrine, this "psychology of poverty" arouses the anger of the affluent toward the poor. Thus, the affluent can avoid the necessity to alter the social situation of the poor by assuming that the poor are bad and deserve their situation. This additional meaning of poverty makes rigid the dependency aspects of the social situation of the poor, and, to some extent, the poor accept the prevalent view of themselves. However, since the poor are not together in an unambiguously clear social category, they, at the same time, may reject being placed in such a category subject to the assumption of their dependency and inferiority. For example, persons eligible to live in public housing are not affected only by the convenience, space, and other physical characteristics of their living quarters. A large proportion seem to prefer dilapidated private housing operated by an indifferent landlord to better maintained, less crowded, less expensive quarters in a public housing project in which the management is concerned with tenant needs. The meaning of living in such a project may offset the superiority of the physical living arrangements.

(d) Over time the dependency relationship of the poor becomes institutionalized and habits, traditions, and organizations arise in both the affluent community and in the neighborhoods of poverty, maintaining the relationship between them. The poor react in part to the institutionalization itself. For example, "lower class" delinquency does not only stem from the fact that the poor have few and drab job opportunities. There is also the perception that the conforming poor tend to remain indefinitely in low social positions as well as the angry rejection by the adolescent poor of attempts, through law enforcement and social agencies, to control and manipulate them without altering their situation.

Consequences of this social process for the poor have been indicated at several points in the preceding discussion; we will only briefly recapitulate some of them here.

First, people tend either to retreat from or to attack forces controlling their lives which they cannot affect and which are not inescapable. For this reason the poor typically stand aloof from settlement houses, get minimally involved with social workers, drop out of school. Only forces too omnipresent to be escaped may ensure normative affiliation through identification with aggressors. It is easy to see the poor as paranoid since they are so often hostile to and suspicious of powerful objects which they may perceive in a distorted fashion. However, paranoia presumably requires origins in early childhood, while the hostility and suspicion of the poor naturally arise from their social position and their necessarily oversimplified and naturally personified perceptions of it.

Second, with less of their selves bound up in their self-conceptions than is the case with other groups, the poor do not entirely accept these definitions of themselves, but protect themselves by various psychological strategies from fully accepting the implications of their situation. The impact of the definitions then is primarily indirect; the definitions have consequences by creating the situation of the poor through the meaning of poverty to those who possess power. The situation gives rise to the typical absence of that hope which is associated with action and which gives salience to intentions and attitudes. Thus, the poor frequently verbalize middle-class values without practicing them. Their verbalizations are useful in protecting their self-conceptions and in dealing with the affluent rather than in any pronounced relationship to non-verbal behavior. This does not imply deliberate falsification; a poor person may have the necessary sincerity, intention, and skill to embark on a course of action but there is so much unconscious uncertainty about achieving psychological returns through success that the action may never be seriously attempted. As has been discovered in social surveys, the poor may not only pay lip service to middle-class notions, but may, for similar reasons, say to any powerful person what they believe he wants to hear. That is, much of the behavior of the poor does not relate primarily to their own basic values, beliefs and perceptions held by others about the poor. The poor are normally involved in partly involuntary self-diminution; their behavior may therefore be remarkably transformed when, as has happened through social action, they begin to acquire a sense of power, of ability to realize *their* aspirations. Thus, the so-called differential values of the poor, which are ill-defined at best, are more nearly comprehensible as the psychological consequences of a long continued situation of perceived powerlessness in contemporary industrial society. They become a subculture to the extent that the traditions, orientations, and habits of dependency become internalized.

Third, the situation of the poor, the inability of the poor to act in their own behalf, creates a less complex personality structure for them than is the case with affluent persons with more linguistic skills. This does not necessarily mean that the poor have less effective personalities, or are unsocialized in comparison, since the personalities of more highly educated persons are often partly constituted by social elaborated fantasies which conceal reality and rationalize avoidance of problem solving.

Fourth, awareness of their common fate typically leads the poor to engage in mutual aid activities, activities which, in spite of involving only very minor skills, are precursors to the joint social action which develops naturally as the poor acquire organizational skills and confidence in using them.

Fifth, because of the social situation of the poor and the fact that the majority society has relatively little normative basis for social control in areas of poverty, these areas are often characterized by high rates of publicly discernible types of deviance: juvenile delinquency, school dropouts, alcoholism, illegitimacy, mother-centered families, and the like.

Finally, there are differential consequences of institutionalized, uncompensated powerlessness for the poor who have various social positions within areas of poverty. For example, because of the greater expectation for men to be powerful and to be sources of power, the consequences of powerlessness for "lower class" men is usually greater than that for women.

All of this suggests that the problems of the poor are not so much of poverty as of a particularly difficult variety of situational dependency, a helplessness to affect many important social factors in their lives, the functioning or purpose of which they do not understand, and which are essentially unpredictable to them.

Not Enough Money versus Situational Dependency

With increased money the poor could at least be better able to cope with such forces, could be less dependent on some. What, then, is the relationship between the poverty of the poor and their situational dependency?

Money is a generalized source of power over people through a right to control over goods and services. As such, money is one of many kinds of power. Poverty, therefore, is one of many kinds of powerlessness, of being subject to one's social situation instead of being able to affect it through action, that is, through behavior which flows from decisions and plans. Since there are several varieties of generalized power, an absence of money is often replaceable *insofar as the psychological reactions to powerlessness are concerned.* An American Indian who lives in poverty may have considerable influence through authority relationships traditional in his culture. Members of religious orders who have taken vows of poverty remain able to exercise influence through their order and through relationships of interdependence with colleagues. The college student with a very low income has influence through the expectations of his future social position. When the poor engage in successful social action they gain power, even when their incomes remain unchanged.

In other words, when social scientists have reported on the psychological consequences of poverty it seems reasonable to believe that they have described the psychological consequences of powerlessness. And many persons without money have, or get, other varieties of power, or else identify with powerful persons or groups and therefore fail to exhibit these consequences. Even the poor do not react entirely on the basis of the social definition of them. There are counter institutions and traditions (churches, unions, and clubs) which deflect the impact of the majority definition. Primary groups (family and peer) also mediate and modify the community definitions they transmit. The behavior of the poor may not, therefore, reflect their self-conceptions; we should not suppose that the poor feel as would middle class persons in their situations, or as their behavior suggests they feel. This very resistance of the poor makes it possible to attempt the otherwise herculean task of trying to get the major society to alter its relationship to poverty by helping the poor themselves to build a backfire, to become strong and effective enough to challenge the invidious definitions that have been made of them.

Human personality is a process of decisions and actions on the basis of decisions. One becomes fully human only through acting in important areas of one's life. All social arrangements which take responsibility out of the hands of the poor, which make decisions and action more difficult or operative over a more restricted area, feed the psychology of powerlessness which is so widely (and correctly) regarded as undesirable. For example, it is often noted that the poor lack a time perspective. But only through action (important decisions and behavior on their basis) does one acquire a history and, with the history, a practical concern with the future.

What consequences does the social situation of the poor have for programs to help the poor? We will next consider some general answers to this question.

Redefining the Social Situation of the Poor

We can reject two possible alternatives.

First, the solution most frequently suggested is to help the poor secure more money without otherwise changing present power relationships. This appears to implement the idea of equality while avoiding any necessary threat to established centers of power. But, since the consequences are related to *powerlessness*, not to the absolute supply of money available to the poor, and since *the amount of power purchasable with a given supply of money decreases as a society acquires a larger supply of goods and services,* the solution of raising the incomes of the poor is likely, unless accompanied by other measures, to be ineffective in an affluent society. Where the poor live in serious deprivation of goods and services, an increase in the supply of those goods and services would be an important source of power, that is, of access to resources which satisfy crucial needs. However, when the poor do not live in actual deprivation, increases in money make relatively little impact on the dependency relationships in which they are entangled. The opportunity to participate in *interdependent* relationships, as a *member* of the majority society, requires an increase in *power*.

Second, the *self-help* doctrine is normally related to conventional criteria of success, and persons who have not met these conventional criteria therefore are threatened with feelings of guilt and shame. One theoretically possible solution would seem to involve redefinition of success, allowing social support to lives which are now viewed as failures. This, however, presupposes an ability to meet some alternative criteria of success through action, a possible solution for philosophers, poets, or beatniks, but not now generally possible for the poor. It may, however, be that the meaning of the self-help doctrine could be adequately extended to reward the social action of the poor who can act successfully through their own organizations.

Along these lines the criteria for an effective solution are reasonably clear. In order to reduce poverty-related psychological and social problems in the United States, the major community will have to change in relationship to neighborhoods of poverty in such fashion that families in the neighborhoods have a greater stake in the broader society and can more successfully participate in the decision-making process of the surrounding community.

It is frequently said that we must provide opportunities for the poor. To render more than lip service to this objective demands more power and more skill and more knowledge than we now possess for the bureaucratic provision of such opportunities. For example, there are a finite number of jobs available, fewer than the number of people looking for work. There are severe limits to the extent to which the adult poor can be trained for existing openings. A large proportion of the poor have jobs which do not remove them from the ranks of the powerless. Any great shift in opportunities made available to the poor within the structure of the majority community will threaten more powerful groups with vested interests in those limited opportunities, and the proponents of creating opportunities for the poor cannot themselves affect the political or economic process enough to implement their good intentions.

It is important to develop opportunities in sensitive relation to the perception by the poor of their own needs. When this is not done, the poor are not likely to be able to use efficiently the opportunities created for them. And, most central of all, rather than to provide opportunities for the "lower class," the poor must as a group be helped to secure opportunities for themselves. Only then will motivation be released that is now locked in the silent and usually successful battle of the neighborhoods of poverty to maintain themselves in an alien social world. This motivation which will enable them to enter the majority society and make it as nurturant of them as it is at present of the more prosperous population.

The involvement of the poor in successful and significant social action provides both immediate and compelling psychological returns and also the possibility of initiative to help the bureaucratic organizations related to the poor to fulfill their officially stated purposes. The institutions of the major community can be forced to establish relationships of interdependence, not of dependence, with the poor; professionals can help by accepting professional roles as employees of the organizations of the poor.

In our society inner worth as expressed in action, striving, the struggle is held eventually to result in attainment of aspirations. If one is not successful, one is viewed as worthwhile so long, and only so long, as one struggles. The poor tend to be regarded as failures and not struggling, and hence as worthless. This perception of worthlessness is incorporated in the conception which others have of the poor and also, to some extent, in the conceptions which the poor have of themselves. One way in which the poor can remedy the psychological consequences of their powerlessness and of the image of the poor as worthless is for them to undertake social action that redefines them as potentially worthwhile and individually more powerful. To be effective, such social action should have the following characteristics:

1. the poor see themselves as the source of the action;
2. the action affects in major ways the preconceptions, values, or interests of institutions and persons defining the poor;
3. the action demands much in effort and skill or in other ways becomes salient to major areas of the personalities of the poor;
4. the action ends in success; and
5. the successful self-originated important action increases the force and number of symbolic or nonsymbolic communications of the potential worth or individual power of individuals who are poor.

The result of social action of this kind is a concurrent change in the view which the poor have of themselves and in the view of the poor by the outside world. There is a softening of the destructive social reality and immediate psychological returns to the poor, although not without hostile reactions from advantaged persons and organizations with known or hidden vested interests in maintenance of the areas of poverty.

The only initial additional resources which a community should provide to neighborhoods of poverty should be on a temporary basis: organizers who will enable the neighborhoods quickly to create powerful, independent, democratic organizations of the poor. These organizations will themselves then seek from the rest of the community resources necessary to the neighborhoods for the solution of the problems they perceive. Agencies for the provision of training and education and opportunities can be developed under the control of the neighborhoods of poverty, thereby ensuring that the poor are in interdependent rather than dependent positions in relation to the agencies. This would meet the professed objectives of most communities since it would effectively motivate the poor to maximum use of opportunities, since the requirements of professional practice will ensure the quality of services rendered, and since the communities state their intention not to allow their help to become an instrument of domination.

The comment that "We know the needs of the poor" is accurate in a very general sense. But there is a great distance between this observation and a knowledge of how, in practice, those needs can be met. If a community is not merely giving lip service to meeting them, if a community wants to be effective as well as to have good intentions, then the way of meeting needs must be appropriate to the personal and social characteristics of those being helped. In this case, effectiveness requires that the only *unilateral* additional help be given at the outset and in the form of temporary assistance in the creation of democratic and powerful organizations of the poor. Through such organizations, the poor will then negotiate with outsiders for resources and opportunities without having to submit to concurrent control from outside. The outcome will be maximal motivation to take advantage of resources and opportunities which are sensitively tailored to their needs.

Part two
Facts

4
Counting Up the Poor

The United States spends more money than any other nation in the world upon statistical investigations, yet we know less about the poverty of the people than almost any other great nation of the Western World.
—Robert Hunter (1904)

Our President is now focusing attention on poverty in the United States. But unfortunately we are ill prepared to act because we have been out of touch ... All we have is a handful of crude data, mostly on family income, and they tell us very little.
—Theodore W. Schultz (1964)

The ruminations of philosophers and poets provide insights into the nature of poverty; scientific understanding, however, can come only through measurement. "In this life," thunders schoolmaster Thomas Grad-grind in Dickens' novel *Hard Times*, "we want nothing but Facts sir; nothing but Facts." Statistics are dull and often wrong; but they are necessary if scholars are to go beyond value judgments and impressionistic appraisals in their thinking about poverty.

The selections in this chapter depict the problems of definition and measurement of poverty. No hard and fast line separates the poor from the rich, just as no line separates the sick from the well, the happy from the depressed, or the sensitive from the vulgar. Poverty, like other conditions of man, can best be described as a continuum rather than a point.

An arbitrary poverty line must be drawn if it is to be measured, but where and how? A student of poverty could take a vote as Gallup has done and establish the poverty line by consensus. On this basis, in 1964 the poverty line was set at $3,800 for a family of four. Note, however, that the line was set well below this amount by the bottom income groups and well above it by those nearer the top. In any consensus, the views of the middle class would probably prevail—as perhaps they do anyway.

The poverty line has also been established on the basis of the judgments of a panel of experts. They defined the contents of a minimum budget, which was then priced. Families were called poor if their incomes were below the cost of this budget. Even this procedure has many short-comings, some of which are discussed in the excerpts from the Council of Economic Advisers and from Rose Friedman.

Early in 1964, when the current attack on poverty got under way, the nation had neither a good estimate of the poverty line nor a consensus on how to establish one. Available evidence on the cost of an economy food budget suggested that a nonfarm family of four persons might need about $3,000 in order to purchase a minimum adequate standard of living. On this basis the Council of Economic Advisers, in its 1964 *Economic Report of the President,* made a study of poverty in the United States, using families of two or more persons with cash incomes under $3 000 and persons living alone (or with nonrelatives) with incomes under $1,500. Despite many shortcomings, which are pointed out by the Council, the report contains much valuable information on the problems of measuring poverty, the number and composition of the poor, and the changes in poverty over a period of time.

The limitations of "official" estimates of poverty in the United States are explored in some detail by Rose Friedman. She makes much of the inadequacy of the budget standard, the failure to take size of family into account, and the omission of noncash income and assets from the income measure. She concludes that there are only half as many poor in the nation as the Council alleges.

In January 1965, revised estimates of poverty were issued in the *Social Security Bulletin.* They were based on an income concept which took into account size of family, age of family head, and noncash income. These revised estimates corrected some, but by no means all, of the defects in the original estimates. The results of this revision, summarized in the article by Miller, suggest that the Council of Economic Advisers used the right number but the wrong kinds of poor people in their estimates.

George Gallup
Poverty by Consensus

President Johnson's appeal for "doubling the war against poverty this year" focuses attention on the problem America's lowest income families face in trying to make ends meet.

In the Gallup Poll's latest "standard of living index," persons interviewed whose family income, before taxes, is under $3,000 a year say a family of four needs a minimum of $73 a week to get along on in their communities.

On this basis, families in this income group need a minimum of $3,800 per year just to meet the barest living expenses. Because this sum is considerably greater than the total annual gross income of these families, their plight is evident.

For nearly three decades, the Gallup Poll has maintained an index of the minimum amount which the public believes a family of four needs each week.

By their own personal appraisal of present living costs, Americans figure it costs $81 to "get along" today. In 1937—when this index was started—$30 was the average amount specified.

The Federal Government maintains its own index of consumer prices for urban families. Admittedly, however, this does not measure the standard of living, nor many other factors that go today to make up the "cost of living."

To establish the public's own "cost of living" index, the Gallup Poll has regularly asked this question of a sample of persons from all walks of life and from all areas of the country:

"What is the SMALLEST amount of money a family of four (husband, wife, and two children) needs each week to get along in this community?"

Highest Income Groups
Say $99 Is Minimum

The minimum amount of money believed to be needed to meet expenses varies by the family income bracket of persons interviewed.

From "Family of Four Needs $81 per Week to Get Along," (Princeton: American Institute of Public Opinion [The Gallup Poll], January 1, 1965). Copyright © 1965 by the American Institute of Public Opinion. Reprinted by permission. George Gallup is Director of the American Institute of Public Opinion.

Those whose annual family income, before taxes, is over $7,000 say that a minimum of $99 a week is needed for a family of four.

Here are the results by income groups, based on annual gross income:

Minimum Amount Needed for Family of Four

(Median average)

Over $10,000	$99 wk.
$7,000–$9,999	$99 wk.
$5,000–$6,999	$80 wk.
$3,000–$4,999	$78 wk.
Under $3,000	$73 wk.

Far West Is Most Expensive Area

The minimum amount needed also varies by regions of the country. The sum is highest in the Far West, where the median average was $101 a week.

Here are the results of the public's "standard of living index" by regions of the country:

Minimum Amount Needed for Family of Four

(Median average)

Far West	$101 wk.
East	$100 wk.
Midwest	$ 82 wk.
South	$ 62 wk.

Cost of Food Was $11 a Week in 1942

Another question in this survey brought out the fact that the average non-farm family spends approximately $27 a week for food, including milk. By way of comparison, the comparable sum in 1942 was $11, less than one-half the amount spent today.

The question:

"*On the average, about how much does your family spend on food, including milk, each week?*"

The amount spent for food varies by region of the country and bears a close relationship to the first question on the smallest amount of money needed for a family of four per week.

The results, by region:

Amount Spent on Food per Week

East .... $32 wk.
Midwest .... $26 wk.
South .... $24 wk.
Far West .... $29 wk.

Income is also a factor, as seen below:

Over $10,000 .... $35 wk.
$7,000–$9,999 .... $33 wk.
$5,000–$6.999 .... $28 wk.
$3,000–$4,999 .... $25 wk.
Under $3,000 .... $20 wk.

United States Department of Agriculture
Poor Man's Crumbs: A Low-Cost Diet

For more than 30 years, the Department of Agriculture has pre-pared food plans based on the National Research Council's estimates of nutritional adequacy. The following plan reflects the food-consumption patterns of families in the lowest third of the income range. This diet was estimated to cost, by 1964 prices, $5.90 per person per week.

Low-Cost Menus for One Week

SUNDAY

Orange juice
Pancakes   Syrup   Butter or margarine
Bacon

Fried chicken
Browned potatoes   Snap beans
Lettuce salad—cottage cheese dressing
Ready-to-serve rolls   Butter or margarine
Apple brown betty

From *Family Food Plans and Food Costs*, U. S. Department of Agriculture Home Economics Research Report #20, November 1962, p. 18. For a description of the methods used to compare food expenditure to income and thus establish a poverty line, see Mollie Orshansky, "Counting the Poor: Another Look at the Poverty Profile," *Social Security Bulletin* (January 1965).

Baked beans with cheese
Toasted rolls
Celery, carrot strips
Plums

MONDAY

Orange juice
Oatmeal   Sugar   Milk
Toast   Butter or margarine

Split-pea soup
Deviled egg sandwiches
Raw relishes

Meat loaf
Scalloped potatoes   Carrots
Green salad
Cornbread   Butter or margarine
Peach upside-down-cake

TUESDAY

Bananas
Ready-to-eat cereal   Sugar   Milk
Toast   Butter or margarine

Tomato juice
Peanut butter and lettuce sandwiches
Apples

Frankfurters and boiled potatoes
Coleslaw with shredded carrots
Bread   Butter or margarine
Peach upside-down cake (left from Monday)

WEDNESDAY

Farina
Sugar   Milk
Toast   Butter or margarine

Meat loaf sandwiches
(meat loaf left from Monday)
Apple-celery-raisin salad

Chili con carne with beans
Crackers
Rice   Raw carrot strips
Oranges

THURSDAY

Grapefruit and orange juice
Omelet
Toast   Butter or margarine

Corn chowder   Crackers
Spiced beet salad
Oatmeal cookies

Braised steak and onions
Boiled potatoes
Green salad
Bread   Butter or margarine
Vanilla pudding

FRIDAY

Grapefruit juice
Fried mush (farina left from Wednesday)
Syrup
Toast   Butter or margarine

Vegetable soup   Crackers
Coleslaw
Oatmeal cookies

Broiled fish
Potatoes   Spinach
Bread   Butter or margarine
Pineapple and cottage cheese salad

SATURDAY

Tomato juice
French toast   Syrup
Butter or margarine
Bacon

Cheese rarebit on toast
Green peas
Cookies

Ragout of beef
Noodles   Chopped broccoli   Celery sticks
Biscuits   Butter or margarine
Cherry crisp

NOTE: There will be milk to drink at each meal for the children, and at one meal a day for parents. Also coffee or tea as desired.

Council of Economic Advisers
What Is Poverty? Who Are the Poor?

The Nature and Extent of Poverty

Measurement of poverty is not simple, either conceptually or in practice. By the poor we mean those who are not now maintaining a decent standard of living—those whose basic needs exceed their means to satisfy them. A family's needs depend on many factors, including the size of the family, the ages of its members, the condition of their health, and their place of residence. The ability to fulfill these needs depends on current income from whatever source, past savings, ownership of a home or other asets, and ability to borrow.

Needs and resources. There is no precise way to measure the number of families who do not have the resources to provide minimum satisfaction of their own particular needs. Since needs differ from family to family, an attempt to quantify the problem must begin with some concept of average need for an average or representative family. Even for such a family, society does not have a clear and unvarying concept of an acceptable minimum. By the standards of contemporary American society most of the population of the world is poor; and most Americans were poor a century ago. But for our society today a consensus on an approximate standard can be found. One such standard is suggested by a recent study, described in a publication of the Social Security Administration, which defines a "low-cost" budget for a nonfarm family of four and finds its cost in 1962 to have been $3,955. The cost of what the study defined as an "economy-plan" budget was $3,165. Other studies have used different market baskets, many of them costing more. On balance, they provide support for using as a boundary a family whose annual money income from all sources was $3,000 (before taxes and expressed in 1962 prices). This is a weekly income of less than $60.

These budgets contemplate expenditures of one-third of the total on food, i.e., for a $3,000 annual budget for a 4-person family about $5 per person per week. Of the remaining $2,000, a conservative estimate for housing (rent or mortgage payments, utilities, and heat) would be another $800. This would leave only $1,200—less than $25 a week—for clothing, transportation, school supplies and books, home furnishings and supplies, medical care, personal care, recreation, insurance, and

From "The Problem of Poverty in America," in *Economic Report of the President, January 1964*, pp. 57–62, 64, 66–73.

everything else. Obviously it does not exaggerate the problem of poverty to regard $3,000 as the boundary.

A family's ability to meet its needs depends not only on its money income but also on its income in kind, its savings, its property, and its ability to borrow. But the detailed data (of the Bureau of the Census) available for pinpointing the origins of current poverty in the United States refer to money income. Refined analysis would vary the income cutoff by family size, age, location, and other indicators of needs and costs. This has not been possible. However, a variable income cutoff was used in the sample study of poverty in 1959 conducted at the University of Michigan Survey Research Center. This study also estimates the overall incidence of poverty at 20 percent; and its findings concerning the sources of poverty correspond closely with the results based on an analysis of Census data.

A case could be made, of course, for setting the overall income limit either higher or lower than $3,000, thereby changing the statistical measure of the size of the problem. But the analysis of the sources of poverty, and of the programs needed to cope with it, would remain substantially unchanged.

No measure of poverty as simple as the one used here, would be suitable for determining eligibility for particular benefits or participation in particular programs. Nevertheless, it provides a valid benchmark for assessing the dimensions of the task of eliminating poverty, setting the broad goals of policy, and measuring our past and future progress toward their achievement.

If it were possible to obtain estimates of total incomes—including nonmoney elements—for various types of families, those data would be preferable for the analysis which follows. The Department of Commerce does estimate total nonmoney incomes in the entire economy in such forms as the rental value of owner-occupied dwellings and food raised and consumed on farms, and allocates them to families with incomes of different size. Because of statistical difficulties, these allocations are necessarily somewhat arbitrary, and are particularly subect to error for the lower income groups. No attempt is made to allocate them by other characteristics that are meaningful for an analysis of poverty. Of course, the total of money plus nonmoney income that would correspond to the limit used here would be somewhat higher than $3,000.

The changing extent of poverty. There were 47 million families in the United States in 1962. Fully 9.3 million, or one-fifth of these families—comprising more than 30 million persons—had total money incomes below $3,000. Over 11 million of these family members were children, one-sixth of our youth. More than 1.1 million families are now raising 4 or more children on such an income. Moreover, 5.4 million families, containing more than 17 million persons, had total incomes below $2,000. More than a million children were being raised in very large families (6 or more children) with incomes of less than $2,000.

Serious poverty also exists among persons living alone or living in nonfamily units such as boardinghouses. In 1962, 45 percent of such "unrelated individuals"—5 million persons—had incomes below $1,500, and 29 percent—or more than 3 million persons—had incomes below $1,000. Thus, by the measures used here, 33 to 35 million Americans were living at or below the boundaries of poverty in 1962—nearly one-fifth of our Nation.

The substantial progress made since World War II in eliminating poverty is shown in table 1. In the decade 1947–56, when incomes were growing relatively rapidly, and unemployment was generally low, the number of poor families (with incomes below $3,000 in terms of 1962 prices) declined from 11.9 million to 9.9 million, or from 32 percent to 23 percent of all families. But in the period from 1957 through 1962, when total growth was slower and unemployment substantially higher, the number of families living in poverty fell less rapidly, to 9.3 million, or 20 percent of all families.

Table 1.—Money Income of Families, 1947 and 1950–62

Year	Median money income of all families (1962 prices)		Percent of families with money income	
	Dollars	Index, 1947—100	Less than $3,000 (1962 prices)	Less than $2,000 (1962 prices)
1947	4,117	100	32	18
1950	4,188	102	32	19
1951	4,328	105	29	17
1952	4,442	108	28	17
1953	4,809	117	26	16
1954	4,705	114	28	17
1955	5,004	122	25	15
1956	5,337	130	23	14
1957	5,333	130	23	14
1958	5,329	129	23	14
1959	5,631	137	22	13
1960	5,759	140	21	13
1961	5,820	141	21	13
1962	5,956	145	20	12

The progress made since World War II has not involved any major change in the distribution of incomes. The one-fifth of families with the highest incomes received an estimated 43 percent of total income in 1947 and 42 percent in 1962. The one-fifth of families with the lowest incomes received 5 percent of the total in 1947 and 5 percent in 1963.

Even if poverty should hereafter decline at the relatively more rapid rate of the 1947–56 period, there would still be 10 percent of the Nation's families in poverty in 1980. And, if the decline in poverty proceeded at the slower rate achieved from 1957 on, 13 percent of our families would still have incomes under $3,000 in 1980. We cannot leave the further wearing away of poverty solely to the general progress of the economy. A faster reduction of poverty will require that the lowest fifth of our families be able to earn a larger share of national output.

The composition of today's poor. To mount an attack on poverty we must know how to select our targets. Are the poor concentrated in any single geographical area? Are they confined to a few easily identifiable groups in society? Conclusions drawn from personal observation are likely to be misleading. Some believe that most of the poor are found in the slums of the central city, while others believe that they are concentrated in areas of rural blight. Some have been impressed by poverty among the elderly, while others are convinced that it is primarily a problem of minority racial and ethnic groups. But objective evidence indicates that poverty is pervasive. To be sure, the inadequately educated, the aged, and the nonwhite make up substantial portions of the poor population. But as table 2 shows, the poor are found among all major groups in the population and in all parts of the country. . . .

Using the income measure of poverty described above, we find that 78 percent of poor families are white. Although one-third of the poor families are headed by a person 65 years old and over, two-fifths are headed by persons in the 25- to 54-year range. Although it is true that a great deal of poverty is associated with lack of education, almost 4 million poor families (39 percent) are headed by a person with at least some education beyond grade school. The data show that less than half the poor live in the South. And the urban poor are somewhat more numerous than the rural poor. . . .

Yet there are substantial concentrations of poverty among certain groups. For example, families headed by persons 65 years of age and older represent 34 percent of poor families. Moreover, they appear among the poor 2½ times as frequently as they appear among all families. The last two columns of table 2 show five additional major categories of families that appear more than twice as often among the poor as among the total population: nonwhite families, families headed by women, families headed by individuals not in the civilian labor force, families with no wage earners, and rural farm families. Of course, some

Table 2.—Selected Characteristics of All Families and of Poor Families, 1962

Selected characteristic	Number of families (millions)		Percent of total	
	All families	Poor families	All families	Poor families
Total	47.0	9.3	100	100
Age of head:				
14–24 years	2.5	.8	5	8
25–54 years	30.4	3.9	65	42
55–64 years	7.3	1.4	16	15
65 years and over	6.8	3.2	14	34
Education of head:[1]				
8 years or less	16.3	6.0	35	61
9–11 years	8.6	1.7	19	17
12 years	12.2	1.5	26	15
More than 12 years	9.3	.7	20	7
Sex of head:				
Male	42.3	7.0	90	75
Female	4.7	2.3	10	25
Labor force status of head:[2]				
Not in civilian labor force ..	8.4	4.1	18	44
Employed	36.9	4.6	78	49
Unemployed	1.7	.6	4	6
Color of family:				
White	42.4	7.3	90	78
Nonwhite	4.6	2.0	10	22
Children under 18 years of age in family:				
None	18.8	4.9	40	52
One to three	22.7	3.3	48	36
Four or more	5.5	1.1	12	11
Earners in family:				
None	3.8	2.8	8	30
One	21.1	4.3	45	46
Two or more	22.1	2.2	47	23
Regional location of family:[3][4]				
Northeast	11.5	1.6	25	17
North Central	13.1	2.3	29	25
South	13.5	4.3	30	47
West	7.0	1.0	16	11
Residence of family:[4][5]				
Rural farm	3.3	1.5	7	16
Rural nonfarm	9.9	2.7	22	30
Urban	31.9	5.0	71	54

[1] Based on 1961 income (1962 prices).
[2] Labor force status relates to survey week of March 1963.
[3] Based on 1960 residence and 1959 income (1962 prices).
[4] Data are from 1960 Census and are therefore not strictly comparable with the other data shown in this table, which are derived from *Current Population Reports*.
[5] Based on 1959 residence and 1959 income (1962 prices).

NOTE.—Data relate to families and exclude unrelated individuals. Poor families are defined as all families with total money income of less than $3,000.

of these groups overlap considerably; but the data help to identify prospective targets for an antipoverty attack. The next section pinpoints these targets further.

The Roots of Poverty

Poverty is the inability to satisfy minimum needs. The poor are those whose resources—their income from all sources, together with their asset holdings—are inadequate. This section considers why those in poverty lack the earned income, property income and savings, and transfer payments to meet their minimum needs.

Earned income. Why do some families have low earned incomes? Some are unemployed or partially unemployed. High overall employment is a remedy of first importance. It would provide earned income for those unemployed who are able to accept jobs and greater earnings for many presently working part time. Yet it is clear that this is only a partial answer. Even for those able and willing to work, earnings are all too frequently inadequate, and a large number of the poor are unable to work. An analysis of the incidence of poverty helps one understand the reasons for low earnings.

The incidence of poverty for any specified group of families is the percentage of that group with incomes below $3,000. For all families,

Table 3.—Incidence of Poverty, by Characteristic Relating to Labor-Force Participation, 1962

Selected characteristic	Incidence of poverty (percent)
All families	20
Earners in family:	
None	76
1	20
2	10
3 or more	8
Labor force status of head: [1]	
Not in civilian labor force	50
Employed	12
Unemployed	34
Age of head:	
14 to 24 years	31
25 to 54 years	13
55 to 64 years	19
65 years and over	47
Sex of head:	
Male	17
Wife in labor force	9
Female	48

[1] Status relates to survey week of March 1963.

NOTE.—Data relate to families and exclude unrelated individuals. Poverty is defined to include all families with total money income of less than $3,000; these are also referred to as poor families. Incidence of poverty is measured by the percent that poor families with a given characteristic are of all families having the same characteristic.

the incidence in 1962 was 20 percent. An incidence for a particular group higher than 20 percent, or higher than the rates for other similar groups, suggests that some characteristics of that group are causally related to poverty. The basic cause may not be the particular characteristic used to classify the group. But an examination of groups with high incidence should throw light on the roots of poverty. . . .

Table 3 shows that the incidence of poverty is 76 percent for families with no earners. From other data, it appears that the incidence rate is 49 percent for families headed by persons who work part time. A family may be in either of these situations as a result of age, disability, premature death of the principal earner, need to care for children or disabled family members, lack of any salable skill, lack of motivation, or simply heavy unemployment in the area.

The problem of another group of families is the low rates of pay found most commonly in certain occupations. For example, the incidence of poverty among families headed by employed persons is 45 percent for farmers, and 74 percent for domestic service workers.

The chief reason for low rates of pay is low productivity, which in turn can reflect lack of education or training, physical or mental disability, or poor motivation. Other reasons include discrimination, low bargaining power, exclusion from minimum wage coverage, or lack of mobility resulting from inadequate knowledge of other opportunities, or

Table 4.—Incidence of Poverty by Education, Color, and Residence, 1962

Selected characteristic	Incidence of poverty (percent)
All families	20
Education of head: [1]	
8 years or less	37
9 to 11 years	20
12 years	12
More than 12 years	8
Color of family:	
White	17
Nonwhite	44
Residence of family:	
Farm	43
Nonwhite	84
Nonfarm	18

[1] Data relate to 1961, and money income in 1962 prices.

NOTE.—Data relate to families and exclude unrelated individuals. Poverty is defined to include all families with total money income of less than $3,000; these are also referred to as poor families. The incidence of poverty is measured by the percent that poor families with a given characteristic are of all families having the same characteristic.

unwillingness or inability to move away from familiar surroundings. The importance of education as a factor in poverty is suggested by the fact that families headed by persons with no more than 8 years of education have an incidence rate of 37 percent (table 4). Nonwhite and rural families show an even higher incidence of poverty.... The heads of these families are typically less well educated than average. For example, nonwhite family heads have completed a median of 8.7 years of school, compared to 11.8 for whites. In 1959 the median education of all males over 25 with incomes below $1,000 and living on a farm was slightly above 7 years in school; those with incomes above $5,000 had completed over 10 years in school.

...The severely handicapping influence of lack of education is clear. The incidence of poverty drops as educational attainments rise for nonwhite as well as white families at all ages. The high frequency of poverty for nonwhites is not, however, fully explained by their educational deficit. The incidence of poverty among nonwhites is almost invariably higher than among whites regardless of age, family type, or level of educational attainment....

Some families are forced into poverty by society's own standards. Their potential earners, otherwise able to hold a job, cannot free themselves from the family responsibilities which they must fulfill. Such is the case, for example, with families headed by women with small children.

Customary or mandatory retirement at a specified age also limits earnings by some healthy, able-bodied persons. However, retirement is often associated with deteriorating health, and poverty among the aged is greatest at ages over 70 or 75 and for aged widows—persons for whom employment is not a realistic alternative.

Property income and use of savings. Some families with inadequate current earnings from work can avoid poverty thanks to past savings—which provide an income and, if necessary, can be used to support consumption. Savings are particularly important for the elderly. More than half of those over 65 have money incomes above $3,000, and many also own homes. Others, although their money incomes are below $3,000, have adequate savings that can be drawn upon to support a decent standard of consumption.

But most families with low earnings are not so fortunate. If avoiding poverty required an income supplement of $1,500 a year for a retired man and his wife, they would need a capital sum at age 65 of about $19,000 to provide such an annuity. Few families have that sum. The median net worth for all spending units (roughly equivalent to the total of families and unrelated individuals) was only $4,700 in 1962.

For all spending units whose head was 65 years or more, the median net worth was $8,000. Meeting contingencies caused by illnesses is often a crucial problem for older people. About half of the aged, and about three-fourths of the aged poor, have no hospital insurance, although their medical care costs are 2½ times as high as those of younger persons. Their resources are typically inadequate to cover the costs of a serious illness.

The median net worth of the fifth of all spending units having the lowest incomes was only $1,000. Much of what property they have is in the form of dwellings. (About 40 percent of all poor families have some equity in a house.) Although this means that their housing costs are reduced, property in this form does not provide money income that can be used for other current expenses.

Most families—including the aged—whose incomes are low in any one year lack significant savings or property because their incomes have always been at poverty levels. This is clear in the results of the Michigan study already cited. Among the reporting families classified in that study as poor in 1959, 60 percent had never earned disposable income as high as $3,000, and nearly 40 percent had never reached $2,000. The comparable figures for all families were 17 and 10 percent, respectively. Among the aged poor reporting, 79 percent had never reached $3,000, and fully one-half had never earned $2,000. While nearly 60 percent of all families have enjoyed peak incomes above $5,000, among all poor families only 14 percent had ever reached that level; and a mere 5 percent of the aged poor had ever exceeded $5,000.

The persistence of poverty is reflected in the large number who have been unable to accumulate savings. The Survey Research Center study found that more than one-half of the aged poor in 1959 had less than $500 in liquid savings (bank deposits and readily marketable securities), and they had not had savings above that figure during the previous 5 years. Less than one-fifth of all poor families reported accumulated savings in excess of $500. The mean amount of savings used by poor families in 1959 was $120; and only 23 percent of the poor drew on savings at all.

It is clear that for most families property income and savings do not provide a buffer against poverty....

Transfer payments and private pensions. Poverty would be more prevalent and more serious if many families and individuals did not receive transfer payments. In 1960, these payments (those which are not received in exchange for current services) constituted only 7 percent of total family income, but they comprised 43 percent of the total income of low-income spending units. At the same time, however, only about half of the present poor receive any transfer payments at all. And, of course, many persons who receive transfers through social insurance programs are not poor—often as a result of these benefits.

Transfer programs may be either public or private in nature and may or may not have involved past contributions by the recipient. Public transfer programs include social insurance—such as unemployment compensation, workmen's compensation, and old-age, survivors', and disability insurance (OASDI); veterans' benefits; and public assistance programs, such as old-age assistance (OAA) and aid to families with dependent children (AFDC).

Private transfer programs include organized systems such as private pension plans and supplementary unemployment benefits, organized private charities, and private transfers within and among families.

It is important to distinguish between insurance-type programs and assistance programs, whether public or private. Assistance programs are ordinarily aimed specifically at the poor or the handicapped. Eligibility for their benefits may or may not be based upon current income; but neither eligibility nor the size of benefits typically bears any direct relationship to past income. Eligibility for insurance-type programs, on the other hand, is based on past employment, and benefits on past earnings.

The Federal-State unemployment insurance system covers only about 77 percent of all paid employment and is intended to protect workers with a regular attachment to the labor force against temporary loss of income. Benefits, of course, are related to previous earnings.

While the largest transfer-payment program, OASDI, now covers approximately 90 percent of all paid employment, there are still several million aged persons who retired or whose husbands retired or died before acquiring coverage. Benefits are related to previous earnings, and the average benefit for a retired worker under this program at the end of 1963 was only $77 a month, or $924 a year. The average benefit for a retired worker and his wife, if she is eligible for a wife's benefit, is $1,565 a year.

Public insurance-type transfer programs have made notable contributions to sustaining the incomes of those whose past earnings have been adequate, and to avoiding their slipping into poverty as their earnings are interrupted or terminated. These programs are of least help to those whose earnings have never been adequate.

Public assistance programs are also an important support to low-income and handicapped persons. Money payments under OAA average about $62 a month for the country as a whole, with State averages ranging from $37 to about $95 a month. In the AFDC program the national average payment per family (typically of 4 persons) is about $129 a month, including services rendered directly. State averages range from $38 a month to about $197 a month.

Private transfers within and between families are included in the total money income figures used in this chapter only to the extent that they are regular in nature, e.g., alimony or family support payments, and are excluded when they take the form of casual or irregular gifts or bequests. While data are lacking on the value of such gifts, they are clearly not a major source of income for the poor.

Private pensions, providing an annuity, are additional resources for some persons and families. In 1961 the beneficiaries of such plans numbered about 2 million (as against about 12 million receiving OASDI benefits), and total benefits paid were about $2 billion. While the combination of OASDI and private pensions serves to protect some from poverty, most persons receiving OASDI receive no private pension supplement. In any case, benefits under private pension plans range widely, and since they are typically related to the individual's previous earnings, they are low when earnings have been low.

Thus, although many families do indeed receive supplements to earnings in the form of pensions, social insurance benefits, and incomes from past saving, those families with a history of low earnings are also likely to have little of such supplementary income. And since most poor families have small amounts of property, they cannot long meet even minimum needs by depleting their assets.

The vicious circle. Poverty breeds poverty. A poor individual or family has a high probability of staying poor. Low incomes carry with them high risks of illness; limitations on mobility; limited access to education, information, and training. Poor parents cannot give their children the opportunities for better health and education needed to improve their lot. Lack of motivation, hope, and incentive is a more subtle but no less powerful barrier than lack of financial means. Thus the cruel legacy of poverty is passed from parents to children.

Escape from poverty is not easy for American children raised in families accustomed to living on relief. A recent sample study of AFDC recipients found that more than 40 percent of the parents were themselves raised in homes where public assistance had been received. It is difficult for children to find and follow avenues leading out of poverty in environments where education is deprecated and hope is smothered. This is particularly true when discrimination appears as an insurmountable barrier. Education may be seen as a waste of time if even the well-trained are forced to accept menial labor because of their color or nationality.

The Michigan study shows how inadequate education is perpetuated from generation to generation. Of the families identified as poor in that study, 64 percent were headed by a person who had had less than an eighth grade education. Of these, in turn, 67 percent had fathers who had also gone no further than eighth grade in school. Among the children of these poor families who had finished school, 34 percent had not gone beyond the eighth grade; this figure compares with 14 percent for all families. Fewer than one in two children of poor families had graduated from high school, compared to almost two out of three for all families.

Of 2 million high school seniors in October 1959 covered by a census study, 12 percent did not graduate in 1960. Of these dropouts, 54 percent had IQ's above 90, and 6 percent were above 110. Most of them had the intellectual capabilities necessary to graduate. The dropout rate for nonwhite male students, and likewise for children from households with a nonworking head, was twice the overall rate, and it was twice as high for children of families with incomes below $4,000 as for children of families with incomes above $6,000. Moreover, many of the children of the poor had dropped out before reaching the senior year.

A study of dropouts in New Haven, Conn., showed that 48 percent of children from lower class neighborhoods do not complete high school. The comparable figure for better neighborhoods was 22 percent.

Other studies indicate that unemployment rates are almost twice as high for dropouts as for high school graduates aged 16 to 24. Moreover, average incomes of male high school graduates are 25 percent higher than those of high school dropouts, and nearly 150 percent higher than those of men who completed less than 8 years of schooling.

There is a well-established association between school status and juvenile delinquency. For example, in the New Haven study cited above, 48 percent of the dropouts, but only 18 percent of the high school graduates, had one or more arrests or referrals to juvenile court.

Low-income families lose more time from work, school, and other activities than their more fortunate fellow citizens. Persons in families with incomes under $2,000 lost an average of 8 days of work in the year 1960–61, compared to 5.4 for all employed persons. They were restricted in activity for an average of 30 days (compared to 16.5 for the whole population) and badly disabled for 10.4 days (compared to 5.8 for the whole population).

Recent changes in the pattern of poverty. In spite of tendencies for poverty to breed poverty, a smaller proportion of our adult population has been poor—and a smaller fraction of American children

Table 5.—Number of Families and Incidence of Poverty,
by Selected Family Characteristics, 1947 and 1962

Selected characteristic	Number of families			Incidence of poverty (percent)[1]		Percentage change in number of poor families,
	1947	1962	Percentage change, 1947 to	1947	1962	1947 to 1962
	Millions		1962			
All families 37.3		47.0	26	32	20	−22
Earners in family:						
None 2.2		3.8	68	83	76	54
1 .... 21.9		21.1	−4	35	20	−45
2 .... 9.9		17.0	73	20	10	−13
3 or more 3.3		5.1	56	10	8	29
Labor force status of head:[2]						
Not in civilian force 5.5		8.4	52	61	50	23
Unemployed 1.2		1.7	49	49	34	2
Employed 31.9		36.9	16	28	12	−48
Age of head:						
14 to 24 years 1.8		2.5	39	45	31	−6
25 to 54 years 25.0		30.4	22	27	13	−41
55 to 64 years 6.1		7.3	19	32	19	−28
65 years and over 4.4		6.8	54	57	47	27
Sex of head:						
Male 33.5		42.3	26	30	17	−30
Female 3.8		4.7	26	51	48	19
Color of family:						
White 34.2		42.4	24	29	17	−27
Nonwhite 3.1		4.6	46	67	44	−3
Children under 18 years of age in family:						
None 16.2		18.8	16	36	26	−16
1 .... 8.9		8.7	−2	30	17	−46
2 .... 6.4		8.5	33	27	13	−33
3 or more 5.7		10.9	92	32	17	2
Regional location of family:[3]						
Northeast 10.1		11.5	14	26	14	−42
North Central 11.5		13.1	14	30	18	−31
South 11.5		13.5	17	49	32	−24
West 5.1		7.0	37	28	15	−26
Residence of family:						
Farm[4] 6.5		3.2	−51	56	43	−62
Nonfarm[5] 30.8		43.8	42	27	18	−5

[1] The incidence of poverty is measured by the percent that poor families with a given characteristic are of all families having the same characteristic.

[2] Labor force status is for April survey week of 1949 and March survey week of 1963. Income data (1962 prices) are for 1948 and 1962.

[3] Income data for 1949 and 1959. Since regional location data are from 1950 and 1960 censuses, they are not strictly comparable with other data shown in this table, which are derived from Current Population Reports.

[4] The 1960 census change in definition of a farm resulted in a decline of slightly over 1,000,000 in the total number of farm families. Therefore, the incidence figures for 1947 and 1962 may not be strictly comparable.

[5] Since 1959, nonfarm data are not available separately for rural nonfarm and urban.

NOTE.—Data relate to families and exclude unrelated individuals. Poverty is defined to include all families with total money income of less than $3,000 (1962 prices); these are also referred to as poor families.

exposed to poverty—in each succeeding generation. But, at least since World War II, the speed of progress has not been equal for all types of families, as is shown in table 5.

The incidence of poverty has declined substantially for most categories shown in the table. But there are some notable exceptions—families (1) with no earner, (2) with head not in the civilian labor force, (3) with head 65 years of age or older, (4) headed by a woman, and (5) on farms. It is also striking that in these classes poverty is high as well as stubborn. Poverty continues high also among nonwhites, although there has been a large and welcome decline in this incidence.

With the sole exception of the farm group, the total number of all families in each of these categories has remained roughly the same or has increased. Hence the high-incidence groups, including the nonwhites, have come to constitute a larger proportion of the poor (table 6).

Table 6.—Selected Characteristics of Poor Families, 1947 and 1962

Selected characteristic	Percent of poor families with characteristic	
	1947	1962
Family head:		
65 years of age and over	20	34
Female	16	25
Nonwhite families	18	22
Rural farm families	30	20 [1]
No earners in family	16	30

[1] Data are from Current Population Reports and are for 1959, based on income in 1962 prices. See table 5, footnote 4, for comparability problem.
NOTE:—Data relate to families and exclude unrelated individuals. Poor families are defined as all families with total money income of less than $3,000 (1962 prices).

This tabulation shows that certain handicapping characteristics, notably old age, or absence of an earner or of a male family head, have become increasingly prominent in the poor population. This is both a measure of past success in reducing poverty and of the tenacity of the poverty still existing. Rising productivity and earnings, improved education, and the structure of social security have permitted many families or their children to escape; but they have left behind many families who have one or more special handicaps. These facts suggest that in the future economic growth alone will provide relatively fewer escapes from poverty. Policy will have to be more sharply focused on the handicaps that deny the poor fair access to the expanding incomes of a growing economy.

But the significance of these shifts in composition should not be exaggerated. About half of the poor families are still headed neither by an aged person nor by a woman, and 70 percent include at least one earner. High employment and vigorous economic growth are still of major importance for this group. And it is essential to remember that one-third of the present poor are children. For them, improvements in the availability and quality of education offer the greatest single hope of escaping poverty as adults. . . .

Rose D. Friedman
The *Official* Estimates Are Wrong

. . . the Council of Economic Advisers in its report to the President, transmitted to Congress in January 1964 . . . did not initiate the current concern with poverty; but its prestige has lent an aura of authenticity to the precise figure of $3,000 of money income per family which it uses to separate the poor from the not-poor. The same aura attaches now to one-fifth, the fraction of the total population that the Council Report calculates to be "poor." These have now become the basic statistics of the poverty literature of 1964.

How does the Council arrive at its figure of $3,000? Are the families and individuals it classifies as the bottom one-fifth, the poorest one-fifth of the population?

The Council itself cautions that its measure of poverty is too simple to be "suitable for determining eligibility for particular benefits or participation in particular programs." But the Council nonetheless uses it to pinpoint the sources of poverty and thereby to indicate the programs needed to cope with poverty. Is it a valid measure for this purpose?

The Council's Concept of Poverty

In its qualitative discussion, the Council characterizes the poor as "those who are not now maintaining a *decent* standard of living—

From *Poverty: Definition and Perspective* (Washington: American Enterprise Institute for Public Policy Research, 1965), pp. 29–36, 38–42. Copyright © 1965 by American Enterprise Institute for Public Policy Research. Reprinted by permission of the publisher.

those whose *basic* needs exceed their means to satisfy them" (italics added). Can these two definitions provide us with an objective criterion for determining who and how many are poor? Standards of decency, like fashions, change from year to year, and mean different things to different people. How do we decide what wants are "needs" and what "needs" are basic, and in what amount? The Council, of course, recognizes that "there is no precise way to measure the number of families who do not have the resources to provide minimum satisfaction of their *own* particular needs." (A third definition of poverty.) Hence, for its objective criterion the Council uses a fourth definition of poverty. A family with less than $3,000 a year of money income is defined as poor. This figure is said to constitute an "approximate standard" of "an acceptable minimum" "for our society today" for which "a consensus . . . can be found."

The Basis for the Council's Figure of $3,000

What is the basis for the Council's "approximate standard" of $3,000? The Council says that "one such standard is suggested by a recent study, described in a publication of the Social Security Administration, which defines a 'low-cost' budget for a nonfarm family of four and finds its cost in 1962 to have been $3,955. The cost of what the study defined as an 'economy-plan' budget was $3,165." . . .

The "recent study" referred to by the Council is "Children of the Poor" by Mollie Orshansky. It appeared in the *Social Security Bulletin* of July 1963. Miss Orshansky's study is not devoted to establishing criteria for determining the poverty level. As its title suggests, it is devoted to counting and classifying the children of the poor. To estimate the number of families with children who are poor and the number of children in those families, the author uses two "crude" criteria of "income adequacy":

(1) "that the low-cost food plan priced by the Department of Agriculture in January, 1962 represents no more than one-third of total income." (In other words, Miss Orshansky estimates that an income is adequate if it is three times the cost of the low-cost food plan.)

(2) three times the "cost of the more restricted but still adequate diet suggested in the economy plan." Since the cost of the economy plan was roughly estimated as four-fifths of the cost of the low-cost food plan, the income level defined by the second criterion is four-fifths that defined by the first.

In counting the poor, Miss Orshansky herself computes the income levels defined by these criteria separately for each size of family, and separately for farm and nonfarm families. However, "by way of suggesting" to the reader "the level of living implied by the present approximation" she notes that "the income required for a husband, wife and two children not on a farm would be $3,165 by the more conservative measure, or $3,955 by the more liberal." These are the numbers quoted by the Council.

Let us examine in some detail the two elements of Miss Orshansky's crude criteria of income adequacy: (a) the food plans; and (b) the fraction of income spent on food.

a. The food plans. The food plans Miss Orshansky uses are two of the five food plans described in Home Economics Research Report #20. . . . These five plans are the latest revisions of plans first developed in the 1930's. They were not then and are not now presented as the minimum cost at which nutritional needs can be met but rather as guides to help families get better nutrition for less money than they actually spend. . . .

Food consumption data from selected income classes of nonfarm families in the 1955 survey were used "to study the current food patterns of families and to obtain basic data for estimating the cost of food for the plans. . . . These representative classes are the ones containing the median income of the low, middle, and high third, respectively, of the income distribution." The median income for the lowest third was $2,258 and fell in the income class $2,000–$2,999. While the low-cost food plan was based on the food patterns for this class, the cost of the low-cost plan is not equal to the average amount spent on food in this income group. Over two-thirds of the families in this income class spent more on food than the $5.40 per person per week estimated as the cost of food for the low-cost plan (in 1955). "In other words, by careful food management, many families can have nutritionally adequate diets for less money than they now spend."

I have not been able to find an explicit statement about precisely how the cost of the low-cost food plan was calculated. However, there is considerable circumstantial evidence to suggest that it was set roughly equal to the cost at which, in fact, 75 percent of the families surveyed met two-thirds of the recommended allowances of the National Research Council. For example, in discussing per person food costs at which adequacy so defined was achieved, Janet Murray says: "This 75 percent level seemed to represent those households on whose food patterns the low-cost food plans were based. The per person food costs [at this level] fall well within the range of the costs of the low-cost food plans in 1955. . . ."

b. The fraction of income spent on food. To get the income corresponding to the specified food costs, Miss Orshansky multiplies by three. The basis for this multiplier is the same survey on which the food plans are based. According to that survey, average expenditures for food by all families in the sample, farm and nonfarm, and all income levels combined, amounted to 33 percent of their average money income after taxes. In addition, it should be noted, these families received some food without money payment—mostly by providing it for themselves.

In using the multiplier of three, Miss Orshansky implicitly assumed that the multiplier for all families should be used for families with low incomes even though she stated explicitly that "poorer families generally devoted more than one-third of income to food, and those better off used less of their income in this way." For the particular 1955 Food Consumption Survey she used, the percentage spent on food varied from 131 percent at incomes under $1,000 to 60 percent at incomes of $1,000–$1,999, to 48 percent at incomes of $2,000–$2,999 to 21 percent at incomes of $8,000 and over. The fact that the families in the bottom income class reported expenditures for food (based on one week's expenditure) that were higher than reported income strongly suggests that a single year's reported income is not a valid measure of the real income status of many of these families. In any event, it appears difficult to justify using the multiplier applicable to all families to compute the income corresponding to a poverty level of living.

To sum up: Miss Orshansky's crude criteria of income adequacy correspond neither to the minimum cost at which families *could* get an adequate diet nor to the income level at which three-fourths of the families do in fact achieve adequate nutrition. Her criteria yield incomes that are far higher than the first and 20 to 50 percent higher than the second.

The Council uses a money income of $3,000 per family to define poverty. This is presumably based on Miss Orshansky's "more conservative measure" for a family of four (four-fifths of the low-cost criterion) rounded to the nearest thousand dollars. Though originally introduced as applying to a family of four, the Council uses $3,000 as the dividing line for families of all sizes.

The Council's Estimate That One-Fifth Are Poor

The Council estimates that nine million families or 20 percent of all families in the United States, were poor in 1962, according to the Council's definition.

I estimate that 4.8 million families, or roughly 10 percent of all families in the United States were poor in 1962, according to the nutritive adequacy definition of poverty. . . . This definition gives an income of $2,200 as the poverty line for a nonfarm family of four. The cost of food implied by the $3,000 income for a family of four, says the Council, is $5.00 per person per week. The amount actually spent for food, on the average, by a family of four with an income of $2,200 was over $6.00 per person per week, because the fraction of income spent on food at this level was about 60 percent and not 33 percent.

It should be emphasized that the difference between the Council's estimate that 20 percent of families were poor in 1962 and my estimate that 10 percent were poor results neither from a different basic criterion of poverty nor from the use of different data. Both use nutrition to separate the poor from the not-poor; both use the same standard of nutritive-adequacy; both use the same statistical data.

The high estimate by the Council simply reflects the crudity of its analysis. First, the Council accepted an estimate of a poverty line that is not valid, according to the criterion on which that estimate is supposed to be based. Second, the Council estimated the percentage of families who are poor by using the same income level to define poverty for all families regardless of their size, composition, or residence.

My estimate of 4.8 million families should not be taken as a precise estimate of the number of poor families even on the particular criterion of poverty for which it is derived. The data on income at which nutritive-adequacy is attained are now nearly a decade old, the adjustments for price changes are at best rough, the income distributions used, though for a more recent date, are based on a concept of income and methods of estimation that differ from those used in the Consumption Survey. The chief importance of this new estimate is to show how much the results depend on the way in which the same criterion is applied.

Does the Council Correctly
Characterize the Poor?

The Council recognizes that "A family's ability to meet its needs depends not only on its money income but also on its income in kind, its savings, its property, and its ability to borrow. . . . Refined analysis would vary the income cut-off by family size, age, location. A case could be made . . . for setting the over-all income limit either higher or lower than $3,000." Nevertheless, says the Council, "the analysis of the sources of poverty, and of the programs needed to cope with it, would remain substantially unchanged." The Council therefore neglects the refinements in estimating the characteristics of the poor. It concludes that "there are substantial concentrations of poverty among certain groups. For example, families headed by persons 65 years of age and older represent 34 percent of poor families. Moreover, they appear among the poor 2½ times as frequently as they appear among all families. . . . Five additional major categories of families that appear more than twice as often among the poor as among the total population [are]: non-white families, families headed by women, families headed by individuals not in the civilian labor force, families with no wage earners, and rural farm families. Of course, some of these groups overlap considerably; but the data help to identify prospective targets for an anti-poverty attack."

This characterization is seriously misleading because of the inadequacy of the Council's definition of poverty. The indiscriminate use of the same income level for families of all sizes leads to a significant overestimate of the relative incidence of poverty among the aged and the young. This overestimate is reinforced by the inadequacy of money income as an index of real income status—a defect common to both the Council's and the nutritive-adequacy definition. This defect also leads to an overestimate of the relative incidence of poverty among farm families and Southern families.

a. Neglect of size of family. . . . By using the same poverty line for large and small families, the Council neglects one very important cause of poverty, namely, large families. Next to economic growth, there is probably no single factor that has contributed more to raising the standard of living of families at the bottom of the income scale than a reduction in size of family.

As a corollary, one of the factors contributing to the lower standard of living of nonwhite families is the larger size of the average nonwhite family. In *Children of the Poor,* Mollie Orshansky points out that "nonwhite families in general, despite their smaller incomes, are considerably larger. Three out of every five mother-child families with six or more children are nonwhite, but only one out of five among those with one child. A fourth of the husband-wife families with six or more children are nonwhite, in contrast to 7 percent of those with a single child."

Young families and aged families both tend to be small in size— the young because they have not completed their families, the aged because their children have left to set up their own households. The neglect of size of family in the Council's estimate therefore means that it overestimates the incidence of poverty in these two groups.

b. Concept of money income. The defects of one year's money income as a measure of resources available for consumption tend to produce a significant overstatement of the incidence of poverty among the young, the aged, farm families, and Southern families. For the young and the aged, this overestimate magnifies the error resulting from the neglect of size of family.

For the young, the chief defect of money income is that it neglects long-run income status. Families with young heads are just beginning their income cycle. It is expected that their permanent income over a longer period of time will be higher than it is at the beginning. Some have married while still in school and are completing their education. Others may be in apprenticeship. Some have not found their niche in the economy. Many are still being helped by their parents. The real income status of these young families on the basis of a longer term estimate of their income is higher than the status indicated by their current money income.

For the aged, the chief defect of money income is the neglect of income from property. The aged are at the opposite end of the income cycle from the young families. They have passed their peak earnings, and are on their way down. Anticipating this well-established pattern of earnings over the life cycle, many older families have accumulated assets in the form of an owned home, stocks, bonds, savings accounts, insurance policies, as well as a share in the Social Security benefits and other pension funds. These assets accumulated during the period of higher earnings can be used to supplement lower earnings in three ways: (1) through the nonmoney income derived from an owned home, (2) through money income in such forms as interest, dividends, social security benefits, and other pension payments, and (3) through funds obtained by selling assets.

The definition of money income in the statistics used . . . includes item (2) above. But it excludes completely items (1) and (3)—nonmoney income derived from an owned home and receipts from the sale of assets.

This restricted definition of funds available for current living is particularly misleading for families with head over 65. According to the 1963 survey of the aged, "Home ownership (farm and nonfarm) at the end of 1962 was reported by three-fourths of the couples with head or wife aged 65 or over." Excluding receipts from the sale of assets similarly misrepresents the level of living of some aged. If, instead of accumulating assets in earlier years, families used their savings to purchase a pension, the proceeds from the pension are included in money income. If the families accumulated assets but sold them and used the proceeds to buy a life annuity, the income from the annuity is likewise included in the definition of income. But if a family chooses to supplement its current income to the same amount by selling assets piecemeal, this supplement is excluded. There are no data, to my knowledge, from which a more realistic estimate of funds available for current living can be made for the aged. But there is little doubt that such an estimate would indicate that too large a fraction are classified as poor by any definition which uses money income alone.

For farm families, money income is defective because it omits nonmoney income in the form of home-produced food and services of an owned home. In addition, because money income varies much more from year to year for farm than for nonfarm families, one year's income may be highly misleading. We can make a crude estimate of the effect of the first defect; we have no data to do so for the second.

According to the 1955 Department of Agriculture Food Consumption Survey, 40 percent of the food used by farm families comes from the home farm or garden. Using this figure, we can make nutritive-adequacy income estimates for farm families alone. Using these, in turn, we can get a rough estimate of the fraction of farm families who should be characterized as poor. My estimate is about 13 percent or 1.3 times the average incidence of poverty in the population as a whole. If no allowance is made for home-produced food, the incidence appears to be 25 percent as compared with 10 percent for the population as a whole. The Council estimates the incidence of poverty among farm families as 44 percent as compared with an incidence of 20 percent for the population as a whole.

For Southern families, a given level of money income will give a higher standard of living than for Northern families for two main reasons: first, the climatic difference; second, lower food prices and a pattern of food habits that can be satisfied at lower costs. The Bureau of Labor Statistics estimates that the second factor alone produces a 20 percent lower food cost in the South than in the North for the same nutritive adequacy.

c. *How important are the errors?* Even the rough estimates that can be made show that the Council's characterization of the poor gives a seriously distorted picture of the problem of poverty. The Council divides those whom it classifies as poor into white and Negro, old and young, farm and city, schooled and unschooled, employed and unemployed. But the group the Council so divides is the wrong group. The error contaminates every one of the Council's divisions. Of the families it designates poor, over 50 percent are two-person families, and less than 20 percent are families of five or more persons. Of the families designated poor by the nutritive-adequacy definition of poverty, less than one-third are two-person families and more than 36 percent are families of five or more persons, and even these percentages overstate the importance of the small family and understate the importance of the large because small families tend to be unusually young or old.

Or, take another classification for which alternative estimates can be constructed: farm vs. nonfarm families. Of the families the Council classifies as poor, 15 percent are farm families; on the alternative estimate, less than 9 percent.

Rougher estimates yet, by age of family head, show differences of a similar order of magnitude: Of the families the Council classifies as poor, 9 percent have a head aged 14–24, and 34 percent, a head aged 65 or over, or 43 percent all together in these two groups. Of the families classified as poor by the nutritive-adequacy definition, 6 percent have a head aged 14–24 and 21 percent a head aged 65 and over, or 27 percent all together.

Clearly, differences of this magnitude can hardly be shrugged off as refinements which, if made, would leave "the analysis of the sources of poverty, and of the programs needed to cope with it . . . substantially unchanged." On the contrary, they are so large that little confidence can be placed in the Council's characterization of the poor.

Herman P. Miller
Facts about Poverty, Revised

When the Council of Economic Advisers made its study of poverty several years ago it used a cash income of less than $3,000 (in 1962 prices) as the poverty line for families of two or more persons and an income of less than $1,500 for persons living alone. The figures were criticized for the failure to take various factors like size of family, age of the family head and farm residence into account. Since then new statistics were prepared by the Department of Health, Education and Welfare in which rough adjustments were made for these factors. A flexible poverty line was used ranging from about $1000 for an elderly person living alone on a farm to over $5000 for a family of seven persons. The value of goods and services obtained without specific payment by farm families was also taken into account. The modest nature of this budget is suggested by the fact that the assumed need of $3130 for a nonfarm family of four persons permits a daily expenditure of 70 cents per person

From "Who Are the Poor?" *The Nation* (June 7, 1965). Reprinted by permission of the publisher.

for food and $1.40 per person for all other needs—housing, medical care, transportation, etc.

The new figures show that in 1963 about 34.5 million persons were in families with incomes insufficient to purchase a minimum budget. They constituted nearly one-fifth of all persons in the United States. About 5 million lived alone and 30 million were members of family groups. One-half of the 30 million were children. The following are some of the key facts about families living in poverty:

(1) About 7 million families and 5 million persons living alone had incomes below the poverty line in 1963. Their aggregate income was about $12 billion below their estimated minimum requirements. This number can be regarded as the poverty gap—that is, the amount required to bring all families and individuals above the poverty line. Annual increases in productivity will simultaneously reduce the poverty gap and increase average income per family. At present, the poverty gap is about 3 percent of the cash income reported to the Census Bureau.

(2) About 2 million families without a father are included among the poor. They account for about one-fourth of the poor and nearly half of the poverty gap. At a cost of about $5 billion, all families headed by women could be provided with incomes sufficient to meet minimum requirements.

(3) About 2 million families (one-fourth of all the poor) were headed by a person who worked full time throughout the year. This group includes 1.3 million families (about 20 percent of the total) headed by a white man who was fully employed throughout the year. These figures dramatize the fact that low wages are still a major cause of poverty in the United States.

Increases in aggregate demand and a full-employment economy probably would not benefit these families, except perhaps by providing work for wives, many of whom are already overburdened with large families.

(4) About 1.5 million family heads worked at full-time jobs, but did not work throughout the year. The poverty of these families was due to a combination of low wage rates, unemployment or illness. Although today's poor are frequently presented as psychologically or spiritually handicapped, the fact is that about 50 percent of them are headed by a person oriented to full-time work whose wages are simply too low to support a family.

(5) The official estimates show that about 2 million (about one-fourth) of the poor families are nonwhite. These figures, however, understate the dynamic role of nonwhites (Negroes) in the drive against poverty. The nonwhites constitute about one-third of the non-aged poor and a much larger proportion of the chronically poor.

(6) The original estimates published by the Council of Economic Advisers showed that the aged were the major group among the poor, accounting for about one-third of the total. The revised figures call for a reappraisal of this view. It now appears that the aged constitute only about one-fifth of the total.

Table 1. Persons in Poverty in 1963
(Numbers in millions)

Type of unit	Total U.S. population	Persons in poverty	
		Number	Percent of total
All persons	187.2	34.6	18
Farm	12.6	3.2	25
Nonfarm	174.6	31.4	18
Unrelated individuals	11.2	4.9	44
Members of families	176.0	29.7	17
Children under 18	68.8	15.0	22

Source: *Social Security Bulletin*, January 1965.

Table 2. Selected Characteristics of Families in Poverty in 1963
(Numbers in millions)

Selected characteristics	All families	Families in poverty	
		Number	Percent of total
Total	47.4	7.2	15
Residence			
Farm	3.1	0.7	23
Nonfarm	44.3	6.5	15
Color			
White	42.7	5.2	12
Nonwhite	4.7	2.0	42
Age of Head			
14 to 24 years	2.7	0.7	26
25 to 64 years	38.0	5.0	13
65 years and over	6.7	1.5	24
Type of Family			
Male head	42.5	5.2	12
Female head	4.9	2.0	40
Employment Status of Family Head			
Not in labor force	8.8	3.0	34
In the labor force	38.6	4.1	11
Work Experience of Family Head in 1963			
Worked in 1963	40.7	4.6	11
Worked at full-time jobs	37.9	3.6	10
50–52 weeks	30.7	2.0	7
Worked at part-time jobs	2.8	1.0	36
Did not work	6.7	2.6	38

Source: *Social Security Bulletin*, January 1965.

The Reduction in Poverty during the Postwar Years

Although poverty remains an urgent national problem, we have been successful in whittling away at it and have good reason to be optimistic about the prospects for future progress. Using the $3000 poverty line, employed by the Council of Economic Advisers, we find that between 1947 and 1963 the proportion of families in poverty dropped from 32 percent to 19 percent (in 1962 dollars). Between 1947 and 1956 the proportion dropped from 32 percent to 23 percent or at the rate of one percentage point per year. There was no change between 1956 and 1958. Since that time the proportion dropped once again from 23 percent to 19 percent or at just under one percentage point per year. In other words, the experience in the reduction of poverty during the past five years has not been appreciably different from the experience during the decade immediately following the second World War.

The maintenance of a constant rate in the reduction of poverty in recent years is no mean accomplishment in view of the many factors tending to depress that rate. It was much easier to reduce poverty by one percentage point when one-third of the families were below the poverty line than it is at present when fewer than one-fifth are at that level. Also, the closer we get to the very bottom of the income distribution, the more we find the hard-core poor whose incomes largely arise outside of the labor market and are not necessarily responsive to economic growth. Finally, although economic growth tends to reduce poverty by pushing families above the poverty line, it also tends to increase it in a statistical sense by making it possible for the young and the old to maintain their own residences, thereby creating low-income families that might not otherwise exist as independent units. Although the undoubling of families acts as a brake on the reduction in poverty, those families that choose to live alone on a lower income are generally "better off" than those who live with others and have a higher combined income as a result. Despite these obstacles, poverty continued to drop at the rate of one percent per year throughout the postwar period.

5
How the Poor Get Along

So long as there shall exist, by virtue of law and custom, a social damnation artificially creating hells in the midst of civilization, and complicating the destiny which is Divine with a fatality which is human; so long as the three great problems of the age —the degradation of man through poverty, the ruin of woman through hunger, the crippling of children through ignorance—are not solved; so long as in certain regions social asphyxia is still possible—in other words, and from a still wider point of view, so long as ignorance and wretchedness exist on earth, books like this [*Les Miserables*] cannot be useless.
—Victor Hugo

What happens to a dream deferred?
Does it dry up
Like a raisin in the sun?
Or fester like a sore—
And then run?
Does it stink like rotten meat?
Or crust and sugar over—
Like a syrupy sweet?
Maybe it just sags
Like a heavy load.
Or does it explode?
—Langston Hughes

Poverty is many different things—a sick old man on welfare, a drunk beating his wife, cockroaches in the kitchen and the stench of urine in the corridor, a dirt farmer fighting an unwilling soil, an unwanted Negro boy sitting on a stoop, a miner with nothing to do. All of these conditions—and more—are suggested in the statistics on poverty. But numbers are abstractions and people are real. It takes more than numbers to reach the state of knowledge that e. e. cummings described so well:

> Now the ears of my ears awake and
> Now the eyes of my eyes are opened

The articles that follow need little introduction. Each tells its own story about the hardships of poverty. Brecht reminds us not to become too sentimental about the poor, for there is little about poverty that is noble or ennobling. Poverty leads to immorality ("... till you feed us, right and wrong can wait"); and immorality can be very ugly ("ill-treating, beating, cheating, eating some other bloke").

Are the poor really so different from everyone else? Mrs. Lamale's figures say no. They show that the poor spend their money very much like the middle class. They don't "booze it up," nor do they ride in expensive cars. The proportion of income spent on basic necessities like food, shelter, and clothing is much the same for families living on $3,000 a year as it is for those living on $6,000 or $7,000. If the diet of the poor is nutritionally inadequate, so is that of a large section of the middle class (Friedman, Chapter 2). Those who argue that there is a "culture of poverty" might be hard-pressed to prove it on the basis of the official figures on consumer-expenditure patterns.

Caplovitz points out that the poor are tricked by shady sales practices—high-pressure salesmen, easy credit, misleading advertising. No doubt they are, but aren't we all? The problem is more acute for the poor, however, because they are less able to resist the pressures, and the consequences of mismanagement are more serious.

Bertolt Brecht
What Does a Man Live By?

MACHEATH.
Now all you gentlemen who wish to lead us
And teach us to desist from mortal sin
Your prior obligation is to feed us:
When we've had lunch, your preaching can begin
All you who love your paunch and our propriety
Take note of this one thing, for it is late:
You may proclaim, good sirs, your fine philosophy
But till you feed us, right and wrong can wait!
Or is it only those who have the money
Can enter in the land of milk and honey?

VOICE OFF.
What does a man live by?

MACHEATH.
What does a man live by? By resolutely
Ill-treating, beating, cheating, eating some other bloke
A man can only live by absolutely
Forgetting he's a man like other folk.

CHORUS OFF.
So, gentlemen, don't be taken in:
Men live exclusively by mortal sin.

GINNY JENNY.
All you who say what neckline is decreed us
And who decide when ogling is a sin
Your prior obligation is to feed us
When we've had lunch, your preaching can begin
You who insist upon your pleasure and our shame
Take note of this one thing (for it is late);
Your fine philosophy, good sirs, you may proclaim,
But till you feed us, right and wrong can wait!
Or is it only those who have the money
Can enter in the land of milk and honey?

VOICE OFF.
What does a man live by?

GINNY JENNY.
What does a man live by? By resolutely
Ill-treating, beating, cheating, eating some other bloke

From *The Threepenny Opera*, English version by Eric Bentley and Desmond I. Vesey in *The Modern Theatre*, Vol. 1, E. Bentley, ed. (Garden City: Doubleday and Company, Inc., 1955), pp. 167–168. Copyright © 1955 by Eric Bentley.

Bertolt Brecht (1898–1956) was an innovative German playwright and poet.

A man can only live by absolutely
Forgetting he's a man like other folk.
CHORUS OFF.
So, gentlemen, do not be taken in:
Men live exclusively by mortal sin.

James Baldwin
Life in Harlem

There is a housing project standing now where the house in which we grew up once stood, and one of those stunted city trees is snarling where our doorway used to be. This is on the rehabilitated side of the avenue. The other side of the avenue—for progress takes time— has not been rehabilitated yet and it looks exactly as it looked in the days when we sat with our noses pressed against the windowpane, longing to be allowed to go "across the street." The grocery store which gave us credit is still there, and there can be no doubt that it is still giving credit. The people in the project certainly need it—far more, indeed, than they ever needed the project. The last time I passed by, the Jewish proprietor was still standing among his shelves, looking sadder and heavier but scarcely any older. Farther down the block stands the shoe-repair store in which our shoes were repaired until reparation became impossible and in which, then, we bought all our "new" ones. The Negro proprietor is still in the window, head down, working at the leather.

These two, I imagine, could tell a long tale if they would (perhaps they would be glad to if they could), having watched so many, for so long, struggling in the fishhooks, the barbed wire, of this avenue.

The avenue is elsewhere the renowned and elegant Fifth. The area I am describing, which, in today's gang parlance, would be called "the turf," is bounded by Lenox Avenue on the west, the Harlem River on the east, 135th Street on the north, and 130th Street on the south. We never lived beyond these boundaries; this is where we grew up. Walking along 145th Street—for example—familiar as it is, and similar,

Reprinted from *Nobody Knows My Name* by James Baldwin, pp. 56–65. Copyright © 1960, 1961 by James Baldwin and used with the permission of the publisher, The Dial Press, Inc., and Michael Joseph Ltd., London.
James Baldwin is a novelist and playwright; his latest work is *Going to Meet the Man* (Dial Press, 1965).

does not have the same impact because I do not know any of the people on the block. But when I turn east on 131st Street and Lenox Avenue, there is first a soda-pop joint, then a shoeshine "parlor," then a grocery store, then a dry cleaners', then the houses. All along the street there are people who watched me grow up, people who grew up with me, people I watched grow up along with my brothers and sisters; and, sometimes in my arms, sometimes underfoot, sometimes at my shoulder—or on it—their children, a riot, a forest of children, who include my nieces and nephews.

When we reach the end of this long block, we find ourselves on wide, filthy, hostile Fifth Avenue, facing that project which hangs over the avenue like a monument to the folly, and the cowardice, of good intentions. All along the block, for anyone who knows it, are immense human gaps, like craters. These gaps are not created merely by those who have moved away, inevitably into some other ghetto; or by those who have risen, almost always into a greater capacity for self-loathing and self-delusion; or yet by those who, by whatever means—World War II, the Korean war, a policeman's gun or billy, a gang war, a brawl, madness, an overdose of heroin, or, simply, unnatural exhaustion—are dead. I am talking about those who are left, and I am talking principally about the young. What are they doing? Well, some, a minority, are fanatical churchgoers, members of the more extreme of the Holy Roller sects. Many, many more are "moslems," by affiliation or sympathy, that is to say that they are united by nothing more—and nothing less—than a hatred of the white world and all its works. They are present, for example, at every Buy Black street-corner meeting—meetings in which the speaker urges his hearers to cease trading with white men and establish a separate economy. Neither the speaker nor his hearers can possibly do this, of course, since Negroes do not own General Motors or RCA or the A & P, nor, indeed, do they own more than a wholly insufficient fraction of anything else in Harlem (those who *do* own anything are more interested in their profits than in their fellows). But these meetings nevertheless keep alive in the participators a certain pride of bitterness without which, however futile this bitterness may be, they could scarcely remain alive at all. Many have given up. They stay home and watch the TV screen, living on the earnings of their parents, cousins, brothers, or uncles, and only leave the house to go to the movies or to the nearest bar. "How're you making it?" one may ask, running into them along the block, or in the bar. "Oh, I'm TV-ing it"; with the saddest, sweetest, most shamefaced of smiles, and from a great distance. This distance one is compelled to respect; anyone who has traveled so far will not easily be dragged again into the world. There are further retreats, of course, than the TV screen or the bar.

There are those who are simply sitting on their stoops, "stoned," animated for a moment only, and hideously, by the approach of someone who may lend them the money for a "fix." Or by the approach of someone from whom they can purchase it, one of the shrewd ones, on the way to prison or just coming out.

And the others, who have avoided all of these deaths, get up in the morning and go downtown to meet "the man." They work in the white man's world all day and come home in the evening to this fetid block. They struggle to instill in their children some private sense of honor or dignity which will help the child to survive. This means, of course, that they must struggle, stolidly, incessantly, to keep this sense alive in themselves, in spite of the insults, the indifference, and the cruelty they are certain to encounter in their working day. They patiently browbeat the landlord into fixing the heat, the plaster, the plumbing; this demands prodigious patience; nor is patience usually enough. In trying to make their hovels habitable, they are perpetually throwing good money after bad. Such frustration, so long endured, is driving many strong, admirable men and women whose only crime is color to the very gates of paranoia.

One remembers them from another time—playing handball in the playground, going to church, wondering if they were going to be promoted at school. One remembers them going off to war—gladly, to escape this block. One remembers their return. Perhaps one remembers their wedding day. And one sees where the girl is now—vainly looking for salvation from some other embittered, trussed, and struggling boy—and sees the all-but-abandoned children in the streets.

Now I am perfectly aware that there are other slums in which white men are fighting for their lives, and mainly losing. I know that blood is also flowing through those streets and that the human damage there is incalculable. People are continually pointing out to me the wretchedness of white people in order to console me for the wretchedness of blacks. But an itemized account of the American failure does not console me and it should not console anyone else. That hundreds of thousands of white people are living, in effect, no better than the "niggers" is not a fact to be regarded with complacency. The social and moral bankruptcy suggested by this fact is of the bitterest, most terrifying kind.

The people, however, who believe that this democratic anguish has some consoling value are always pointing out that So-and-So, white, and So-and-So, black, rose from the slums into the big time. The existence—the public existence—of, say, Frank Sinatra and Sammy Davis, Jr. proves to them that America is still the land of opportunity and that inequalities vanish before the determined will. It proves nothing of the sort. The determined will is rare—at the moment, in this country, it is unspeakably rare—and the inequalities suffered by the many are in no way justified by the rise of a few. A few have always risen—in every country, every era, and in the teeth of regimes which can by no stretch of the imagination be thought of as free. Not all of these people, it is worth remembering, left the world better than they found it. The determined will is rare, but it is not invariably benevolent. Furthermore, the American equation of success with the big time reveals an awful disrespect for human life and human achievement. This equation has placed our cities among the most dangerous in the world and has placed our youth among the most empty and most bewildered. The situation of our youth is not mysterious. Children have never been very good at listening to their elders, but they have never failed to imitate them. They must, they have no other models. That is exactly what our children are doing. They are imitating our immorality, our disrespect for the pain of others.

All other slum dwellers, when the bank account permits it, can move out of the slum and vanish altogether from the eye of persecution. No Negro in this country has ever made that much money and it will be a long time before any Negro does. The Negroes in Harlem, who have no money, spend what they have on such gimcracks as they are sold. These include "wider" TV screens, more "faithful" hi-fi sets, more "powerful" cars, all of which, of course, are obsolete long before they are paid for. Anyone who has ever struggled with poverty knows how extremely expensive it is to be poor; and if one is a member of a captive population, economically speaking, one's feet have simply been placed on the treadmill forever. One is victimized, economically, in a thousand ways—rent, for example, or car insurance. Go shopping one day in Harlem—for anything—and compare Harlem prices and quality with those downtown.

The people who have managed to get off this block have only got as far as a more respectable ghetto. This respectable ghetto does not even have the advantages of the disreputable one—friends, neighbors, a familiar church, and friendly tradesmen; and it is not, moreover, in the nature of any ghetto to remain respectable long. Every Sunday, people who have left the block take the lonely ride back, dragging their increasingly discontented children with them. They spend the day talking, not always with words, about the trouble they've seen and the trouble—one must watch their eyes as they watch their children—they are only too likely to see. For children do not like ghettos. It takes them nearly no time to discover exactly why they are there.

The projects in Harlem are hated. They are hated almost as

much as policemen, and this is saying a great deal. And they are hated for the same reason: both reveal, unbearably, the real attitude of the white world, no matter how many liberal speeches are made, no matter how many lofty editorials are written, no matter how many civil-rights commissions are set up.

The projects are hideous, of course, there being a law, apparently respected throughout the world, that popular housing shall be as cheerless as a prison. They are lumped all over Harlem, colorless, bleak, high, and revolting. The wide windows look out on Harlem's invincible and indescribable squalor: the Park Avenue railroad tracks, around which, about forty years ago, the present dark community began; the unrehabilitated houses, bowed down, it would seem, under the great weight of frustration and bitterness they contain; the dark, the ominous schoolhouses from which the child may emerge maimed, blinded, hooked, or enraged for life; and the churches, churches, block upon block of churches, niched in the walls like cannon in the walls of a fortress. Even if the administration of the projects were not so insanely humiliating (for example: one must report raises in salary to the management, which will then eat up the profit by raising one's rent; the management has the right to know who is staying in your apartment; the management can ask you to leave, at their discretion), the projects would still be hated because they are an insult to the meanest intelligence.

Harlem got its first private project, Riverton—which is now, naturally, a slum—about twelve years ago because at that time Negroes were not allowed to live in Stuyvesant Town. Harlem watched Riverton go up, therefore, in the most violent bitterness of spirit, and hated it long before the builders arrived. They began hating it at about the time people began moving out of their condemned houses to make room for this additional proof of how thoroughly the white world despised them. And they had scarcely moved in, naturally, before they began smashing windows, defacing walls, urinating in the elevators, and fornicating in the playgrounds. Liberals, both white and black, were appalled at the spectacle. I was appalled by the liberal innocence—or cynicism, which comes out in practice as much the same thing. Other people were delighted to be able to point to proof positive that nothing could be done to better the lot of the colored people. They were, and are, right in one respect: that nothing can be done as long as they are treated like colored people. The people in Harlem know they are living there because white people do not think they are good enough to live anywhere else. No amount of "improvement" can sweeten this fact. Whatever money is now being earmarked to improve this, or any other ghetto, might as well be burnt. A ghetto can be improved in one way only: out of existence.

Ben H. Bagdikian
Ed MacIntosh: Man on a Pension

> "*I ain't had a letter in twelve months.*
> *And that was from the bank.*"

Edmund MacIntosh was depending on the theory that hard-boiled eggs and opened cans of Spam need no refrigeration. And he was sick.

He had also depended on the theory that if you work hard, live frugally, and mind your own business, you'll get by without help. And now he was seventy-four years old and needed help.

Mr. MacIntosh depended on hard-boiled eggs because his hotel room has no refrigerator and he can't afford to eat out. He is trying to live on his $50-a-month Social Security check. Room rent is $38.50 a month, which provides a room with clean linen every two weeks and clean towels every day. The remainder goes for food and chewing tobacco. Every week friends on the same floor buy him two dozen eggs, seven small cans of V-8 juice, two cans of Spam, a carton of dry cereal (because the box says, "Minimum daily requirement of vitamins") and his tobacco. He boils his eggs at once and eats them morning and evening. He stretches a can of Spam for three days or so. It has cost him violent nausea to discover that hard-boiled eggs and opened Spam need refrigeration in warm weather.

He was trying to eat on $11.50 a month, or 38 cents a day. The Department of Agriculture thinks that the cleverest shopper for the minimum needs of an old man has to have a dollar a day.

It came as almost as shattering a blow that his other theory about self-reliance also has flaws. He has worked hard in his time, lived frugally, minded his own business, but somehow at age seventy-four this has not been enough. He is slowly starving to death, hastening the invasion of age.

"*What I need is medical attention,*" he says. But he needs more than that. And so do about 8,000,000 other Americans over sixty-five who are impoverished. Mr. MacIntosh is not unique. He lives on about $600 a year. There are 1,500,000 lone individuals in the United States

From *In the Midst of Plenty* (Boston: Beacon Press, 1964), pp. 103–111. Reprinted by permission of the Beacon Press, copyright © 1964 by Ben H. Bagdikian.

Ben H. Bagdikian is a journalist whose studies have ranged from the American news media to the nation's poor.

who live on less than $500 a year. The 8,000,000 aged poor are a growing segment of the American population who feel in their bones that they are no longer needed or wanted. In some primitive societies the old and sick are placed in a special shelter where they slowly and discreetly die. In the United States there are no such deliberate dwellings for death but there are the acres of crumbling rooming houses and cheap motels in every city where the aged await the end. There used to be 3000 old people on Los Angeles' Bunker Hill alone, and 16,000 inhabitants over sixty in Uptown of Chicago. Every city has districts where the aged sit or lie all day, seldom getting outdoors, eking out a Social Security check or a pension or dwindling savings, but unknown to most of the city. They are known to the Social Security office, which recognizes the cluster of addresses in its card files, or the welfare department, or the Fire Department, which usually has special plans when an alarm flushes the terrified residents out of the geriatric warrens.

When Edmund MacIntosh was a boy there were fewer than 4,000,000 Americans over sixty-five, only one in twenty citizens. At that time a child at birth could expect to live forty-seven years. For those who cheated this statistic by living longer, the usual fate was to remain a part of a large household in a large house, with children and grand-children, in the towns and villages of the turn of the century.

Today there are 16,000,000 Americans over sixty-five, one in every eleven citizens. At birth today a child can expect to live seventy years. Four million of the aged live alone, and millions more as couples by themselves, far from their children who live in small city apartments or in compact suburban cottages.

Science is keeping people alive longer. But it is taking away their jobs sooner. In 1920 over 30 percent of the aged were working. Today only 20 percent have jobs. The simple jobs that used to be the special preserve of the aged are among the first eliminated by automa-tion. It is impolite to call anyone "old" but this is cruel semantics. So-cially, even physically, the extended vigor of Americans makes it natural that these be euphemized as "senior citizens" or the "ageing," or, at worst, "the elderly." But when it comes to work, they are old. Today if a man loses his regular job at age forty-five, the odds that he will never find another steady job are frighteningly high. Medical science has made spectacular gains in keeping human beings alive, but social policy has failed to find a civilized way for them to nourish their sur-viving bodies and spirits. Survival has its price, in high medical costs, in loneliness, and in uselessness. Yet little is done to fill the lengthening empty years. The Department of Health, Education and Welfare says that by the year 2000 there will be 30,000,000 Americans over sixty-five, double the number today. Dr. Herbert S. Robb, of the Wayne College of Medicine, says, "*If we could cure arteriosclerosis, the ordinary life-span except for cancer might be 120 to 130 years.*"

A lot of old Americans will recognize the world of Edmund MacIntosh. He has a solid, dignified manner, even as he lies on his bed, propped on an elbow, his square-jawed face turning ashen. His third-floor room in a Los Angeles hotel is painted a vague green. Torn curtains at the windows are tied in a knot to let in some light and provide a view of an eroding dirt hillside and the side of a concrete bridge.

He was born in North Carolina, was graduated from high school, finished two years of a military institute. During World War I, in the Merchant Marine, he married a girl from Georgia. They had a daughter. The MacIntosh life was never luxurious but he seemed to earn money adequately. After the first war, he bought a newsstand in Times Square for $200 and cleared $2500 a year from it. When the Depression shrank that income below tolerable limits he went to work in a Baltimore hospital and finally to Washington, D.C. where he worked in a newspaper distributing office and made $3000 a year. This was not enough to keep the whole family together happily and his wife and daughter went to live with one of his relatives while he worked things out in Washington. The day after Pearl Harbor, Mr. MacIntosh, then fifty-two, volunteered and because of his World War I experience was shipped out as a merchant seaman. He saw his wife before he left.

"*I kissed her goodby when I left and gave her a hug and went. I was in Midway when I noticed the letters was coming farther and farther apart. First they was once a week, then every two weeks, then once a month. I was on a ship when it finally came. I wasn't surprised. It was a notice she was filing for divorce. I read it once and tore it up into little pieces and dropped the pieces over the side. That was that.*"

After the war Edmund MacIntosh went it alone, working steadily and minding his own business. After his discharge he became a civilian guard at an Oakland air base at $38 a week, room free. He left that to become a railroad guard on the Southern Pacific at $80 a week, the high point of his working career.

"*Ah, those were the best days. The pay was good. The work was good. I was doing what I liked. I had friends and saw shows. I was living in a San Francisco rooming house where railroad men stayed, for a dollar a day. Then in '54 the railroad started laying off men. I came down here to Los Angeles after that. It's warmer and it's supposed to be cheaper living.*"

He went from his pleasant railroadman's rooming house to a Los Angeles flophouse at 60 cents a night. He did odd jobs. By now he was sixty-four and nobody wanted to put him on a regular payroll. Mostly he cut lawns in Los Angeles, and cleaned cellars and garages. He lived on $1.50 a day. "*I could get a good breakfast, eggs and bacon, for half a dollar, I'd have no lunch, and a snack for supper, you know, eggs or a hot dog. I was getting by. I had enough to see a picture show once a week.*"

Then, about a year ago, after almost ten years as the old man who always came around cutting lawns, automation hit Edmund Mac-Intosh. He was made obsolete by power lawn mowers.

"*They was using more and more of them. I couldn't afford one and when I used the people's mower it took only half the time as with a hand mower and by and by my people realized that, hell, they might as well do it themselves. I don't blame them. With a power mower it's no work at all. But I just wasn't getting enough work to stay alive. That's when I went to the Social Security people. I knew I had Social Security coming to me when I reached sixty-five but I was getting along cutting grass so I went to the Social Security people and asked them if I'd lose anything by not taking it right then. They told me no, it would just pile up, so I let it. But when those power mowers came in and I wasn't making enough to eat, I went to the Social Security people. I didn't mind doing that. Now, welfare, that's charity and that's something else. But Social Security, that's yours, you work for that yourself.*

"*So last year I went to the Social Security. They was awfully nice and I picked up my back pay and started my $50 a month. I try living on the $50 but it just doesn't work. Some months it's all right, some months it's not. I hate to use all my money in the bank from my Social Security savings because it's all I've got. But now I need help.*"

Mr. MacIntosh was lucky. Only because he was over 72 did his uncollected Social Security pension accumulate. He was also lucky he could steadily withdraw money from this nest egg to augment his monthly payments.

He spit some tobacco from his reclining position. He didn't quite make it to the green plastic wastebasket on the floor.

"*Well, they've told me about welfare and I didn't much like the idea of that. But I've done about everything I can to cut out my outgo. I moved to a cheaper hotel here and now they're going to tear this one down. I sold my TV for $15.50 and I miss it now. Maybe I'll have to go to welfare. But I don't know where to go and I'm not able to go out any more. If I try walking my head swims and I'm afraid if I got outside I'll fall down and the cops will think I'm a wino.*

"*This is a tough neighborhood. I had a friend, older man like myself, good fellow, didn't drink. He had dizzy spells now and then and one day he had a spell and stopped to lean against a lamppost. Well, the cops picked him up for a drunk. You get one telephone call when they pick you up and I was the only man he knew so he called me.*

He said he needed $21 to make bail but $21 was more than I had or could put my hands on. He spent thirty days in jail. So I've been afraid to try walking much outdoors.

"*The last time I left this city was seven years ago. Last time I left this block was two weeks ago. I took a cab to Third and Main for a haircut that cost me 50 cents. Cab costs 85 cents. I get my hair cut at the barber school. But they don't seem to have no taxi school for a cheap ride.*"

Sometimes in the evening, Edmund MacIntosh will walk to the elevator on his floor and ride down to the "lobby" of his hotel, a corridor of depression where ashen old men sit in torn plush sofas beside a row of orange steel barrels marked "Scrap."

Most of the time he lies on his bed, listening to a cracked plastic radio, mostly to news and discussion programs.

"*I like the radio, though I miss my TV. I don't have the money to buy a newspaper. The janitor here's a nice fellow and he brings me an old one now and then. On the radio I like to hear political talks. Best thing I like is the President's press conference. I'm a Democrat in politics. My Daddy was and my granddaddy was. We believed all Republicans go to hell when they die and I didn't want to go to hell. I voted last year for Governor Brown and Mayor Yorty. I voted for Kennedy. I've voted all my life ever since I was old enough. Fact is, I was accused once of voting before I was old enough. I was nineteen years old, pretty near old enough.*"

He fears the day when even his walking to the elevator will stop and the time when he will not have kind friends. As it is, a couple on the floor look in on him every day. The janitor brings him old papers. Another man does his shopping every week. But the hotel will be torn down and Edmund MacIntosh will be moved among strangers.

"*What I need most is a doctor. But I don't know no doctor I can call. I need something for my eyes. Four years ago I went to the hospital and they scraped them and I could read a newspaper without glasses. Now if I shut my right eye I can't see that doorknob over there. My hearing's going, too.*"

I asked him what things he missed most, now that he is alone in his hotel room. He pulled with his arms against the steel rod of his headboard and let himself look out the window at the bare earth hill and the gray concrete that made his view of the world.

"*Things I miss? You haven't got enough paper.*"

He was silent for awhile. He was good-natured and matter-of-fact.

"*My eyes are getting dimmer. I keep having these dizzy spells. I keep getting sick to my stomach. There's not a thing on my stomach right now. I guess what I want more than anything else is a doctor. Some good medicine.*"

He paused some more.

"*I'd like to go to church. I went a year ago but I don't know if I'll be able to go again. I can't right now and it's a little hard for me to tell when I will again. If I will again. Straight up, that is. I need a suit of clothes. I'd love to go to a picture show. They may sound like asking for everything in sight, but I miss things like that.*"

He chewed some more and spit again. He missed again.

"*All right. A man ain't going to have everything all his life. Sure, I'd like to be able to walk around without getting dizzy. And go to church. And go to a picture show. But maybe if I just had some good company I guess that would be all right, too. I ain't had a letter in twelve months. And that was from the bank about my account.*"

The man referred to in this chapter as "Edmund MacIntosh" died three months after this interview. The coroner's report said death was from "apparent natural causes."

Truman Moore
Shacktown USA: Migrant Farm Labor

Each year when the harvest begins, thousands of buses haul thousands of crews to fields across America as millions of migrant workers hit the road. They ride in flatbed trucks or old condemned school buses patched together for just one more season. They go by car: Hudson bombers with engines knocking, laying a smoke screen of oil; prewar Fords packed with bags, bundles, pots and pans, children crying. They go in pickups made into mobile tents—a home for the season. They ride the rods of the friendly Southern Pacific.

They come from farms in the Black Belt, from closed mines in the mountains of Kentucky and West Virginia, from wherever men are desperate for work. They come by whatever means they can find. These

Condensed from *The Slaves We Rent* by Truman Moore. Copyright © 1965 by Truman Moore. Reprinted by permission of Random House, Inc., and Paul R. Reynolds Inc., 599 Fifth Avenue, New York 17, N. Y.

Truman Moore is a freelance writer and photographer. This article appeared in *The Atlantic Monthly* (May 1965) as "Slaves for Rent—The Shame of American Farming."

are the migrants—the gasoline gypsies, the rubber tramps—crossing and recrossing America, scouring the countryside in a land where the season never ends. There's always a harvest somewhere.

From Florida to Oregon the fruit tramp pursues the orchards. From Texas to Michigan, the berry migrants work from field to field. Two million men, women, and children invade every State of the Union to pick fruit, to chop cotton, to scrape beans, to top onions, to bunch carrots, to pull corn, to fill their hampers with the richest harvest earth ever yielded to man....

Into all these fields, through State after State, the migrants cut a footpath across America. But in spite of their mobility, the migrants are shut off in their own world. Migrant America is a network of side roads, of farm towns and labor camps and riverbanks, of fields and packing sheds. The famous cities are not New York, Boston, and San Francisco, but the capitals of the agricultural empire of the big growers: Homestead and Belle Glade in Florida; Stockton in California; Riverhead on Long Island; and Benton Harbor in Michigan. For the migrants, no roadside motel or tavern offers a neon welcome. The host community sees them not as a potential payroll but as a blight to the community's health and a threat to the relief rolls. Businessmen, dance bands, and tourists making their way across the country find many services and comforts at their disposal. The migrant can hope at most for good weather, a grassy bank, and a filling station that will permit him to use the rest room....

The Tar-Paper Curtain

Across America there are tens of thousands of migrant camps. They are in the valleys and in the fields, on the edges of cities and towns. Some are half deserted. Some are behind barbed wire and even patrolled by armed guards. Migrant camps are within commuting distance of Times Square, under the vapor trails of Cape Kennedy, and surrounded by missile sites in the Southwest. They have names like Tin Top, Tin Town, Black Cat Row, Cardboard City, Mexico City, the Bottoms, Osceola (for whites), Okeechobee (for blacks), and Griffings Path.

Negroes from the Black Belt are dismayed by camps they find up North. Okies and Arkies who migrate today find camps much like those the Joads found in "The Grapes of Wrath." You can drive from New York to California and never see a migrant camp. You have to know where to look. To borrow a popular analogy, a tar-paper curtain separates the migrants from the rest of America.

Let us look at a typical migrant camp which we will call Shacktown. Shacktown is owned by a corporate farm, one of whose foremen is in charge of the camp. "But mostly," he says, "we just turn it over to the people to run for themselves." In other words, no one collects garbage or maintains the camp in any way. The camp is built on the grower's sprawling farm. It cannot be reached without trespassing, and several signs along the road remind the visitor of this fact. Even finding it is difficult. Local residents are suspicious of outsiders who are interested in migrant camps. Requests for directions are met with icy stares.

Shacktown was built about 15 years ago. No repairs to speak of have been made since then. Most of the screen doors are gone. The floors sag. The roofs leak. The Johnsons, a Shacktown family, have a 6-month-old baby and five older children. "When it rains," says Mr. Johnson, "it leaks on our bed and all over the room. At night when it rains, we have to stand up with the baby so he don't get wet and catch pneumonia."

All the rooms in Shacktown are the same size, 8 by 16 feet. When the Johnsons moved in, they found they needed much more space. They sawed through the wall, a single thickness of 1- by 6-inch pine, and made a door to the next cabin, which was not occupied. The exterior walls are unpainted and uninsulated. They keep out neither wind nor rain, sight nor sound. Cracks between the boards are big enough to put your hand through. There is no privacy, and the Johnsons, like most Shacktown families, have learned to live without it. The windows are simple cutouts with a hatch propped open from the bottom. Some have a piece of clothlike screening tacked on.

The only touch of the 20th century in the Johnsons' cabin is a drop cord that hangs down from the ceiling. It burns a single light bulb, plays a small worn radio, and when it works, an ancient television set that Mr. Johnson bought for $10, through which they get their only glimpse of urban, affluent America.

Although there are trees nearby, the camp is built on a barren, red-clay hill, backed by a blazing summer sun. There are four barrack-type frame buildings, divided into single rooms. Behind the barracks are two privies, both four-seaters. The door to the women's privy is missing, but the rank growth of weeds serves as a screen. There are no lights, and no one uses the toilets after dark. The Johnsons use a slop jar at night. It is kept in the kitchen and used for garbage too.

There is virtually no hope of keeping out the flies that swarm around the privies. But one county health inspector found an unusual way of getting the growers interested in the problem. The inspector would drop by the grower's house just before lunch and ask to see the migrant camp. When they came to the privy, the inspector would throw a handful of flour over the seats, which invariably swarmed with flies. On the way back to the house, the inspector would manage to get invited to stay for lunch. At the table he would remark, "Well, I'm sure glad you asked us all to lunch." And there crawling around on the fried chicken would be a floured, white-backed privy fly.

During most of the season in Shacktown there will be several full- or part-time whores. The going price is $3. Prostitution thrives behind open doors. Venereal diseases are sometimes epidemic. In a crew near Morehead City, N.C., 1 woman infected 10 men in the course of 3 days. Six out of eight crews working in the area had at least one syphilitic.

There are two hasps on the Johnsons' door in Shacktown. One is for the family to use. The other is for the grower. If the rent is not paid, the family will find when they return from the field that they have been locked out. Some growers provide cabins free. Some charge according to the number of able-bodied workers. Rents run from as low as $10 a month to as high as $50.

The Johnsons, like most Shacktown families, do their own cooking. But grocery shopping is not easy. There is a small cracker-barrel store near the camp, run by the grower, but the prices are a third higher than in town. "'We got a 10-cent raise,'" says Mr. Johnson, "and everything in the store went up a quarter. He wants us to buy from him or move out. It don't seem right."

Cooking is done on a small, open-flame, unvented kerosene stove which serves as a heater in the cold weather. Fires and explosions are not uncommon. The cabins are not wired for electric heaters; natural gas is not available. Bottle gas requires a deposit and an installation fee. Asked if the tenants did not suffer from the cold nights, the camp manager replied, "Oh, heat's no problem. You would be surprised how hot it gets in one of them little cabins with so many people."

For most of the year the cabins are miserably hot. Refrigeration is nonexistent, and perishable foods seldom find their way to the migrant's table. The baby's milk sours quickly, and he is given warm Coke. Good water is always scarce in Shacktown. Between the long buildings there is a single cold-water tap. The faucet leaks, and there is no drainage. A small pond has developed, and the faucet is reached by a footbridge made of boards propped on rocks. This is the only water in camp.

Just keeping clean is a struggle. Water must be carried in from the spigot, heated over the kerosene stove, and poured into the washtub. In the evening, the oldest children are sent out with buckets to stand in line for water. Sometimes when the line is too long, the Johnsons buy their water from a water dealer, who sells it by the bucket. "We get some of our water down the road about 5 miles," says Mrs. Johnson. "Sometimes I get so tired I would just like to go in and die. We have to boil the water and then take it to the tub to wash the clothes. We

have to boil water for washing dishes. The last camp we was in had a
shower, but you had to stand in line for it half a day, especially in
the summer."

The problem of getting water is widespread in migrant camps.
A Mexican national in California said his camp was without water for
a week. "The contractor said the pump broke. There was a small
rusty pipe that brought enough water for washing the hands and the
face, but we could not wash our clothes, and we could not take a bath
for a week. The inspector ordered the pump be fixed right away. Now
the water from the baths is pumped out of a big hole, and it flows
through a ditch between the bunkhouse and the tents. When it makes
warm weather it smells very bad. To me it looks like the contractor is
not afraid of the inspector."

When several children in a Swansboro, N.C., camp became ill, a
young minister named Jack Mansfield had the water in the camp tested.
It was found to be contaminated. He reported this to the county health
office, but they said nothing could be done since the camp had been
condemned long ago. . . .

As bad as conditions are in the camps where the migrants live,
they are worse in the fields where they work. A Florida Health Department report noted that at times crews refused to harvest fields because
of the human waste deposited there by an earlier crew.

Americans are probably the most dirt-conscious people in the
world. We are a bathroom-oriented society. Chains of restaurants, motels,
and hotels across the country appeal to customers almost solely on the
contention that their establishments are spotlessly clean. In such a society,
it is not pleasant to imagine that beneath the cellophane wrapper lies
a head of lettuce that has been urinated on. A storm of controversy
erupted when a labor union showed a movie of fieldworkers urinating
on a row of lettuce. Growers charged that the picture was posed by
unionmen in old clothes. Perhaps it was, but it need not have been faked.

The fields of the modern factory farm are immense. And there
are no bathrooms. A Catholic priest observed that "most consumers
would gag on their salad if they saw these conditions, the lack of sanitary
conditions, under which these products are grown and processed." . . .

The Children of Harvest

. . . Billy was the youngest of the children. He was not quite 5
but old enough to do a little work. He didn't earn much, but it was
better, his father said, than having him sit around the day-care center
costing them 75 cents every single day. His mother kept the money he

earned in a mason jar. When fall came, he'd get a pair of shoes if there was enough money. He could start school, if there was one nearby, in new shoes.

His brother lay beside him in the clearing. John was 10. In the years that separated Billy and John, a brother and sister had died, unnamed, a day after birth. John kept them alive in his imagination. There were few playmates in the camps and fields that he ever got to know.

"I got two brothers and a sister," he would say. "And they's all in heaven but Billy there."

He called his invisible brother Fred, which is what he wanted to be called instead of John. Faith was the name he gave his sister. He saw her as soft and gentle, wearing a dress with white frills, like a china doll. He played over in his mind a single drama with endless variations. Faith was hurt or being picked up by some bully. He would come to her side to help or defend her. Then he and Faith and Fred would sit beneath a tree, and they would praise him for his bravery, and he would say it was nothing. They would have something cold to drink and maybe some candy to eat. He retreated more and more into this pleasant world. His mother had noticed his blank gaze many times and had heard him say "Faith." She thought he was going to be called to the ministry to be a gospel preacher or a faith healer. . . .

These are the children of harvest. "The kids that don't count" they are sometimes called. "The here-today-gone-tomorrow kids." . . .

The migrant child may never develop any idea of home. His family is never in any place long enough, and home to him is wherever he happens to be. He seldom sees a doctor. It is almost certain that he will have pinworms and diarrhea. Other common ailments untreated are contagious skin infections, acute febrile tonsillitis, asthma, iron deficiency anemia, and disabling physical handicaps. A poor diet condemns the child from the start. A report on a camp in Mathis, Tex., showed that 96 percent of the children had not drunk milk in 6 months. Their diet consisted mainly of cornmeal and rice. A doctor commenting on the report said there was evidence of ordinary starvation. The migrant child is prone to scurvy, rickets, and kwashiokor—a severe protein deficiency. Some reports have put the incidence of dental abnormalities at 95 percent, and others said that bad teeth were universal. . . .

Children have worked on farms since the first farmer had a son, and it has always been considered part of the rural way of life. But there is a difference between the farmer's boy doing his chores and the migrant child topping onions and digging potatoes. The two are blurred together in the minds of people outside agriculture. The blurring gets help from such spokesmen as North Carolina's Congressman COOLEY, who enunciated the Blue Sky Doctrine: "There are no sweat shops on the farms of America," he said. "On the farms of our Nation, children labor with their parents out under the blue skies."

Under the blue skies of Idaho, a 12-year-old girl got her ponytail caught in a potato-digging machine. It ripped off her scalp, ears, eyelids, and cheeks. She died shortly afterward in a hospital. On a farm in California, a 10-year-old girl came back from the fields exhausted from a day's work. She fell asleep on a pile of burlap bags as she waited for her parents. As other workers returned from the fields, they tossed the empty bags on the stack, and the little girl was soon covered up. A 2-ton truck backed across the pile and drove off. They did not find her body until the next day.

If children were mangled in steel mills, there would be a storm of public protest. But death and injury on the mechanized farms seem to pass unnoticed. Under the blue sky of the farm factory is no place for little children. Agriculture is one of the three most hazardous industries. In California alone, more than 500 agricultural workers under the age of 18 are seriously injured every year.

The migrants who follow the harvest are the only people in America who are desperate enough for this work to take it. Their children will be another generation of wanderers, lost to themselves and to the Nation.

Mary W. Wright
The Outskirts of Hope

Are there perhaps some individuals in need in Appalachia who do not now avail themselves of help "already theirs for the asking?" Why are there cases of serious deprivation which are not in contact with appropriate agencies of assistance?

I know a man, I'll call him Buddy Banks. He lives in a ravine in a little, one-room pole-and-cardboard house he built himself, with his wife, their six children, and baby granddaughter. Mr. Banks, 45 years old, is a sober man, a kindly man, and a passive man. He can read and

From "The Outskirts of Hope," *Mountain Life and Work* (Spring 1964), pp. 10–15. Reprinted by permission of the publisher, The Council of the Southern Mountains, Inc.

Mary W. Wright is a caseworker in Appalachia for the Presbyterian Children's Welfare Center, Buckhorn, Kentucky. This article also appeared in the *Journal of Marriage and the Family* (November 1964).

write a little, has worked in the coal mines and on farms, but over the years he's been pretty badly battered up and today is "none too stout." Last fall, when he could no longer pay the rent where he was staying, his mother-in-law gave him a small piece of ground, and he hastened to put up this little shack in the woods before the snow came. If, as you rode by, you happened to glance down and saw where he lives, and saw his children playing among the stones, you would say, "White trash." You would say, "Welfare bums."

When the newspaper announced the new ADC program for unemployed fathers, I thought of Buddy Banks. There is not much farm work to be done in the wintertime, and Mr. Banks has been without a job since summer. Here in their ravine, they can dig their coal from a hole in the hill and dip their water from the creek, and each month he scratches together two dollars for his food stamps by doing odd jobs for his neighbors, who are very nearly as poor as he is. Other than this, there is nothing coming in. I thought, maybe here is some help for Buddy Banks.

Since Mr. Banks does not get a newspaper or have a radio, he had not heard about the new program. He said, yes, he would be interested. I offered to take him to town right then, but he said no, he would have to clean up first, he couldn't go to town looking like this. So I agreed to come back Friday.

On Friday he told me he'd heard today was the last day for signing up. We were lucky, eh? It wasn't true, but it's what he had heard, and I wondered, suppose he'd been told last Tuesday was the last day for signing up, and I hadn't been there to say, well, let's go find out anyway.

Buddy Banks was all fixed up and looked nice as he stepped out of his cabin. His jacket was clean, and he had big rubber boots on and a cap on his head. I felt proud walking along with him, and he walked proud. (Later, in town, I noticed how the hair curled over his collar, and the gray look about him, and the stoop of his shoulders. If you had seen him, you'd have said, "Country boy, come to get his check.")

When we reached the Welfare Office, it was full of people, a crowd of slouchy, shuffly men, standing around and looking vaguely in different directions. I followed Buddy Banks and his brother-in-law, who had asked to come with us, into the lobby, and they too stood in the middle of the floor. Just stood. It was not the momentary hesitation that comes before decision. It was the paralysis of strangeness, of lostness, of not knowing what to do. A girl was sitting at a table, and after a number of minutes of nothing, I quietly suggested they ask her. No, they told me, that was the food stamp girl. But there was no other. So finally, when I suggested, well, ask her anyway, they nodded their heads, moved over, and asked her. I wondered how long they might have gone on standing there if I'd kept my mouth shut. I wondered how long the others all around us had been standing there. I had an idea that if I hadn't been right in the way, Buddy Banks just might have turned around and gone out the door when he saw the crowd, the lines, and that smartly dressed food stamp girl bending over her desk.

Yes, he was told, and after waiting a few minutes, he was shown behind the rail to a chair beside a desk, and a man with a necktie and a big typewriter began to talk with him. They talked a long, long time, while the brother-in-law and I waited in the lobby. (They had asked the brother-in-law if he had brought the birth certificates. No, he hadn't, and so they said there wasn't anything they could do, to come back next Tuesday. He said nothing, stared at them a moment, then walked away. He stood around waiting for us all day long and never asked them another question. He said he would tend to it some other time. Fortunately, they got Mr. Banks sitting down before they inquired about the birth certificates.)

I knew what they were talking about: I have talked long times with Mr. Banks myself, and they were going over it again, and again, and I could imagine Mr. Banks nodding his head to the question he didn't quite understand, because he wanted to make a good impression, and it would be a little while before the worker realized that he hadn't understood, and so they would go back and try again, and then Mr. Banks would explain as best he could, but he would leave something out, and then the worker wouldn't understand, so that, in all, their heads were bent together for almost an hour and a half. It seemed a long time to take to discover Buddy Banks's need—a visit to his home would have revealed it in a very few minutes, but of course 12 miles out and 12 miles back takes time too, and there are all those eligibility rules to be checked out, lest somebody slip them a lie and the editorials start hollering, "Fraud! Fraud!" Actually, I was impressed that the worker would give him that much time. It *takes* time to be sympathetic, to listen, to hear— to understand a human condition.

At last he came out, and, with an apologetic grin, he said he must return on Tuesday, he must go home and get the birth certificates. Then they would let him apply. (How will you come back, Mr. Banks? Where will you get the $3 for taxi fare by next Tuesday? Perhaps you could scrape it up by Monday week, but suppose you come on Monday week and your worker isn't here? Then perhaps you won't come back at all...)

While Mr. Banks was busy talking, I was chatting with one of the other workers. Because I am a social worker too, I can come and go through the little iron gate, and they smile at me and say, "Well, *hello* there!" We talked about all the work she has to do, and one of the things she told me was how, often, to save time, they send people down to the Health Department to get their own birth records. Then they can come back and apply the same day. I wondered why Mr. Banks's worker never suggested this. Maybe he never thought of it. (Maybe he doesn't live 12 miles out with no car, and the nearest bus eight miles from home. And no bus fare at that.) Or perhaps he *did* mention it, and Mr. Banks never heard him, because his head was already filled up with the words that went before: "I'm sorry, there's nothing we can do until you bring us the birth certificates," and he was trying to think in which box, under which bed, had the children been into them . . . ?

So I tried to suggest to him that we go now to the Health Department, but he didn't hear me either. He said, and he persisted, I'm going to the Court House, I'll be right back, will you wait for me? I tried to stop him: let's plan something, what we're going to do next, it's almost lunchtime and things will close up—until suddenly I realized that after the time and the tension of the morning, this was no doubt a call of nature that could not wait for reasonable planning, nor could a proud man come out and ask if there might not be a more accessible solution. And so, as he headed quickly away for the one sure place he knew, I stood mute and waited while he walked the three blocks there and the three blocks back. I wonder if that's something anybody ever thinks about when they're interviewing clients.

Mr. Banks and I had talked earlier about the Manpower Redevelopment Vocational Training Programs, and he had seemed interested. "I'd sure rather work and look after my family than mess with all this stuff, but what can I do? I have no education." I told him about the courses and he said, yes, I'd like that. And so we planned to look into this too, while we were in town. But by now Mr. Banks was ready to go home. "I hate all this standing around. I'd work two days rather than stand around like this." It wasn't really the standing around he minded. It was the circumstances of the standing around. It took some persuading to get him back into the building, only to be told—at 11:30—to come back at ten to one. (Suppose his ride, I thought, had been with somebody busier than I. Suppose they couldn't wait till ten to one and kept badgering him, "Come on, Buddy, hurry up, will you? We ain't got all day!")

I tried to suggest some lunch while we waited, but they didn't want lunch. "We had breakfast late; I'm not hungry, really." So instead, I took him around to the Health Department and the Circuit Court and the County Court, and we verified everything, although he needed some help to figure which years the children were born in.

At ten to one, he was again outside the Welfare Office, and he drew me aside and said that he'd been thinking: maybe he should go home and talk this whole thing over a little more. He felt that before jumping into something, he should know better what it was all about. This startled me, for I wondered what that hour and a half had been for, if now, after everything, he felt he must return to his cronies up the creek to find out what it all meant. So we stood aside, and I interpreted the program as best I could—whom it was for, what is required, and what it would do for him and his family—while he stood, nodding his head and staring at the sidewalk. Finally, cautiously, almost grimly, he once again pushed his way into that crowded, smoke-filled lobby.

"Those who are to report at one o'clock, stand in this line. Others in that line." Mr. Banks stood in the one o'clock line. At 1:15, he reached the counter. I don't know what he asked, but I saw the man behind the desk point over toward the other side of the building, the Public Assistance side, where Mr. Banks had already spent all morning. Mr. Banks nodded his head and turned away as he was told to do. At that point I butted in. "Assistance for the unemployed is over there," the man said and pointed again. So I mentioned training. "He wants training? Why didn't he say so? He's in the wrong line." I don't know what Mr. Banks had said, but what *does* a person say when he's anxious, tired, and confused, and when a crowd of others, equally anxious, are pushing from behind, and when the man at the counter says, "Yes?" I butted in, and Mr. Banks went to stand in the right line, but I wondered what the man behind us did, who didn't have anybody to butt in for him.

While Mr. Banks was waiting, to save time, I took the birth certificates to his worker on the other side. I walked right in, because I was a social worker and could do that, and he talked to me right away and said, "Yes, yes, this is good. This will save time. No, he won't have to come back on Tuesday. Yes, he can apply today. Just have him come back over here when he is through over there. Very good."

At 1:30, Buddy Banks reached the counter again, was given a card and told to go sit on a chair until his name was called. I had business at 2:00 and returned at 3:00, and there he was, sitting on the same chair. But I learned as I sat beside him that things had been happening. He had talked with the training counselor, returned to his welfare worker, and was sent back to the unemployment counselor, after which he was to return once more to his welfare worker. I asked what he had learned about the training. "There's nothing right now, maybe later." Auto mechanics? Bench work? Need too much education. There may be something about washing cars, changing oil, things like that. Later on. Did you sign up for anything? No. Did they say they'd let you know? No. How will you know? I don't know.

At last his ADC (Unemployed) application was signed, his cards were registered, his name was in the file. Come back in two weeks and we'll see if you're eligible. (How will you get back, Buddy? I'll find a way.)

It was four o'clock. "Well, that's over." And he said, "I suppose a fellow's got to go through all that, but I'd sure rather be a-working than a-fooling around with all that mess." We went out to the car, and I took him home. "I sure do thank you, though," he said.

While I'd been waiting there in the lobby, I saw another man come up to the counter. He was small and middle-aged, with a wedding band on his finger, and his face was creased with lines of care. I saw him speak quietly to the man across the desk. I don't know what he said or what the problem was, but they talked a moment and the official told him, "Well, if you're disabled for work, then there's no use asking about training," and he put up his hand and turned away to the papers on his desk. The man waited there a moment, then slowly turned around and stood in the middle of the floor. He lifted his head to stare up at the wall, the blank wall, and his blue eyes were held wide open to keep the tears from coming. I couldn't help watching him, and when suddenly he looked at me, his eyes straight into mine, I couldn't help asking him— across the wide distance of the crowd that for just an instant vanished into the intimacy of human communion—I asked, "Trouble?" Almost as if he were reaching out his hands, he answered me and said, "I just got the news from Washington and come to sign up, and . . ." But then, embarrassed to be talking to a stranger, he mumbled something else I couldn't understand, turned his back to me, stood another long moment in the middle of the crowd, and then walked out the door.

Disabled or not disabled. Employed or not employed. In need or not in need. Yes or no. Black or white. Answer the question. Stand in line.

It is not the program's fault. You have to have questionnaires, and questionnaires require a yes or no. There is no space for a maybe, but . . .

Nor is the people-who-work-there's fault, for who can see—or take time to see—the whole constellation of people and pressures, needs and perplexities, desires and dreads that walk into an office in the person of one shuffling, bedraggled man—especially when there are a hundred other bedraggled men waiting behind him? You ask the questions and await the answers. What else can you do?

Then perhaps it is the fault of the man himself, the man who asks—or doesn't quite know how to ask—for help. Indeed, he's called a lazy cheat if he does, and an unmotivated, ignorant fool if he doesn't. It must be his own fault.

Or maybe it's nobody's fault. It's just the way things are . . .

Yes, there are reasons why some in need among us do not avail themselves of the help that is "already theirs for the asking."

Which of us, I sometimes wonder, will know which counter to go to in Heaven, and after the first few questions, will we too be tempted to turn around and go out the door and try to catch us a ride back home—even if it is just a one-room pole shack buried in a dank ravine?

David Caplovitz
How the Poor Are Bilked

The numerous accounts of exploitation fall under several general headings. Some reveal the high-pressure sales techniques to which these families are subjected. Others relate to the misrepresentation of the price of goods. And still others refer to the substitution of inferior goods for those ordered. Included here are accounts of the sale of reconditioned goods as new.

The repetitiveness of the incidents is quite striking. Some families were victimized by unethical television repairmen, a few by the same company. Another group were victims of the pots-and-pans salesmen; encyclopedia salesmen show up in several of the accounts, as do the peddlers selling sink attachments.

As we shall see, the incidents touch upon a number of themes. These include the role of the mass media in setting off the chain of events with alluring ads; the anonymity of many of the credit transactions to the point where the consumer is not sure who the merchant is; the bewilderment of the consumer in the face of powerful forces brought into play by the merchant; and the hopelessness, frustration, and resignation of many in the face of exploitation.

Bait Advertising and the Switch Sale

A sizable number of the families had been victimized by "bait" advertising. Responding to advertisements for sewing machines, phono-

Reprinted with permission of The Macmillan Company from *The Poor Pay More* by David Caplovitz, pp. 141–154. Copyright © 1963 by The Free Press of Glencoe, a Division of The Macmillan Company.

David Caplovitz is Associate Professor of Sociology, Columbia University.

graphs, washing machines, and other items offered at unusually low prices, they succumbed to the salesmen's "switch-sale" technique by buying a much more expensive model.

The technique is illustrated by the story of a 26-year-old Negro housewife:

> I saw a TV ad for a $29 sewing machine, so I wrote to the company and they sent down a salesman who demonstrated it for me. It shook the whole house, but I wanted to buy it anyway. But he kept saying it would disturb all the neighbors by being so noisy, and *went out to the hall and brought in another model costing $185. . . .*
>
> I actually had to pay $220. He promised if I paid within a certain amount of time I would get $35 back. *But since my husband was out of work, we couldn't pay within the time period,* so I didn't get the refund. . . . *I was taken in by the high-pressure sales talk.*

A middle-aged Puerto Rican husband was victimized by a variant of this racket. Instead of responding to an ad, he received a call from a salesman saying that his wife had won a sewing machine:

> He brought the machine to the house. It was worth $25, and we ended up buying another one for $186. A friend of mine bought a similar machine, maybe better than mine, for $90. *They tricked me into buying the machine for $186 on credit.*

In these cases, the reactions are much the same, the feeling of being tricked by a high-pressure salesman. In each instance, a purchase was made at a price higher than the anticipated one.

The "switch sale" is by no means limited to sewing machines. A 28-year-old Negro housewife told the following story about a phonograph sale:

> I saw an advertisement in the paper *for a $49 Hi-Fi set.* The ad said: "Phone for free demonstration," so I did. The salesman came a few days later, bringing a set that was different from the one I saw advertised. I told him it wasn't the set I saw in the paper, but he said it was, so we hassled for a while. He kept high-pressuring me, saying he had one in the car he knew I would like. So finally, I told him to bring it up. He did, and played it for me.
>
> *I asked him to leave it so my husband could hear it, but he said "no." Then I asked him to come back later when my husband would be home and he said "no" again. Well, I decided to gamble and signed the papers.* [Later they mailed a coupon book. The set came to $175.]
>
> He asked me for a down-payment, so I gave him my old radio and got $10 off. *And right after that, my husband came in. He didn't want the set, but the salesman told him we couldn't return it.* Later my husband examined the set. The salesman had said it contained

four woofers and two tweeters, but my husband found out they didn't exist. We called the store, but they said we couldn't change it, so we had to pay the full amount.

Once the set stopped working. We phoned the store and got free repairs. *But the second time the set broke down, we called the store and were told that the company no longer dealt in Hi-Fi sets, only in sewing machines.*

One law of the commercial jungle facing the low-income consumer is vividly dramatized in this irreversibility of the credit transaction. Tacit in all dealings with ethical merchants is the right to exchange merchandise if the customer is not satisfied. Not so in the low-income market. Once the signature is obtained on the contract, the sale is consummated. It should be noted that the husband returned in time to register his displeasure to the salesman. But the concept of the satisfied customer is foreign to such hit-and-run transactions. Even when the couple discovered that the phonograph did not measure up to the salesman's claims, they were still unable to exchange it. As we shall see, this is not an isolated occurrence. Other families also discovered that the principle of exchange does not apply to them. The "run-around" this couple received when seeking service is also fairly typical. The explanation given seems quite thin, and yet it was apparently enough to free the store from the complaining customer. The incident also illustrates the way "easy credit" breaks through traditional constraints upon consumption. However reluctant at first, this housewife was still able to indulge her impulse to buy without consulting her husband.

Bait advertising was reported by a 37-year-old Negro mother living on welfare. She had seen a newspaper ad, placed by a 125th Street furniture store, announcing the reupholstering of couches with good material for $49.95:

> I phoned them and they sent out a salesman. I told him I saw the ad and wanted my couch covered for $49.95. I asked him to show me the material. He pulled out some patterns and looked at them and said, "These aren't so hot. I really want to give customers something they'll be satisfied with." Then he flipped to the higher-priced patterns—*but I didn't know they were higher-priced then.* I picked out a pattern and asked him how much. He told me $149. *But I only had $49 in cash and wanted to pay only in cash, so I told him that this was too high. He praised the material so much, talking about its quality and durability, that I finally told him that if I could get an account I'd take it. He gave me a contract. I just took a quick look and signed it.* They sent for the couch and returned it two weeks later. The work on the seams of the pillows was awful. . . . Six months later, the wire in the spring popped out the side and the other side had a pointed end on it.

By now the elements of the process are familiar: the "bait ad," the high-pressure salesman, the purchase of a much more expensive item, and, as often happens, dissatisfaction with the merchandise. Of particular interest in this case is the fact that the woman had every intention of paying cash when she responded to the ad but was converted into a credit buyer in spite of her intent. . . .

Misrepresentation of Prices

The preceding incidents illustrate various schemes through which low-income families are pressured into buying. Other incidents exhibit another fairly common form of duplicity: the misrepresentation of price, particularly in credit transactions. Although the merchant is required by law in New York State to enter both the cash price and the finance charges on the installment contract, some circumvent this law either by not explaining the terms of the contract or by not sending the customer his copy of the contract until sometime after the sale is consummated. In several instances we found that the consumer did not learn the full cost of his merchandise until he received the payment coupons some time after the sale. This practice is illustrated by the following typical episodes:

> [41-year-old Puerto Rican husband, welfare family] I was cheated on a TV set I bought. At first the price was supposed to be $220. After I signed the contract I found out that it was really $300. *But then it was too late.*

> [34-year-old Puerto Rican housewife] I was told by the salesman that the credit price for the Hi-Fi set was $299. *When I got the payment book, I found out that I had to pay them $347.*

> [28-year-old Negro housewife] I heard an ad on the radio about a special bargain on washing machines for only $100. After I ordered it and had it installed, I got a bill for $200. I said I wouldn't pay it and they took it away. *I paid a $50 down-payment, and they never gave it back to me. I'm just glad I did not have to pay the balance.*

In the last case, we see that the misleading price appeared in an ad. The consumer made the purchase over the telephone, and therefore the true cost was not revealed until after the installation. It should also be noted that the misleading advertisement led to the loss of a $50 down-payment. The vulnerable position of many low-income consumers is suggested by this woman's feeling of relief that she did not lose even more money.

The manner in which salesmen lie to families about the cost of goods is revealed by another incident involving a door-to-door salesman selling washing machines:

> [Husband and wife, aged 33 and 27, Puerto Rican] A salesman came to the door about three months ago and showed us a pamphlet with pictures of washing machines. He said it would be simple to buy it on credit. We met him at the furniture company, *where he showed us the machine and said it would not cost more than $290. So we signed the papers and didn't have to pay any cash.* When the machine was installed it didn't work.
>
> We called the store three times and were promised a mechanic, but he never came. *And we got a credit-payment book in the mail for $462.66,* saying we were supposed to pay $18 a month. [*They also received a sales slip, and on this bill there is a typed statement to the effect that a down-payment of $29.30 was made by Mr. R. Both Mr. and Mrs. R. deny any cash payments.*] A month later we got a statement saying that payments were overdue and we would have to pay 93¢ more. We don't want this machine and they're going to sue us.

In this incident the true price was almost 60 per cent more than the one quoted by the salesman. Perhaps the mysterious down-payment credited to this family was made by the peddler-intermediary in order to reassure the merchant.

A number of families told us that peddlers frequently misrepresented the price of their merchandise, quoting lower prices initially and then demanding higher ones on later visits. Typical of these accounts is the story of a 36-year-old Puerto Rican mother on welfare:

> In March, 1960, a peddler knocked at my door and *insisted so much that I said I'd take a lamp for $29.* I gave him a $3 deposit. When he came back with the account book the next week, *the price had gone up to $42.* I said I wouldn't pay it. *So he took away the lamp, but he never gave me back the $3.*

Again we see the loss of a down payment as the outcome of this practice.

Substitution of Goods

Not only are prices misrepresented in the low-income market, but so is quality. Some families were sold reconditioned merchandise that had been represented as new, and others received merchandise inferior to that ordered.

The sale of used merchandise as new is of course illegal. Yet, . . . some merchants hinted that their competitors engaged in this practice.

The following reports indicate that this does indeed happen. A 36-year-old Puerto Rican mother on welfare gave this account:

> I bought a TV set from a First Avenue store. *It was a used set which was sold as new.* After seven days it broke down. The store took it back and returned it in two weeks. It broke down again and they took it for thirty days. They brought it back and it broke down one week later. They took it away again and I *asked for a refund because there was a guarantee of ninety days which had not run out. But they wouldn't give me back my $100 or bring me another TV.* I went to the store several times but with no results.

A basic inequality in the merchant-consumer relationship is pointed up by this incident. When the low-income consumer fails to live up to his obligations of payment, the merchant is able to utilize the law to protect his rights. When the merchant fails to respect a guarantee, however, the consumer is more likely to lose his initial investment than to obtain justice. In part, this is due to his ignorance of the laws which protect him and the agencies which can help him. But this inequality also partly stems from the merchant's superior resources. He can turn the job of collecting over to lawyers, collection agencies, and the courts. The consumer, on the other hand, must invest his own time in at least initiating legal action, time which, as we have seen, he cannot easily take from his job.

In another incident the sale of a used TV set as new was confirmed by a repairman. A 39-year-old Puerto Rican mother living on welfare had this experience:

> I got a new TV set and some beds for $452.67. The TV alone was $280. It broke down after two years, and I paid $30 for repairs. *The TV repairman said that the set was a reconditioned one in a new cabinet.*

The substitution of merchandise is illustrated by an incident told by a 26-year-old Negro husband:

> We've spent more money repairing the TV than it cost. *The store sent a different one than we asked for and it didn't look new.* We complained to the store and they offered a trade for $25 on another one.

The Anonymity of Basic Transactions

Several families responded to the question about cheating by describing pots-and-pans salesmen who sold them poor-quality merchandise at exorbitant prices. The details of these stories are similar. The salesman shows up either with the goods or with a catalogue. He stresses the unusually low payments, gets the housewife to sign a contract, extracts a small down-payment, and then disappears. Sometime later the family receives a payment book from a finance company and frequently learns only then that the set of pots and pans will cost as much as $60. What is striking about these accounts is the anonymity of the transaction. Several interviewees reported that they tried unsuccessfully to find out the name of the store from which they had bought the merchandise. The high-pressure techniques of these salesmen as well as the theme of anonymity are illustrated in this report by a 30-year-old Puerto Rican husband:

> This happened about four or five days after we moved in. My wife was home and a man knocked at the door. He was selling pots and he pressured my wife to look at them. He said they would cost only $5 a month and that he would leave her a piggy bank so she could save for other things. Then he told her to "sign here," and when all the payments were made she'd get a present. He then asked her if he could just leave the pots for a second while he went downstairs. But since she was signed up he never came back. We got a coupon book and mailed $5 each month to a bank in New Jersey. . . . *I don't know the name of the store but I guess it's somewhere in Fenway, New Jersey. I have no records of it.*

> [Another young Puerto Rican husband gave a similar account:] A salesman came around selling aluminum pots and pans. They're not worth a damn. I gave him a dollar down and then the bank sent me a book and I had to send in payments. *Some bank in New Jersey. I tried to find out the store's name, but I couldn't.* The set cost $60— $5 a month for twelve months.

These incidents illustrate the various ways in which merchants take advantage of low-income consumers. They show the high pressure tactics, the substitution of goods, the exorbitant prices and the shoddy merchandise that are commonplace in the low-income market. . . .

Helen H. Lamale
How the Poor Spend Their Money

A cartoon which appeared before the Election last fall showed the President patting his head with his left hand, labelled "Prosperity," and rubbing his stomach with his right hand, labelled "Poverty." The caption said, "It's easy once you get the hang of it . . . !" Getting "the hang of it" is the problem which confronts anyone who undertakes to discuss and evaluate levels of living among the poor. It can only be done within the framework of the levels and manner of living of the total population. It requires an understanding of how radically these levels of living have changed—in recent years and since the mid-1930's when widespread national interest was last focused on the problem of poverty. The significant differences in size, age, and other characteristics of families, their participation in the labor force, and place of residence, which have accompanied the greatly improved economic status of families, are all important considerations in appraising levels of living among the poor today. Poverty in the midst of prosperity is quite different from poverty in the midst of general economic depression. A few historical statistics on consumer income and expenditures will give perspective to this discussion of current levels and distributions of income, spending, and saving.

Mid-1930 to 1950

Between the mid-1930's and 1950, average current expenditures of employed city-worker families increased almost 60 percent after allowance for the price increases over the period. The proportion of their total spending used for food, shelter (including fuel and utilities), and clothing declined from a little more than 70 percent in 1934–36, to a little less than 60 percent in 1950. Expenditures for household operation, housefurnishings and equipment, medical care, recreation, and automobile purchase and operation in 1950 were all two to more than three times their level in the mid-1930's. Net increases in expenditures for personal care, education, and tobacco all exceeded the 60-percent average increase in total goods and services. The net increase in food expenditures, though considerably less than the average for all goods and services, was still

From a lecture, "Levels of Living among the Poor," presented in the spring of 1965 before a faculty seminar on poverty at the University of California, Los Angeles.

Helen H. Lamale is Chief of the Division of Living Conditions Studies, Bureau of Labor Statistics, U. S. Department of Labor.

substantial—30 percent. Food consumption surveys, conducted by the Department of Agriculture in the late 1940's, reported a marked improvement in the nutritional adequacy of diets—some of it through the improved processing of foods, e.g., enriching of white bread and flour. Current shelter expenses of renters and homeowners had a net increase of 26 percent from the mid-1930's to 1950, and payments on mortgage principal and down payments on homes averaged four and a half to five times their mid-1930 level—reflecting the increase in homeownership among city-worker families from 30 to 45 percent. The period was characterized by expanding use of insurance and credit to cover current living expenses.

The Gains of the 1950's

These improvements in the level of living continued in the 1950's. In 1960–61, urban families and single consumers (hereafter referred to as families) spent an average of $5,390 for current annual living expenses. After allowance for price increases over the decade, this bought about 14 percent more in goods and services than in 1950. Since their average "real" income (after taxes and price change) was up 22 percent, they used only 91 percent of their after-tax income for current consumption in 1960–61, as compared with 97 percent in 1950. The widened margin between income and current expenditures enabled families to increase their gifts and contributions, to put more in personal insurance, and to save more than in 1950.

The improvement in the level of living of the average family during the decade is also indicated in the continued reduction in the percent of total spending allocated to the three "basics," food, shelter (including fuel, etc.) and clothing, and to food alone. For urban families, the relative importance of spending for the three "basics" declined from 57 to 53 percent, and for food from almost 30 percent in 1950, to 24 percent in 1960–61. These indications of improvements in the level of living observed for the average family also occurred throughout the income distribution and among families of different size, age, occupation, and place of residence. Failure to recognize these changes over the past two decades can lead to understatements of our progress in reducing poverty and misunderstanding with respect to the nature and extent of the present need.

Levels and Patterns of Living in 1960–61

The average income after taxes of all nonfarm families—urban and rural—was $5,634, and their expenditures for current consumption goods and services averaged $5,145 in 1960–61. These averages, however, conceal wide variations in income and spending associated with different socio-characteristics of families. They also conceal wide variations in consumption levels actually achieved by various groups in the population after allowing for differences in consumption needs associated with differences in family size, age, and composition. For example, about 45 percent of 1-person families had incomes under $2,000, while only 7 percent of all families of two or more persons had such incomes. On the other hand, the budgetary requirements of 1-person families, most of whom are elderly, are only about 37 percent of those of a 4-person younger family. To allow for these variations, the following discussion of current levels and patterns of living is based on the income and spending patterns of families of different size which are equivalent to those of 4-person families with after-tax income of $3,000 to $4,000, as reported in the BLS Survey of Consumer Expenditures in 1960–61. All nonfarm families of two or more persons in 1960–61 averaged 3.6 persons and had income and expenditures approximating those of families with incomes after taxes of $6,000–$7,499. This is the income class used for comparison with the selected "equivalent low-consumption" classes. (See Tables 1 and 2.)

1. *Food expenditures.* The percent of total spending used for food is a commonly accepted measure of relative levels of living of various groups in the population—the lower the percentage, the higher the level of living. This has been found to be a reasonably valid measure provided the population groups being compared are generally homogeneous with respect to family characteristics and other factors related to food expenditures, including the relation of food prices to prices of other goods and services.

In 1960–61, food expenditures of nonfarm families, on the average, accounted for 24 percent of total current consumption expenditures; they represented the same proportion of total spending of families in the $6,000–$7,499 class. (See Table 3.) This was approximately 5 percentage points lower than for all urban families in 1950.

In the selected low-consumption classes in 1960–61, the percent spent for food varied from 27 percent for 3-person families to 31 percent for families of 6 or more persons. This is about the same, or slightly less than the percent spent for food by the average urban family in 1950.

Food expenditures as a percent of total spending for families with incomes under the selected classes ranged from 29 percent for 1-person families to 34 percent for families of 6 or more persons, a level approximately the same as that of employed wage- and clerical-worker families of two or more persons in 1950.

Although comparisons of the percent spent for food give an idea of the relative level of living of various groups in the population at a

Table 1—Summary of Family Expenditures, Incomes, and Savings, by Family Size at Selected Income Levels

Total Nonfarm United States, 1960–61 [1]

	Family Size and Annual Money Income after Taxes						
	1 person $1,000–1,999	2 persons $2,000–2,999	3 persons $2,000–3,999	4 persons $3,000–3,999	5 persons $4,000–4,999	6 or more persons $5,000–5,999	Families and single consumers $6,000–7,499
Family characteristics:							
Number of families in sample	523	520	356	149	150	164	1,854
Families in universe							
Estimated number (000)	2,403	2,415	1,691	702	676	752	7,994
Percent in size class	29.4	15.5	18.3	8.4	12.5	15.1	15.4
Average:							
Family size	1.0	2.0	3.1	4.1	5.1	7.0	3.7
Money income before taxes	$1,493	$2,603	$3,324	$3,695	$4,748	$5,734	$7,513
Number of full-time earners	.1	.3	.6	.7	.8	.9	1.0
Age of head (years)	65.6	60.1	42.8	38.7	37.3	38.9	42.9
Education of head (years)	8.2	8.0	8.9	9.2	9.6	9.7	11.3
Number of children under 18 years	—	.1	1.0	2.0	3.0	4.7	1.6
Percent:							
Homeowners, all year	42	57	42	41	52	62	67
Auto owners, end of year	15	57	68	77	84	88	92
Nonwhite	18	13	20	19	15	17	6
With children under 18 years	—	13	77	95	100	100	66
With persons 65 years and over	64	56	19	10	5	7	10
Avg. income, expenditures & savings:							
Money income after taxes and other money receipts	$1,485	$2,543	$3,211	$3,648	$4,564	$5,624	$6,779
Net change in assets & liabilities	−119	−217	−235	−383	−95	−75	+173
Total expenditures, insurance, gifts and contributions	1,664	2,861	3,651	4,411	5,147	6,021	6,875
Account balancing difference	−60	−101	−205	−380	−488	−322	−269

[1] For definitions, see Consumer Expenditures and Income, BLS Report No. 237-93, and Supplement 3-Part A to BLS Report No. 237-38, U.S. Department of Labor.

Table 2—Details of Family Expenditures, Insurance, Gifts and Contributions, Value of Items Received without Expense and Home-Produced Food, by Family Size, at Selected Income Levels

Total Nonfarm United States, 1960–61

	1 person	2 persons	Family Size and Annual Money Income after Taxes 3 persons	4 persons	5 persons	6 or more persons	Families and single consumers
	$1,000–1,999	$2,000–2,999	$2,000–3,999	$3,000–3,999	$4,000–4,999	$5,000–5,999	$6,000–7,499
Expenditures for current consumption	$1,554	$2,659	$3,436	$4,139	$4,773	$5,542	$6,177
Food, total	449	737	941	1,140	1,393	1,733	1,493
Food prepared at home	352	661	812	966	1,208	1,525	1,209
Food away from home	97	76	129	174	185	208	284
Tobacco	20	59	83	95	112	98	117
Alcoholic beverages	17	30	37	39	48	64	103
Housing, total	668	877	1,029	1,151	1,323	1,510	1,782
Shelter	372	422	478	494	557	626	803
Rented dwelling	262	247	301	290	279	237	256
Owned dwelling	105	166	165	194	271	381	502
Other shelter	5	9	12	9	7	8	45
Other real estate	1	2	2	2	11	1	5
Fuel, light, refrigeration, water	132	195	202	224	285	309	292
Household operations	108	150	181	225	236	261	341
Housefurnishings and equipment	55	108	166	207	234	314	341
Clothing, clo. materials and services	87	165	309	413	499	608	641
Personal care	42	80	110	132	150	168	176
Medical care	121	270	240	320	260	318	398
Prepaid care	32	66	63	70	71	91	107
Recreation	31	63	109	142	168	194	258
Reading	18	25	25	29	30	41	56
Education	1	6	22	39	20	42	59
Transportation	86	280	487	560	659	681	969
Automobile	56	242	447	520	621	624	892
Other travel and transportation	30	38	40	40	38	57	77
Other expenditures	14	67	44	79	111	85	125

Table 2, continued—Details of Family Expenditures, Insurance, Gifts and Contributions, Value of Items Received without Expense and Home-Produced Food, by Family Size at Selected Income Levels

Total Nonfarm United States, 1960–61

	1 person $1,000–1,999	2 persons $2,000–2,999	3 persons $2,000–3,999	4 persons $3,000–3,999	5 persons $4,000–4,999	6 or more persons $5,000–5,999	Families and single consumers $6,000–7,499
Personal insurance, total	$ 27	$ 82	$ 133	$ 191	$ 246	$ 317	$ 391
Social security, government and private retirement	10	34	49	92	131	158	219
Gifts and contributions, total	84	120	82	82	128	162	307
to persons	40	63	35	30	53	50	151
to organizations	44	57	47	52	75	112	156
Value of items received without expense	133	151	188	201	206	251	211
Food	15	14	14	27	20	16	12
Housing	47	42	47	47	41	54	37
Clothing	19	31	46	53	79	79	65
Transportation	11	7	14	11	8	13	11
Medical care	24	40	34	40	20	62	39
Other	17	17	33	23	38	27	48
Value of home-produced food	4	30	30	36	48	36	15

Table 3—Percentage Distribution of Expenditures for Current Consumption, by Family Size at Selected Income Levels

	Total Nonfarm United States, 1960–61						
	1 person $1,000–1,999	2 persons $2,000–2,999	3 persons $2,000–3,999	4 persons $3,000–3,999	5 persons $4,000–4,999	6 or more persons $5,000–5,999	Families and single consumers $6,000–7,499
Percent distribution:							
Expenditures for current consumption	100.0	100.0	100.0	100.0	100.0	100.0	100.0
Food, total	28.9	27.7	27.4	27.6	29.2	31.3	24.2
Food prepared at home	22.7	24.9	23.6	23.4	25.3	27.5	19.6
Food away from home	6.2	2.8	3.8	4.2	3.9	3.8	4.6
Tobacco	1.3	2.2	2.4	2.3	2.4	1.8	1.9
Alcoholic beverages	1.1	1.1	1.1	.9	1.0	1.2	1.7
Housing, total	43.0	33.0	29.9	27.8	27.7	27.2	28.8
Shelter	23.9	15.9	13.9	11.9	11.7	11.3	13.0
Rented dwelling	16.9	9.3	8.8	7.0	5.9	4.3	4.2
Owned dwelling	6.7	6.3	4.8	4.7	5.7	6.9	8.1
Other shelter	.3	.3	.3	.2	.1	.1	.7
Fuel, light, refrigeration, water	8.5	7.3	5.9	5.4	6.0	5.5	4.7
Household operations	7.0	5.6	5.3	5.4	4.9	4.7	5.5
Housefurnishings and equipment	3.5	4.1	4.8	5.0	4.9	5.7	5.5
Clothing, clo. materials & services	5.6	6.2	9.0	10.0	10.5	11.0	10.4
Personal care	2.7	3.0	3.2	3.2	3.1	3.0	2.8
Medical care	7.8	10.2	7.0	7.7	5.5	5.7	6.4
Prepaid care	2.1	2.5	1.8	1.7	1.5	1.6	1.7
Recreation	2.0	2.4	3.2	3.4	3.5	3.5	4.2
Reading and education	1.2	1.2	1.3	1.6	1.0	1.5	1.9
Transportation	5.5	10.5	14.2	13.6	13.8	12.3	15.7
Automobile	3.6	9.1	13.0	12.6	13.0	11.3	14.4
Other travel and transportation	1.9	1.4	1.2	1.0	.8	1.0	1.3
Other expenditures	.9	2.5	1.3	1.9	2.3	1.5	2.0
Sum of food, shelter (incl. fuel, etc.) and clothing	66.9	57.1	56.2	54.9	57.4	59.1	52.3
Value of items received without expense as a percent of total current consumption expenditures:							
Food	1.0	.5	.4	.7	.4	.3	.2
Housing	3.0	1.6	1.4	1.1	.9	1.0	.6
Clothing	1.2	1.2	1.3	1.3	1.7	1.4	1.1
Medical care	1.6	1.5	1.0	1.0	.4	1.1	.6
Other							

given time and improvements in levels of living over time, they give no clue as to the quality of living with respect to the content and nutritional adequacy of diets which such food expenditures may provide. For this, expenditures must be compared with food plans which provide nutritional adequacy at different cost levels. Such food plans have been developed and published by the U.S. Department of Agriculture (USDA) for 4 cost levels—Economy, Low-Cost, Moderate-Cost, and Liberal.

In the 1960–61 BLS survey, the annual food expenditures of nonfarm families in the $6,000–$7,499 class averaged $1,493, or $404 per family member. *In the selected low-consumption classes,* food expenditures ranged from $449 for 1-person families to $1,733 for families of 6 or more persons, or from $449 to $248 on a per-family-member basis. These averages were well within the range of 1961 costs for the USDA Low-Cost Food Plan, as estimated for different types of families within size classes and across regions.

Family size	Annual average food expenditure in "low-consumption" classes	Approximate range in annual cost of USDA Low-Cost Food Plan
1 person	$ 449	$305 to $ 450
2 persons	737	450 to 865
3 persons	941	615 to 1,260
4 persons	1,140	760 to 1,630
5 persons	1,393	885 to 1,960
6 or more persons	1,733	995 to 2,240

2. *Percent for the "Basics."* Like the percent spent for food, the percent of total spending allocated to the three "basics"—food, shelter (including fuel and utilities), and clothing—is often used as a measure of relative levels of living. This is based on the assumption that these three expenditure categories are "necessities" and that spending for other goods and services is discretionary. Although the distinction between necessary and discretionary spending is by no means as clearcut today as it was several decades ago, the percent spent for the three "basics" still furnishes some insights into relative levels of living of different groups in the population.

As previously mentioned, the percent spent for food, shelter, and clothing by urban families dropped from 57 percent in 1950 to 53 percent in 1960–61; nonfarm families in the $6,000–$7,499 income class in 1960–61 used 52 percent of their current spending for these "basics." Families in the selected low-consumption classes spent from 55 to 59 percent, except for 1-person families who used 67 percent of their total spending for these three "basics." The proportion spent for food, shelter, and clothing by these low-consumption families in 1960–61, was approximately the same as that spent by the average urban family in 1950. Also except for 1-person families, families with incomes under those of the selected low-consumption classes, used from 58 to 63 percent for food, shelter, and clothing in 1960–61—about the same as spent by wage- and clerical-worker families of two or more persons in 1950.

The percent of total spending used for clothing, both by families in the selected low-consumption classes and with incomes below this level, varied widely across family-size groups—from 6 and 5 per cent, respectively, for 1- and 2-person families to 11 percent for 6 or more-person families, compared with 10 percent at the $6,000–$7,499 income level where the average family size was 3.7 persons. The relatively low clothing spending of these 1- and 2-person families is, in part, a reflection of their age which averaged 60 to 70 years in these family-size and income classes.

The percent spent for shelter also varied widely across family-size classes—from about one-fourth of total current expense for 1-person families to about one-sixth for families of 6 or more persons in the selected low-consumption classes; and from one-third to one-sixth of total current spending, respectively, for families with lower incomes.

However, this pattern of spending for shelter, by families of different size at low-consumption levels cannot be appraised apart from an appraisal of their combined expenditures for shelter and transportation and the pattern of home and auto ownership, which vary widely among families of different size at low-consumption levels, and incidently, among geographical regions and between large cities, small towns, and rural nonfarm areas. When transportation expenditures are added to shelter, the combined expenses represented about 37 percent of total current expense for 1-person families at both the selected low-consumption level and those with incomes under that level. For other family-size classes, the percent spent for shelter and transportation varied between 29 and 34 percent, compared with 33 percent for all nonfarm families with incomes of $6,000–$7,499. Homeownership in the selected low-consumption classes ranged from 41 percent for 4-person families to 62 percent for families of 6 or more persons, and auto ownership from 15 percent for 1-person families to 88 percent for families of 6 or more persons. In the $6,000–$7,499 income class, homeownership was 67 percent and auto ownership, 92 percent.

The quality of the housing occupied by these low-consumption families cannot be discerned from the available tabulations of the BLS survey data. Generally, the space provided and the condition of owned dwellings are better than those of rented dwellings, and better inside than outside metropolitan areas for low-income families, as reported in the 1960 Census of Housing. In 1960, about one-third of all U.S. families

(Census definition) with income under $3,000 lived in housing that was dilapidated or lacked plumbing (i.e. hot and cold running water, or private toilet, or bathing facilities inside the structure), compared with about one-fourth living inside metropolitan areas and about one-half of "under $3,000 income" families living outside metropolitan areas. Thirty percent of all U.S. low-income owners, compared with 42 percent of renters with income under $3,000, were living in such housing. For owners and renters with income over $3,000, only 6 and 13 percent, respectively, occupied such housing.

Although the household inventory data obtained in the BLS survey have not yet been tabulated by level of income and tenure, the high average level of ownership by all urban families of such items as vacuum cleaners (70 percent), televisions (84 percent), washing machines (66 percent), refrigerators (81 percent), etc., makes it evident that a majority of all nonfarm families at the selected low-consumption levels, particularly homeowning families, have these items.

The presence of a telephone in the home, or substantial expenditures for such service, is also a clue to the nature of the household inventory. In 1960–61, 81 percent of the families in the selected equivalent low-consumption classes reported expenditures for telephone and telegraph services which average $63 annually per family buying, compared with reports of such expense by 97 percent of all nonfarm families with incomes from $6,000 to $7,499, and with annual average expenditure of $101 per family buying.

The great variety of expenditures for shelter, transportation and household equipment, coupled with differences in patterns of home and auto ownership among various types of families in different localities, raises serious doubts as to how "discretionary" such spending really is for families at low economic levels.

3. *Discretionary spending.*   Most discussions of the buying habits of the poor eventually get around to the question of whether the poor are spending their incomes for "luxuries" at the expense of "necessities"; and its corollary—whether they pay more for their purchases than do higher income families. Undoubtedly, some poor families, like some rich families, spend foolishly, and there is much evidence that poor families are often victims of unfair selling practices. On balance, however, the 1960–61 survey data seem to indicate that families at the lower end of the income scale were buying the same goods and services as the average family, but at a rate and/or price level commensurate with the difference in their financial status. For example, six percent of the selected low-consumption families bought refrigerators at an average cost of $176, compared with an average of $266 for the 8 percent of families in the

$6,000–$7,499 class who bought. For washing machines, the comparable figures were 7 percent at $140, and 9 percent at $197; for vacuum cleaners, 4 percent at $68, compared with 9 percent at $85.

Average expenditures per family buying for many items represent multiple purchases of such items during the year, for example, women's shoes, and thus are not unit prices. They do, however, seem to reflect the same buying pattern with respect to purchases of the average family, as data for household durables. About three-fourths of the low-consumption families reported expenditures for women's shoes which averaged $18 per family buying, compared with 88 percent of the families at the $6,000–$7,499 level buying at an average expenditure of $31.

The data also show pretty much the same pattern of relationships between the buying of low-consumption families and the average family for such diverse items as: meals out, snacks, laundry and cleaning sent out, auto purchase (reflecting both new and used car purchases), men's haircuts, purchase and care of pets, and televisions.

4. What about Use of Credit and Insurance. In addition to their expenditures for current consumption, families in, and below, the equivalent, low-consumption classes typically made some payments into health and life insurance, Social Security or retirement funds, and made some gifts to persons outside the family and contributions to religious, welfare, and other organizations.

Families in the low-consumption classes spent about one-fourth to one-third of their total medical care expenditures for insurance, compared with about one-fourth of total medical care expenditures for insurance by families at the average level. Forty-eight percent of the low-consumption families spent an average of $111 for life, endowment, annuity, etc. insurance (excluding veterans and group insurance deducted from pay), compared with 71 percent of the $6,000–$7,499 income families at $198 for those buying.

Gifts and contributions to organizations ranged from $44 for 1-person low-consumption families to $112 for families of 6 or more persons, compared with $156 for families at the $6,000–$7,499 level.

Nonfarm families on the average, had an annual net savings (increase in assets or decreases in liabilities) of $177 in 1960–61. Fifty-two percent of the families reported an increase in savings; 42 percent, a decrease; and 7 percent, no change. Families in all size classes both in and below the selected "low-consumption" classes reported net decreases in savings. At the selected low-consumption levels, these ranged from a $75 deficit for families of 6 or more persons to $−383 for 4-person families. Available tabulations of the data do not show the percent of savers and dissavers in these equivalent low-consumption classes, but the data for all U.S. nonfarm families indicate that some families at all current money income levels managed to save during 1960–61, as the following summary shows:

After-tax income	Average net change in assets and liabilities	Percent of families reporting:		
		savings increase	savings decrease	no change
All nonfarm families	$ 177	52	42	7
Under $1,000	−495	15	59	26
$1,000–$1,999	−181	28	48	24
2,000– 2,999	−173	39	49	12
3,000– 3,999	−203	42	50	8
4,000– 4,999	−36	53	44	3
5,000– 5,999	+31	57	40	2
6,000– 7,499	+173	62	37	2
7,500– 9,999	+461	66	33	1
10,000–14,999	+963	68	31	1
15,000 and over	+4,788	77	20	3

How Adequate Are the Levels of Living of the Poor?

Throughout this discussion, I have tried to introduce some qualitative appraisal of the expenditures of families at the lower end of the economic scale, e.g. food expenditures, comparison with 1950 and the average pattern, etc. However, there is much yet to be done before any real appraisal can be made of the adequacy of the levels of living of the poor today. Basic research tools, such as standard budgets and equivalence scales, need to be extended and brought up to date. No real appraisal of adequacy can be made without consideration of the wide variations in prices and living costs which exist between regions and between different types of places within regions. Analysis of family spending and saving for welfare purposes is, primarily, micro-economic research. Statistically, as well as conceptually speaking, "poverty has many faces."

Part three
Solutions

6
Conventional Programs to Combat Poverty

> If to do were as easy as to know what were good to do, chapels had been churches and poor men's cottages princes' palaces.
> —William Shakespeare

Before the depression of the thirties, primary responsibility for combating poverty was left to the individual and his family. Private charities helped where they could, particularly in the large cities, and many states had developed special programs of aid for the blind, for children, and for the aged. In most states, however, these programs were entirely local or were restricted to limited groups in need of institutional care.

The catastrophic impact of the depression made it clear to most Americans that the formulas and clichés developed in a rural society, with an abundance of good land and ever widening horizons, no longer applied and that joint action by the individual, the employer, and the state would be required to meet the hazards of industrial life. In this context, the Social Security Act was passed in 1935, with provisions (1) to protect wage earners and their dependents from loss of income because of unemployment, old age, disability, or death; (2) to protect children from health hazards of infancy and early childhood, from crippling illness, and from social maladjustments; and (3) to help groups of people least able to protect themselves from the effects of want.

Although the Social Security Act was, and still is, the bulwark of our welfare program, other legislation was enacted to meet special needs. Farm programs were created to help the rural poor; minimum wage laws were passed to bolster the incomes of the nonfarm-working poor; and public-housing programs were put into effect to improve living conditions and environment of the home.

All of these programs have been attacked at one time or another during the past thirty years. Our farm policies have long been criticized as a well-to-do farmer's income-maintenance program that does virtually nothing for the poor. The minimum-wage laws have repeatedly been attacked by economists because they tend to eliminate the jobs of marginal workers, particularly youthful ones, who might otherwise be employed. Public-housing laws are criticized most vociferously by experts, who once favored them, because they create new ghettos. And now the welfare programs have come under attack because they are alleged to do little for the poor.

In a recent article in *Fortune*, Charles E. Silberman summarized the growing disenchantment of economists, social workers, and other social scientists with "welfarism": "The massive public and private social-work, social-welfare apparatus that has developed in the United States over the past forty years or so fails to relieve and sometimes even aggravates the problems of poverty. Government welfare expenditures have risen to perhaps $30 billion a year, but scarcely anyone believes today that these vast sums do much to reduce poverty."

The articles in this chapter show the kinds of programs that are included in the conventional anti-poverty toolbag and the recent criticism of these programs as well.

Sar A. Levitan
The American Welfare System

...Over the past 30 years the United States has developed an intricate though far from comprehensive welfare system. The underlying assumption of this system is that special programs are needed to take care of the diverse needs of the poor. It has been suggested that in practice these programs are more a series of make shift measures than tailor

From *Programs in Aid of the Poor* (Kalamazoo, Michigan: The W. E. Upjohn Institute for Employment Research, 1965). Reprinted by permission of the author.

Sar A. Levitan is an economist at the W. E. Upjohn Institute for Employment Research and is author of *Federal Aid to Depressed Areas* (Johns Hopkins, 1964).

made programs, and that millions of needy receive little or no aid. And the assistance offered in most cases is inadequate to raise the beneficiaries above the poverty level.

The welfare system consists of three types of programs:

1. Programs which offer cash assistance mainly to those outside the labor force. These programs include Old Age, Survivors and Disability Insurance; public assistance programs under the Social Security Act; pensions for needy veterans; and general assistance for needy persons not covered by the Social Security Act financed exclusively by states and localities.

2. Programs to aid those in the work force. These programs include training to equip the poor with skills saleable in the labor market, aid to depressed areas, unemployment insurance, minimum wage protection, job creation, and work relief.

3. Programs that provide services and goods to the poor on the basis of need regardless of labor force status. Included in this group of programs are child care, subsidized housing, medical services and drugs, and several forms of food distribution.

The distinction between programs aimed for the working poor and for those outside the labor force is useful and in accordance with the prevailing values of our society. This distinction is reflected in existing programs and is likely to be a controlling factor in developing further programs in aid of the poor.

It is assumed that special tailor made programs are needed to bolster the level of living of the working poor. This might be accomplished best by providing them with services and goods which are not likely to diminish the incentive to work, and by equipping them for more productive jobs whenever feasible. For those outside the labor force, burdened with impediments which preclude gainful employment, society's help to the poor must consist of providing a combination of services and income; in some cases, however, as conditions of individual and family responsibilities change, training may also be appropriate. . . .

Income Maintenance Programs for the Poor outside the Labor Force

The Social Security Act, now the product of three decades of evolution, is the basic instrument for providing income maintenance for persons outside the labor force. This Act has created two distinct groups of beneficiaries: some receive payments regardless of the economic resources of individual recipients; others qualify for benefits only upon the determination of individual need. The distinction between the two types of programs is made on the basis of prior contributions. Those who made payroll contributions qualify to receive benefits for themselves, their dependents, and their survivors as a matter of right; they are not required to establish personal need.

Old Age, Survivors, and Disability Insurance. In reality, the insurance features of Old Age, Survivors and Disability Insurance are partially based on government fiat rather than hard-cash contributions. OASDI benefits are heavily weighted in favor of low earners, and only minimum qualifications are needed to entitle a person to receive benefits. A beneficiary with qualifying dependents may receive twice the amount of another person who may have made identical contributions. The monthly payments to a primary beneficiary who made maximum contributions based on annual earnings of $4,800 (prior to the 1965 amendments to the Social Security Act) were only about double the payments made to an individual who paid Social Security taxes on earnings of only $1,320 a year, though the former had contributed nearly four times as much in taxes. Whether the above ratio holds true for lifetime benefits is not known since longevity data based on income are inadequate to form any conclusive opinion on this matter.

Average annual benefits for a single retiree in 1965, including the 7 percent increase provided by the 1965 amendments to the Social Security Act, amount to less than $1,000; the benefits for an aged couple are 50 percent higher. This average level of benefits is just about sufficient to meet the minimum requirements of aged beneficiaries residing on farms; those living in urban areas must live in poverty if they depend upon social security payments as the sole means of support.…

Public assistance. In addition to supplying income to beneficiaries under OASDI, the Social Security Act provides monetary support for four impoverished groups: old persons, blind, permanently and totally disabled, and families with dependent children. A total of $3.4 billion cash benefits was paid under these four programs in 1964 to a monthly average of nearly 7 million beneficiaries. The following tabulation presents the average number of beneficiaries and the cost of these programs in fiscal 1964:

Program	Number (Thousands)	Benefits* (Millions)
Total	6,955	$3,446.0
Old Age (OAA)	2,176	1,610.1
Blind	97	85.7
Permanently and Totally Disabled	505	335.1
Families with Dependent Children	4,177	1,415.1

* Excludes payments to suppliers of medical care (vendor payments).

. . . Though the federal government contributes nearly 60 percent of the total cost of the public assistance programs under the Social Security Act, the administration of these programs, within broad Federal standards, is left to the states; they determine qualifications, eligibility, and the level of benefits. The last-mentioned item is determined on the basis of minimum needs required by applicants for public assistance, a figure which varies widely among the states. For example, the median annual cost of basic needs calculated by the states for a mother with three children on AFDC in 1963 was $2,436, and ranged from $1,560 in Arkansas to $3,540 in Alaska. But in two of every three states, actual benefits were below the predetermined minimum needs. . . .

Public assistance for those destitute who fail to qualify under any of the above four categories may be paid by some states and localities without federal participation. In 1964, such general assistance provided income maintenance for an average of about 800,000 persons at an annual cost of $273 million—an average of less than $7 a week per recipient.

The public assistance programs which provide some income to less than one of every four classified as poor have been under increasing attack from foes and friends alike. There is little controversy about Old Age Assistance, Aid to the Blind, and Aid to the Permanently and Totally Disabled, though the level of benefits varies widely among the states. OAA, the costliest of these programs, helps support about one of every eight persons aged 65 and over (the median age of the beneficiaries is about 77 years). Four of every ten OAA recipients were also receiving aid from OASDI, but their income from the latter program was even below the meager minimum predetermined needs to qualify for OAA. With average annual cash benefits meeting barely half the minimum requirements of aged people under the Social Security Administration criteria, even critics of the welfare state find little fault with the benefits for the neediest aged population.

Controversy has focused on AFDC, particularly in those states where unemployed parents could qualify for benefits. The program has grown constantly since World War II in terms of cost and number of beneficiaries.

A number of factors have contributed to the rise in AFDC recipients over the past 25 years. First and most obviously, the population under age 18 has increased by some 29 million. Second, the proportion as well as the number of broken homes has increased. . . . There has also been a steady increase in the number of illegitimate children during the past decade. Families headed by a female, particularly with illegitimate children, are likely candidates for AFDC. . . .

Finally, liberalization of state and federal laws has increased the number of persons qualifying for AFDC. Particularly significant are the 1961 amendments to the Social Security Act which qualified unemployed parents with dependent children to receive AFDC benefits. Eighteen states have accepted this provision, which has added some 350,000 AFDC beneficiaries during the past four years.

Quite apart from the mounting number of recipients, AFDC is vulnerable to attack on the grounds of certain socially unacceptable reasons which may qualify persons to receive AFDC benefits. In 1961, AFDC family characteristics showed that nearly one of every five children were illegitimate; 7 percent of the fathers were in jail; the parents of nearly two-fifths of the children receiving benefits were estranged. The high incidence of illegitimacy and broken homes has served as a basis for attack on the relief system.

Programs for the Poor in the Work Force

"Give a man a fish," an old proverb moralizes, "and you feed him for a day. Teach him to catch a fish and you feed him for life." This maxim is an apt text for the Great Society's war on poverty. The current emphasis in the war on poverty is providing opportunity rather than subsistence for the poor. The underlying assumption is that in our highly productive economy there are places for all who are properly motivated and well-equipped to participate in the world of work. The problem of the poor, according to this reasoning, is that they are isolated from the mainstream of American life. . . .

This means adapting existing institutions so that they can minister to the special needs of the poor: it means equipping the poor with skills needed in the free labor market and providing them with jobs when none exist under free market conditions; it further means inducing private industry to bring jobs to unemployed workers stranded in depressed areas, and assuring them adequate earnings to rise above the threshold of poverty.

Labor market services. An examination of existing public labor market operations indicates, regrettably, that despite some improvements in recent years they are not geared to minister to the special needs of many of the poor and disadvantaged. Statistics of the United States Employment Service (USES) and its state affiliated organizations are not available in sufficient detail to develop a comprehensive picture of their services to poverty groups. Whatever the record of the public employment service in placing the poorly educated and unskilled, its services are necessarily responsive to the needs of employers who naturally tend to seek the best qualified employees to fill existing job vacancies. Thus the USES has devised techniques to select the most qualified applicants. The General Aptitude Test Battery (GATB), given to nearly one of every four applicants for nonfarm placement, is designed to screen and test the literate. But unfortunately, the vast majority of the unemployed poor have a limited education, and many are illiterate. In 1963, 15 percent of all family heads had less than eight years education, but they accounted for 36 percent of all families with an annual income of less than $3,000. The USES has recognized that if it is to provide for the needs of this group, it will have to adopt new techniques. In recognition of this fact, the employment service recently developed a nonreading measure of general learning ability. This nonreading test is designed to determine whether low scores of certain individuals reflect limited ability, inadequate reading ability, or cultural limitations. In addition, research is under way to develop a non-reading edition of all nine GATB aptitudes.

To service more adequately the illiterate and poorly educated, the public employment service would need to expand its functions and activities. Since rendering special services to disadvantaged workers is costly, it would naturally lead to the neglect of other unemployed workers unless Congress allocates additional funds to the USES for this purpose. Of course, expansion of services to the disadvantaged by the USES must not be achieved at the cost of neglecting its regular functions.

Important steps have been taken recently to expand the services to disadvantaged youth by the establishment of some 60 Youth Opportunity Centers operated by the public employment service, and the number of these centers is scheduled to double. These Youth Opportunity Centers offer special counseling, testing, and placement services to improve the employment prospects of youths who are poorly equipped to compete for jobs in the open market. A total of $30 million has been appropriated in fiscal 1966 for the operation of these centers and the expansion of other services to youth, including special assistance offered to selective service rejectees.

In 1963 Congress recognized the special needs of uneducated and unemployed workers by adding basic education to the vocational course for those who lacked a rudimentary education, and by extending the maximum training period for these students from 52 weeks to 72 weeks. In 1965 the maximum duration of training was extended to two years. Officials in charge of MDTA apparently found it difficult to develop adequate training techniques which would service the least educated, for by the end of 1964 only about 2 percent of the MDTA trainees were selected for experimental and demonstration projects designed to help poorly educated unemployed workers. Whether MDTA training can be adapted to equip large numbers of these persons to fill existing job vacancies in the future remains in doubt.

Job creation and work relief. The New Deal placed major reliance on two programs—public works and work relief—for income maintenance of the unemployed and impoverished. The former program, designed to fulfill needed public facilities, relied on normal market processes under which the government contracted with private enterprise to construct the facilities. Work relief, on the other hand, emphasized job creation; considerations of labor efficiency and project need were secondary. In both cases, the wages paid to the workers were those prevailing in the local labor market. These programs, whose total cost amounted to $17 billion, remained in effect as long as mass unemployment prevailed, tapered off sharply after Pearl Harbor; and were abandoned completely shortly thereafter when full employment conditions were achieved in the wartime economy.

The current war on poverty places little emphasis upon job creation, except for unemployed and impoverished youth. The 1962 amendments to the Social Security Act, while presumably designed to rehabilitate relief recipients, remained largely an exhortation as far as providing work to recipients of assistance, even though a number of states and communities conducted some projects providing work to reliefers. During 1964 about 9,000 AFDC recipients found employment following participation in public assistance work and training programs. The Economic Opportunity Act provides expanded work or training programs for unemployed parents (especially fathers) whose families are on relief rolls. It was estimated in 1964 that 130,000 relief recipients were available for work, if jobs could be found for them. A total of $112 million was allocated in fiscal 1965 to provide work relief—or work experience, according to the current euphemism—to aid 89,000 relief recipients. The program started slowly, yet by June 30, 1965, 16,000 persons had actually gained employment. Meanwhile, the Department of Health, Education, and Welfare, which administers the program, had signed contracts to provide work experience for another 73,000 persons.

Initially the program offered no monetary inducements to participants and limited their earnings to the benefits that they were entitled to receive under the relief program. Beginning in July 1965, however, persons selected for work experience became entitled to receive 100 percent of the basic needs. As mentioned earlier, the majority of the states pay AFDC recipients less than 100 percent of their total basic needs. The work experience projects provide funds for special training, guidance, counseling, and remedial medical treatment, in addition to work experience, to help rehabilitate the relief recipients.

The 1965 amendments to the Economic Opportunity Act expanded the scope of the work-experience program by including workers in farm families with an income of less than $1,200. A total of $150 million was authorized to be expended during fiscal 1966.

Current appropriations allow only a small proportion of AFDC recipients to participate in the work-experience program. It was recognized that the bulk of AFDC recipients could not benefit from this program because many AFDC mothers were either unemployable or fully occupied with home responsibilities. In some cases day-care facilities might be provided to free a greater number of mothers for work. Some experts might argue, however, that it would be wiser as a matter of public policy to permit a mother to devote all her energies to the rearing of her children, rather than work at what is most likely to be a low-paying and unskilled job.

The Economic Opportunity Act has been more generous in providing employment opportunities for youth. In fiscal 1965, a total of $379 million was appropriated for youth employment programs, divided as follows: $190 million for Job Corps, $132 million for Neighborhood Youth Corps, and the balance for college work-study programs. The expenditures authorized for 1966 are $700 million. . . .

Unemployment insurance.   The object of the unemployment insurance program is to provide essential aid, during periods of forced idleness, to unemployed workers, who have substantial recent attachment to the labor force. It limits the income plunge of those who become unemployed and minimizes or staves off poverty for many. Reasonable people may disagree as to the proper level or duration of benefits. But it can hardly be argued that the unemployment insurance system should be markedly altered to serve as a major means of income support for the poor.

Unemployment insurance makes up about half of the net wage loss (take-home pay) of those forced into idleness, but many workers are not covered by the system or exhaust their benefits before they regain employment. Half of the 9.5 million persons who were unemployed for five weeks or longer during 1962 did not receive any unemployment insurance benefits. Available evidence suggests that unemployment insurance serves those who are classified as poor to a lesser extent than other unemployed. About 15 million workers are not currently protected by unemployment insurance, including more than 6 million employed in those categories where the working poor tend to concentrate—agriculture, domestic service, and small firms with three or less workers. On the other hand, nearly half the states use a formula weighted in favor of low-wage earners, and 12 states pay additional benefits for dependents.

Aside from the restricted coverage, it would appear that unemployment benefits have a limited applicability to many of the poor. A person receiving unemployment benefits must have a recent history of work and be currently available for work in order to collect benefits. A large percentage of the idle poor are not available for work because of disability, illness, or home responsibilities. Moreover, to qualify for unemployment insurance a worker must earn a minimum of wages and/or be employed in a covered industry for a minimum of about 15 weeks (the exact minimum earnings and duration of employment vary from state to state). The repeated spells of unemployment which the poor experience would therefore normally entitle them to only the most temporary relief, or disqualify them.

Current proposals to extend unemployment benefits to 39 or 52 weeks from the normal prevailing 26 weeks would probably have only limited applicability to the poor, though the added benefits may prevent some long-term unemployed from falling below the poverty line. These proposals would restrict the extended duration of benefits to unemployed persons with considerable past work experience. The Johnson Administration plan for extended benefits, financed jointly by employers and the federal government, would be limited to workers with at least 78 weeks of employment during the preceding three years. Many of the poor do not have such work experience.

Whatever the merits of current proposals to raise unemployment benefits and extend their duration, they can hardly be justified on the ground that they would substantially combat the current prevalence of poverty. Probably an extension of coverage, particularly to domestic and agricultural workers, would have a greater impact for the poor. The Johnson Administration proposals to extend unemployment insurance coverage would apply to about 40 percent of all agricultural workers. Whether Congress will adopt this proposal cannot be foretold.

Minimum Wages. The image of the destitute, idling through life on relief or eking out a living from old age receipts, is only partially correct. . . . The fact is that a substantial number of those living below the threshold of poverty are actually "fully employed." About half of the 7.2 million impoverished household heads in 1963 were in the work force, including 2 million heads of families who worked full-time during the entire year. Another 1.6 million family heads worked on part-time or full-time jobs during part of the year.

More than 10 million jobs in the United States currently pay less than $1.50 an hour. These jobs, although most typically found in trade and service industries, are widespread throughout our economy. The majority of the low-paying jobs are held by youngsters who have just entered the work force or by women who are supplementing family incomes. But for the 2 million family heads (95 percent male), low-paying jobs represent not starting wages but a way of life. And 5.7 million children were being raised by these working-poor who were fully employed during 1963. . . .

It is quite apparent that present wage levels are inadequate to permit millions of steady workers particularly those with large families to escape poverty. Yet the elimination of substandard wages was one of the basic goals of the New Deal and was expressed in the Fair Labor Standards Act of 1938.

The objective of the Fair Labor Standards Act is to achieve as rapidly as practicable minimum wage levels that will maintain the health, efficiency, and general well-being of workers. Congress was understandably concerned that an unduly high minimum wage might price many low-productivity jobs out of existence. Applying the reasonable assumption that a low-paying job is better than no job at all, Congress thus provided that minimum wages should not be so high as to curtail employment and earning power substantially.

In order to achieve these dual but frequently conflicting objectives, Congress has acted cautiously in applying the law over the years. It has established minimum wages which directly affect only a limited number of employees at the bottom of the economic ladder. Only three of every five non-governmental wage and salary earners are covered; excluded from protection are the bulk of workers in the lowest paid industries, including those engaged in service, trade and all farm and domestic workers.

Congress has, nevertheless, raised the statutory minimum wage rates on three occasions since the end of World War II, and the rise in minimum wages has more than kept pace with the increase in average wages of American industry. The current minimum hourly rate on jobs covered by the federal minimum wage law is $1.25. Under the prodding of President Kennedy, Congress in 1961 took the first step to extend protection of minimum wages. Brought under minimum wage protection that year were some 3.7 million employees, mostly in retail and service industries and covering about a fourth of the total workers in these industries. The House Committee on Education and Labor, in September 1965 approved a bill to expand coverage to 6 million additional workers engaged in retail, service, and agricultural enterprises and to raise wages of those previously covered to $1.75 by 1968. Action on the proposed legislation has been deferred to 1966.

In addition, a number of states have enacted minimum wage laws for employees not affected by the federal legislation. These laws cover some 5 million employees in 34 states. Minimum hourly rates under these laws range from 16 cents in Arkansas (originally enacted in 1915) to a $1.75 in Alaska; in 12 of these states the minimum wage is $1.25 or higher.

Since low wages are a major factor accounting for poverty, the role of minimum wages in the war against poverty has been a matter of debate. Would it be feasible to speed up increases in minimum wages and extensions of coverage? There is no doubt that existing minimum wage legislation has succeeded in raising the earnings of millions of workers. The last boost in federal minimum wages, raising hourly rates in two stages from $1.00 to $1.25 an hour and covering an additional 3.7 million workers, increased the wages of some 3 million workers. There is, however, wide disagreement upon the number of jobs which minimum wage legislation may have eliminated.

In a dynamic economy it is impossible to isolate the effects of the statutory minimum wage legislation from other developments. Opponents have argued that minimum wage legislation is a significant obstacle to youth employment, but convincing evidence is hard to come by.... Since only fragmentary data are available showing comparative youth unemployment rates, no conclusive judgment can be made on the impact of minimum wage legislation upon youth unemployment. The impediments to youth employment are the result of a complex series of factors, and there is little evidence that minimum wage legislation is a controlling factor in the high level of unemployment which has existed among youths throughout the United States....

Economists would appear to be at a loss to advise policy-makers on the impact of minimum wage legislation upon aggregate employment and disemployment. In the final analysis, an economist's conclusions will depend upon what he believes deep down in his heart to be true; and whatever his conclusions, it is likely that he will find some relevant supporting facts. Those who favor minimum wage legislation voice social and humanitarian objections to substandard wages and stress the economic need to widen the base of consumer purchasing power. Opponents retort that minimum wage legislation extends the evils of governmental interference with free market forces and that arbitrary meddling with the determination of minimum wages may cause disemployment, thus causing results opposite from those intended by the proponents of minimum wage legislation. Some observers advocate that employers of labor with low productivity be subsidized by the government so that they can pay a socially acceptable minimum wage....

During the four years following September 1961, the effective date for the latest amendments to the Fair Labor Standards Act, average wage rates in manufacturing, exclusive of fringe benefit costs, rose about

15 percent, while minimum wages increased 25 percent. This fact alone should indicate the need for exercising caution in considering any further increases in minimum wages over the next few years, assuming the continuation of recent trends in overall productivity and consumer prices. The wisdom of using statutory minimum wages to upset existing wage differentials may also be questioned. If movements in average manufacturing wages are taken as a guide, it would appear that federal minimum wage rates have about kept pace with wage changes in American industry. Since 1939, every boost in federal minimum wages has been geared to setting minimum wage rates at about half the average wage rates in manufacturing. While there is nothing sacrosanct about existing wage differentials, a significant realignment due to excessive boosts in minimum wages might lead to accelerated elimination of low-paying jobs.

Moreover, the most acute unemployment problem we are now facing is found among teenagers who normally enter the labor force in lower-paid jobs. Additional boosts in minimum wages might tend to impede further the hiring of new entrants into the labor force. But some have questioned whether high youth unemployment should be a controlling consideration in raising minimum wages. They emphasize that widespread poverty among heads of families who work on full-time jobs suggests that for millions of adult workers statutory minimum rates are not entry wages but continuing wages of these workers throughout their lifetime. Cogent as this argument might appear, it leaves unanswered a more basic issue, namely, whether the low-paying jobs would exist at all if minimum rates were raised above levels justified by the productivity of the affected workers. At best, therefore, it would appear that minimum wage legislation is only another tool in the war on poverty.

On the other hand, it should be recognized that some forced adjustment of the price structure may be used to effect public policy. The recent experience with the elimination of imported farm labor is a case in point. Secretary of Labor W. Willard Wirtz took the position that adjustments in the price structure for certain agricultural commodities would enable food growers to raise wages of farm labor sufficiently to make jobs in agriculture attractive to American workers. It was estimated, for example, that raising the cost of lettuce by about a penny a head would make it possible for growers to hike wages by about 50 percent. Similar small increases in the cost of other fruits and vegetables to consumers would enable growers to pay "minimum decent" wages to their laborers.

But there are limits to which price adjustments can be used to boost wage costs. Some liberal spokesmen who are fond of asserting that an affluent society should not tolerate a $1.25 minimum wage have proposed legislation to raise the hourly minimum to $2. Regrettably, such pronouncements are more rhetoric than serious policy alternatives. Reasonable people may differ over whether the current minimum wage should be extended to additional millions of workers, and whether it should be kept for a while at the present level or raised by a few cents. But there can be little doubt that too rapid boosts in the minimum wage would cause serious economic dislocations and disemployment. It would be a case of killing the goose that laid the egg, for the way to fight poverty is not by the elimination of jobs. The proposed raise in minimum wages by 40 percent, from $1.25 to $1.75, over a three-year period, due to be considered by Congress in 1966, is therefore fraught with danger and may lead to the elimination of many jobs. If the bill is enacted into law, it should therefore be accompanied by a work relief program which would provide employment to displaced workers.

Without negating or minimizing the past achievements of minimum wage legislation, it would be unrealistic to place excessive reliance upon such legislation as a tool to combat poverty. Moreover, except for the youth employment measures, existing programs for improving labor market services, training the unemployed and helping depressed areas apparently are not geared to minister aid to a significant proportion of the poor. If society is determined to reduce poverty at a more rapid rate than in the past, other tools will have to be relied upon.

Provision of Services and Goods

In our society the state has assumed the responsibility of providing many social services to its citizens. Most of these benefits are made available without regard to the recipients' level of income, and the cost of these services exceeds manyfold the total outlay in aid of the poor. Governmental expenditures in providing education to the nation's children and youth are twice as costly as all the programs aimed directly at aiding the poor. In addition to direct public services, there are what Richard M. Titmuss of the London School of Economics has called the "iceberg phenomena of social welfare." This refers to the revenue system which exempts certain types of expenditures from income taxes. One example of this "fiscal welfare" system is the provision allowing for deduction of interest paid on home mortgages from regular income subject to taxation. Many other examples could be cited. It may be noted that many direct public services, as well as the "fiscal welfare" provisions, tend to favor the affluent members of society over the poor. . . .

We are concerned here with services and goods which the government makes available to the poor on the basis of need, though these are not always separable from overall government services and fiscal aids. Child services are combined for poor and affluent families, while separate housing programs are provided on the basis of need. Two other programs—food distribution and medical assistance—are also discussed in this section. As a rule, the benefits of these programs are available to the needy regardless of their labor force status.

Services for children. Programs to aid children were the earliest social welfare services provided by the federal government, dating back to the Taft Administration. The Social Security Act provides grants to states on a matching basis for four types of programs:

1. Welfare services to help children in difficulty vary from community to community, but they generally include social services to children in their own home, protective services to neglected and abused children, foster care, day-care, and related services.

2. Maternal and child health services include maternity clinics and clinics for mentally retarded children.

3. Services for crippled children provide diagnostic and other care needed by these children.

4. Health care for needy children has been added by the 1965 amendments to the Social Security Act with the purpose of providing comprehensive health care in areas where low-income families tend to concentrate.

Total costs of these programs in 1964 amounted to about half a billion dollars, with the federal government contributing about a fifth of the total costs. However, federal contributions to child welfare programs have been increasing in recent years, and current legislation provides for additional expansion of federal aid. Under existing legislation, annual federal grants to states for maternal and child welfare programs amount to about $170 million and are due to rise to about $250 million before the end of the decade.

Except for health care for needy children, added in 1965, these service programs are not aimed exclusively at the children of poor families, though most beneficiaries of maternal and child health services are from low-income families. An official government brochure describing the child welfare services announces that the program is designed "for troubled children and children in trouble." Problems of child neglect, abuse, and emotional disturbance are not limited exclusively to impoverished homes, though it is not at all surprising that poor children have more than their share of such problems. Consequently, children from impoverished homes are likely candidates for assistance offered by child-welfare programs. A 1963 study found that while AFDC children constitute less than a twentieth of the total child population, they accounted for nearly a fifth of the children receiving child welfare services. Altogether, more than one of every four recipients of child welfare services administered by public agencies were members of families which receive some type of public assistance. In addition, many other poor children who are not public assistance recipients may be beneficiaries of child welfare services. . . .

Food distribution programs. Without decrying the goals or potential of the recent war on poverty, the admonition of a social worker from an earlier generation is still applicable today: "Social services never filled an empty stomach." While outright starvation may be rare in the United States, millions of persons do not have the means to purchase food for a well-balanced and adequate diet. To help improve the diet of needy persons and to help dispose of surplus agricultural foods, the federal government has subsidized the food stamp program and operates a direct food distribution program. In addition, the national school lunch program and the special milk program are designed for the purpose of improving the nutritional well-being of all children, with a built-in mandate to provide free or reduced price lunches to needy children in schools where the programs operate.

More than 17 million elementary and secondary school children— 35 percent of the total number of school children—regardless of their family income level, benefited from the school lunch program in the 1964–1965 academic year; and all levels of government combined contributed nearly half of the $1.6 billion expended by the school lunch and milk programs. The federal share amounted to $483 million, including $130 million cash disbursements for the lunch program and $98 million for the special milk program, with the balance coming from surplus commodities. State and local governments contributed $324 million, and the remainder ($788 million) was paid by the children.

The National School Lunch Act of 1946 requires schools participating in the program to provide free or reduced-cost lunches for needy children, and nearly 1 of every 10 lunches provided under the program were made available to children free or at reduced prices. These lunches were served to over a million needy children. However, a 1962 study by the Department of Agriculture found that another 1.2 million needy children, or on the borderline of need, were not receiving these lunches. Nearly half a million of these impoverished school children attended public schools which participated in the program; but because of the heavy concentration of needy children, school authorities in these areas lacked the resources to provide free lunches for all who needed them. Another 700,000 needy children attended public schools which had no lunch service because of the schools' relative isolation or lack of facilities. Gunnar Myrdal's observation that welfare legislation tends to favor the more affluent is well illustrated by these programs.

This is one of the costs of poverty: Because many needy children are concentrated in impoverished areas, they are denied free lunches; at the same time more affluent students receive the benefits of governmentally subsidized meals. . . .

The federal government also makes food available to needy persons through a program dating from the 1930's. The Department of Agriculture distributes processed and packaged foods to designated state agencies. In 1965, 48 states, including more than half of the counties in the nation, participated in the program. The food donated by the government is acquired under the price support and surplus removal programs; the commodities include butter, lard, cheese, flour, cereals, dry eggs and milk, livestock products, beans, and rice.

Participating in the program in 1965 were an average of 5.3 million people, about equally divided between public assistance recipients and other needy persons. The total cost to the government to acquire, process and ship these commodities amounted to $225 million, or $42.50 per recipient. The retail cost of these commodities would be nearly double this amount. Since the Department of Agriculture calculates that the annual food budget per person in a low-income family amounts to about $250, it may be estimated that the commodities distributed by the department account for about a third of the total food costs of those who participate in the program. Thus the direct food distribution program provides a socially acceptable outlet for surplus agricultural commodities.

Direct food distribution has enormous advantages to the government. Except for the cost of packaging and transportation, there is no additional cost to the government because the donated commodities have already been acquired to achieve a social goal unrelated to food distribution, namely: providing price supports for surplus agricultural commodities. Nevertheless, the program has been criticized on several grounds. Not only do the available surplus commodities fail to supply adequate food for a balanced diet, but the procedures involved in distributing the food show little concern for the self-respect of recipients, who normally have to line up at government warehouses or relief agencies to receive their "commodities." In addition, direct food distribution fails to utilize existing retail outlets.

Shortly after assuming office, President Kennedy instructed the Secretary of Agriculture to revive on a pilot basis, the food stamp plan which was in operation between 1939 to 1943. Enabling legislation for the plan had been enacted during the Eisenhower Administration, but the Secretary of Agriculture had not implemented it. Under the food stamp plan, eligible families—public assistance recipients and other needy persons as determined by the states—may exchange money they would normally spend on food for stamp coupons whose value is greater than the amount paid. The coupons may then be exchanged in retail stores for domestically produced food (imported caviar is out). The value of the bonus coupons decreases as income increases. For example, a family of four with a monthly income of $40 receives $3 worth of coupons for each $1 of food purchased. The amount which a family is required to pay for the coupons increases as income approaches the maximum permitted for recipients to remain eligible. The upper income limit for a family of four is about $3,000 annually, at which point the bonus is about one-fifth of the family's total allotment of coupons.

As initiated in May 1961, the program was limited to impoverished residents in only eight depressed areas. The program has expanded so that by mid-1965 needy families in 29 states, including 110 areas, were eligible to participate. The total number of participants at that time was 633,000. Food coupons issued during fiscal 1965 were valued at $85.5 million, involving a bonus of $32.5 million to the participants. Thus the participants received about $1.60 worth of food in retail stores for every dollar they paid. Current plans would expand the food stamp plan during 1966 to include a million persons, and eventually to a total of four million people at an annual cost to the government of about $360 million.

The major purposes of the food stamp program are to upgrade the quality of diet, increase food consumption, and allow the poor free selection of food purchases. Studies conducted by the Department of Agriculture in the initial eight pilot areas seemed to indicate that food purchases by participating families increased significantly. In Detroit, where half the original participants were located, food expenditures of recipients increased 34 percent. In rural areas increases were smaller.

A major criticism of the program, aside from its costs, is that it tends to make the recipients dependent upon the government and thus destroys self-reliance. Most observers would agree that reliance upon the government for basic needs is undesirable. However, one may also consider whether the alternative, a deficient and debilitating diet, is not less conducive to self-reliance.

Housing. The federal government is heavily involved in the housing business. The magnitude of its involvement is reflected by the 1965 Housing Act, which carries a multi-billion dollar price tag in a combination of insured loans, grants, and subsidies to be expended over a four-year period. Several of the housing programs are designed exclusively to provide adequate shelter for the poor. These include public housing, rent subsidies, grants to help rehabilitate homes for poor families displaced by urban renewal or public transportation projects, and special housing programs for older persons and farm laborers.

The rationale for providing government assistance to shelter the poor is the well-established fact that unsubsidized private enterprise cannot profitably provide adequate housing to low-income groups. In the absence of government subsidies or grants, the poor are confined to slum and substandard shelter—housing that is dilapidated or lacking plumbing facilities. The shortage of adequate housing for the poor appears almost insurmountable in the short-run. According to the 1960 Census, 5.3 million families with an annual income of less than $3,000 lived in substandard housing. Only 1,750,000 of the nation's standard (adequate) housing units rented at less than $50 a month; therefore, with an annual income of less than $3,000, most of the impoverished resided in substandard or overcrowded housing. Thus far government housing programs have filled only a small portion of the housing needs of poor families.

The oldest government measure designed to provide shelter for the poor is the public housing program which dates from 1937. During nearly three decades the federal government has provided some 600,000 housing units for impoverished families. Attempts to accelerate the construction of public housing during the post-World War II period have not materialized; in recent years an average of about 25,000 units have been completed each year. Some major cities have added no new public housing during recent years. In mid-1965, more than 100,000 units for which funds were available had been approved by the federal government, but construction on most of these projects had not started. A major barrier to the construction of public housing is the unavailability of sites. Even where sites are available, organized community groups have frequently raised effective opposition to locating public housing for impoverished families in the midst of more affluent neighborhoods. Racial prejudice is another obstacle to construction, since a large proportion of public housing residents are Negroes.

Public housing is constructed at no cost to the local community, though the community may incur expenses in providing services to the project after it is built. No taxes are paid on public housing. The initial planning and development are financed through loans from the federal Public Housing Administration. When the project is sufficiently advanced, the community floats federally-guaranteed bonds in the open market to cover the cost of the project and repays the initial federal loan. The loan is then amortized by the federal government over a period of 40 years. The federal government also pays an annual contribution of $120 for each unit occupied by aged or handicapped persons. Rental fees cover upkeep of the project; payments to the community in lieu of taxes amount to about 10 percent of the rent collected on the project, which is normally less than the full amount of taxes paid by private owners on comparable facilities. Residents are charged rents amounting to 20 percent of their monthly income. According to a survey made in 1963, the median income of new occupants was $205 a month. The average monthly rent was therefore $40, regardless of the true cost of the space occupied by a new family.

Authorized contributions to subsidize the public housing program amounted to $366 million in fiscal 1965 and $413 million for each of the subsequent four years. The 1965 law authorizes the construction of 35,000 new units a year, and the lease or purchase, including renovation when necessary, of an additional 25,000 units.

In 1965 the government also undertook to pay part of the rent for impoverished families living in substandard housing or displaced by government action, such as urban renewal, and for impoverished families with aged or handicapped members. Under this program private nonprofit organizations, limited dividend corporations, or cooperatives were authorized to borrow funds, guaranteed by the federal government, in the open market to build or acquire homes at an anticipated average cost of $12,500 per unit. The monthly rent paid by the occupants would be no more than 25 percent of their income. A family with a monthly income of $240 would be required to pay $60. Assuming that a fair economic rent for the housing unit is $90, the government would pay the difference between the true cost of the housing and the amount the occupant would be required to pay.

The major innovation of the new program is that it will enable impoverished families to live side by side with more affluent neighbors. If the family's income increases, the rent subsidy will decline. Under the new program a family will not be displaced if its income rises above the subsidy level, as is now the practice in public housing. While controversy over this new program centered around the direct subsidies feature, the idea of special provisions to cover costs of housing is hardly new: subsidies have been offered for a period of 28 years to cover the cost of public housing, and are also part of the federal tax structure which permits income tax deductions for mortgage interest. The mortgage guarantee program is another subsidy to homeowners. Alvin L. Schorr, an authority on public housing, has estimated that in 1962 federal subsidies, via income tax deductions, to homeowners in the upper 20 percent of income distribution amounted to $1.7 billion, compared to $820 million of federal subsidies for poor people....

In the 1965 legislation Congress authorized the commitment of $30 million in rent subsidies for fiscal 1966 but appropriated only $450,-000 for fiscal 1966 to enable the Housing and Urban Development Department to prepare plans for the program. The level of subsidies is to be increased during the subsequent three years, and the total annual commitment will reach $150 million in fiscal 1969. It was estimated that the total originally authorized expenditures (assuming that funds would actually be appropriated and expended) would provide an additional 250,000 to 300,000 housing units for the poor over the next four years, depending upon the extent of subsidies that will be paid per unit. At this early stage it is, of course, impossible to predict whether the program will be viable. Experience with public housing has indicated the difficulty of providing impoverished families with adequate shelter, even when funds are available.

Medical services. In addition to food and shelter, certain medical services are now considered by our society as essential ingredients for a minimum standard of living. Public assistance programs include medical services as part of a basic need budget. In fiscal 1964 nearly one-quarter of the $4.9 billion expended for public assistance went to suppliers of medical care (that is, vendor payments). Among the medical services are hospitalization, nursing-home care, physicians' services, and prescribed drugs.

The federal government has, since 1960, contributed directly to medical care for indigent aged persons. States participating in this program are required to provide qualified beneficiaries with institutional and noninstitutional medical care. Thirty-seven states participate, and federal contributions range from 55 percent to 83 percent of total cost, depending upon the state's per capita income—the lower the income, the higher the share of federal contributions. This formula differs from other public assistance programs where federal contributions are included as part of the grants and are subject to the maximum limitations discussed earlier. In fiscal 1964 total payments to suppliers of medical care amounted to $1.1 billion. . . .

The 1965 enactment of Medicare will have a profound effect upon medical services offered to the entire aged population, including the poor. . . . The new legislation will not only provide needed medical services for the aged, but will also release available funds to expand medical services to other groups receiving public assistance. . . . More than two-thirds of total public assistance medical expenditures have been allocated to the aged poor. The medical assistance for the aged program (Kerr-Mills) will continue, but most of the present costs of old age medical assistance will be covered from Medicare funds. To provide more adequate medical services to other needy persons, the legislation extends the same services—now available only to the aged—to all federally-subsidized public assistance recipients as well as to other needy persons who do not receive cash assistance.

The implementation of this legislation will, of course, require state action; the medical assistance for the aged program enacted in

1960 had not been adopted by 13 states five years later. However, the 1965 Social Security Act amendments specify that all federal contributions for the payment of medical care under public assistance programs will be terminated by the end of this decade. This should be an adequate incentive for all states to join in the federally-subsidized programs and provide expanded medical care to all recipients of public assistance. . . .

Milton Friedman
Critics of Welfare Programs: The Welfare Grab Bag

The humanitarian and egalitarian sentiment which helped produce the steeply graduated individual income tax has also produced a host of other measures directed at promoting the "welfare" of particular groups. The most important single set of measures is the bundle misleadingly labeled "social security." Others are public housing, minimum wage laws, farm price supports, medical care for particular groups, special aid programs, and so on.

I shall first discuss briefly a few of the latter, mostly to indicate how different their actual effects may be from those intended, and shall then discuss at somewhat greater length the largest single component of the social security program, old age and survivor's insurance.

Miscellaneous Welfare Measures

1. *Public housing.* One argument frequently made for public housing is based on an alleged neighborhood effect: slum districts in particular, and other low quality housing to a lesser degree, are said to impose higher costs on the community in the form of fire and police protection. This literal neighborhood effect may well exist. But insofar as it does, it alone argues, not for public housing, but for higher taxes

Reprinted from *Capitalism and Freedom* (pp. 177–189) by Milton Friedman by permission of The University of Chicago Press. Copyright © 1962 by the University of Chicago.

Milton Friedman is Paul Snowden Russell Distinguished Service Professor of Economics, University of Chicago.

on the kind of housing that adds to social costs since this would tend to equalize private and social cost.

It will be answered at once that the extra taxes would bear on low-income people and that this is undesirable. The answer means that public housing is proposed not on the ground of neighborhood effects but as a means of helping low-income people. If this be the case, why subsidize housing in particular? If funds are to be used to help the poor, would they not be used more effectively by being given in cash rather than in kind? Surely, the families being helped would rather have a given sum in cash than in the form of housing. They could themselves spend the money on housing if they so desired. Hence, they would never be worse off if given cash; if they regarded other needs as more important, they would be better off. The cash subsidy would solve the neighborhood effect as well as the subsidy in kind, since if it were not used to buy housing it would be available to pay extra taxes justified by the neighborhood effect.

Public housing cannot therefore be justified on the grounds either of neighborhood effects or of helping poor families. It can be justified, if at all, only on grounds of paternalism; that the families being helped "need" housing more than they "need" other things but would themselves either not agree or would spend the money unwisely. The liberal will be inclined to reject this argument for responsible adults. He cannot completely reject it in the more indirect form in which it affects children; namely, that parents will neglect the welfare of the children, who "need" the better housing. But he will surely demand evidence much more persuasive and to the point than the kind usually given before he can accept this final argument as adequate justification for large expenditures on public housing.

So much could have been said in the abstract, in advance of actual experience with public housing. Now that we have had experience, we can go much farther. In practice, public housing has turned out to have effects very different indeed from those intended.

Far from improving the housing of the poor, as its proponents expected, public housing has done just the reverse. The number of dwelling units destroyed in the course of erecting public housing projects has been far larger than the number of new dwelling units constructed. But public housing as such has done nothing to reduce the number of persons to be housed. The effect of public housing has therefore been to raise the number of persons per dwelling unit. Some families have probably been better housed than they would otherwise have been—those who were fortunate enough to get occupancy of the publicly built units. But this has only made the problem for the rest all the worse, since the average density of all together went up.

Of course, private enterprise offset some of the deleterious effect of the public housing program by conversion of existing quarters and construction of new ones for either the persons directly displaced or, more generally, the persons displaced at one or two removes in the game of musical chairs set in motion by the public housing projects. However, these private resources would have been available in the absence of the public housing program.

Why did the public housing program have this effect? For the general reason we have stressed time and again. The general interest that motivated many to favor instituting the program is diffuse and transitory. Once the program was adopted, it was bound to be dominated by the special interests that it could serve. In this case, the special interests were those local groups that were anxious to have blighted areas cleared and refurbished, either because they owned property there or because the blight was threatening local or central business districts. Public housing served as a convenient means to accomplish their objective, which required more destruction than construction. Even so, "urban blight" is still with us in undiminished force, to judge by the growing pressure for federal funds to deal with it.

Another gain its proponents expected from public housing was the reduction of juvenile delinquency by improving housing conditions. Here again, the program in many instances had precisely the opposite effect, entirely aside from its failure to improve *average* housing conditions. The income limitations quite properly imposed for the occupancy of public housing at subsidized rentals have led to a very high density of "broken" families—in particular, divorced or widowed mothers with children. Children of broken families are especially likely to be "problem" children and a high concentration of such children is likely to increase juvenile delinquency. One manifestation has been the very adverse effect on schools in the neighborhood of a public housing project. Whereas a school can readily absorb a few "problem" children it is very difficult for it to absorb a large number. Yet in some cases, broken families are a third or more of the total in a public housing project and the project may account for a majority of the children in the school. Had these families been assisted through cash grants, they would have been spread much more thinly through the community.

2. *Minimum wage laws.* Minimum wage laws are about as clear a case as one can find of a measure the effects of which are precisely the opposite of those intended by the men of good will who support it. Many proponents of minimum wage laws quite properly deplore extremely low rates; they regard them as a sign of poverty; and they hope, by outlawing wage rates below some specified level, to reduce

poverty. In fact, insofar as minimum wage laws have any effect at all, their effect is clearly to increase poverty. The state can legislate a minimum wage rate. It can hardly require employers to hire at that minimum all who were formerly employed at wages below the minimum. It is clearly not in the interest of employers to do so. The effect of the minimum wage is therefore to make unemployment higher than it otherwise would be. Insofar as the low wage rates are in fact a sign of poverty, the people who are rendered unemployed are precisely those who can least afford to give up the income they had been receiving, small as it may appear to the people voting for the minimum wage.

This case is in one respect very much like public housing. In both, the people who are helped are visible—the people whose wages are raised; the people who occupy the publicly built units. The people who are hurt are anonymous and their problem is not clearly connected to its cause: the people who join the ranks of the unemployed or, more likely, are never employed in particular activities because of the existence of the minimum wage and are driven to even less remunerative activities or to the relief rolls; the people who are pressed ever closer together in the spreading slums that seem to be rather a sign of the need for more public housing than a consequence of the existing public housing.

A large part of the support for minimum wage laws comes not from disinterested men of good will but from interested parties. For example, northern trade unions and northern firms threatened by southern competition favor minimum wage laws to reduce the competition from the South.

3. *Farm price supports.* Farm price supports are another example. Insofar as they can be justified at all on grounds other than the political fact that rural areas are over-represented in the electoral college and Congress, it must be on the belief that farmers on the average have low incomes. Even if this be accepted as a fact, farm price supports do not accomplish the intended purpose of helping the farmers who need help. In the first place, benefits are, if anything, inverse to need, since they are in proportion to the amount sold on the market. The impecunious farmer not only sells less on the market than the wealthier farmer; in addition, he gets a larger fraction of his income from products grown for his own use, and these do not qualify for the benefits. In the second place, the benefits, if any, to farmers from the price-support program are much smaller than the total amount spent. This is clearly true of the amount spent for storage and similar costs which does not go to the farmer at all—indeed the suppliers of storage capacity and facilities may well be the major beneficiaries. It is equally true of

the amount spent to purchase agricultural products. The farmer is thereby induced to spend additional sums on fertilizer, seed, machinery, etc. At most, only the excess adds to his income. And finally, even this residual of a residual overstates the gain since the effect of the program has been to keep more people on the farm than would otherwise have stayed there. Only the excess, if any, of what they can earn on the farm with the price-support program over what they can earn off the farm, is a net benefit to them. The main effect of the purchase program has simply been to make farm output larger, not to raise the income per farmer.

Some of the costs of the farm purchase program are so obvious and well-known as to need little more than mention: the consumer has paid twice, once in taxes for farm benefit payments, again by paying a higher price for food; the farmer has been saddled with onerous restrictions and detailed centralized control; the nation has been saddled with a spreading bureaucracy. There is, however, one set of costs which is less well known. The farm program has been a major hindrance in the pursuit of foreign policy. In order to maintain a higher domestic than world price, it has been necessary to impose quotas on imports for many items. Erratic changes in our policy have had serious adverse effects on other countries. A high price for cotton encouraged other countries to enlarge their cotton production. When our high price led to an unwieldy stock of cotton, we proceeded to sell overseas at low prices and imposed heavy losses on the producers whom we had by our earlier actions encouraged to expand output. The list of similar cases could be multiplied.

Old Age and Survivor's Insurance

The "social security" program is one of those things on which the tyranny of the status quo is beginning to work its magic. Despite the controversy that surrounded its inception, it has come to be so much taken for granted that its desirability is hardly questioned any longer. Yet it involves a large-scale invasion into the personal lives of a large fraction of the nation without, so far as I can see, any justification that is at all persuasive, not only on liberal principles, but on almost any other. I propose to examine the biggest phase of it, that which involves payments to the aged.

As an operational matter, the program known as old age and survivor's insurance (OASI) consists of a special tax imposed on payrolls, plus payments to persons who have reached a specified age, of amounts determined by the age at which payments begin, family status, and prior earning record.

As an analytical matter, OASI consists of three separable elements:

1. The requirement that a wide class of persons must purchase specified annuities, i.e., compulsory provision for old age.

2. The requirement that the annuity must be purchased from the government; i.e., nationalization of the provision of these annuities.

3. A scheme for redistributing income, insofar as the value of the annuities to which people are entitled when they enter the system is not equal to the taxes they will pay.

Clearly, there is no necessity for these elements to be combined. Each individual could be required to pay for his own annuity; the individual could be permitted to purchase an annuity from private firms; yet individuals could be required to purchase specified annuities. The government could go into the business of selling annuities without compelling individuals to buy specified annuities and require the business to be self-supporting. And clearly the government can and does engage in redistribution without using the device of annuities.

Let us therefore consider each of these elements in turn to see how far, if at all, each can be justified. It will facilitate our analysis, I believe, if we consider them in reverse order.

1. *Income redistribution.*   The present OASI program involves two major kinds of redistribution; from some OASI beneficiaries to others; from the general taxpayer to OASI beneficiaries.

The first kind of redistribution is primarily from those who entered the system relatively young, to those who entered it at an advanced age. The latter are receiving, and will for some time be receiving, a greater amount as benefits than the taxes they paid could have purchased. Under present tax and benefit schedules, on the other hand, those who entered the system at a young age will receive decidedly less.

I do not see any grounds—liberal or other—on which this particular redistribution can be defended. The subsidy to the beneficiaries is independent of their poverty or wealth; the man of means receives it as much as the indigent. The tax which pays the subsidy is a flat-rate tax on earnings up to a maximum. It constitutes a larger fraction of low incomes than of high. What conceivable justification is there for taxing the young to subsidize the old regardless of the economic status of the old; for imposing a higher rate of tax for this purpose on the low than on the high; or, for that matter, for raising the revenues to pay the subsidy by a tax on payrolls?

The second kind of redistribution arises because the system is not likely to be fully self-financing. During the period when many were covered and paying taxes, and few had qualified for benefits, the system appeared to be self-financing and indeed to be having a surplus. But this appearance depends on neglecting the obligation being accumulated with respect to the persons paying the tax. It is doubtful that the taxes paid have sufficed to finance the accumulated obligation. Many experts assert that even on a cash basis, a subsidy will be required. And such a subsidy generally has been required in similar systems in other countries. This is a highly technical matter which we cannot and need not go into here and about which there can be honest differences of opinion.

For our purpose, it is enough to ask only the hypothetical question whether a subsidy from the general taxpayer could be justified if it is required. I see no grounds on which such a subsidy can be justified. We may wish to help poor people. Is there any justification for helping people whether they are poor or not because they happen to be a certain age? Is this not an entirely arbitrary redistribution?

The only argument I have ever come across to justify the redistribution involved in OASI is one that I regard as thoroughly immoral despite its wide use. This argument is that OASI redistribution on the average helps low-income people more than high-income people despite a large arbitrary element; that it would be better to do this redistribution more efficiently; but that the community will not vote for the redistribution directly though it will vote for it as part of a social security package. In essence, what this argument says is that the community can be fooled into voting for a measure that it opposes if the measure is presented in a false guise. Needless to say, the people who argue this way are the loudest in their condemnation of "misleading" commercial advertising!

2. Nationalization of the provision of required annuities. Suppose we avoid redistribution by requiring each person to pay for the annuity he gets, in the sense of course, that the premium suffices to cover the present value of the annuity, account being taken both of mortality and interest returns. What justification is there then for requiring him to purchase it from a governmental concern? If redistribution is to be accomplished, clearly the taxing power of the government must be used. But if redistribution is to be no part of the program and, as we have just seen, it is hard to see any justification for making it part, why not permit individuals who wish to do so to purchase their annuities from private concerns? A close analogy is provided by state laws requiring compulsory purchase of automobile liability insurance. So far as I know, no state which has such a law even has a state insurance company, let alone compels automobile owners to buy their insurance from a government agency.

Possible economies of scale are no argument for nationalizing the provision of annuities. If they are present, and the government sets up a concern to sell annuity contracts, it may be able to undersell competitors by virtue of its size. In that case, it will get the business without compulsion. If it cannot undersell them, then presumably economies of scale are not present or are not sufficient to overcome other diseconomies of governmental operation.

One possible advantage of nationalizing the provision of annuities is to facilitate the enforcement of compulsory purchase of annuities. However, this seems a rather trivial advantage. It would be easy to devise alternative administrative arrangements, such as requiring individuals to include a copy of a receipt for premium payments along with their income tax returns; or having their employers certify to their having met the requirement. The administrative problem would surely be minor compared with that imposed by the present arrangements.

The costs of nationalization seem clearly to outweigh any such trivial advantage. Here, as elsewhere, individual freedom to choose, and competition of private enterprises for custom, would promote improvements in the kinds of contracts available, and foster variety and diversity to meet individual need. On the political level, there is the obvious gain from avoiding an expansion in the scale of governmental activity and the indirect threat to freedom of every such expansion.

Some less obvious political costs arise from the character of the present program. The issues involved become very technical and complex. The layman is often incompetent to judge them. Nationalization means that the bulk of the "experts" become employees of the nationalized system, or university people closely linked with it. Inevitably, they come to favor its expansion, not, I hasten to add, out of narrow self-interest but because they are operating within a framework in which they take for granted governmental administration and are familiar only with its techniques. The only saving grace in the United States so far has been the existence of private insurance companies involved in similar activities.

Effective control by Congress over the operations of such agencies as the Social Security Administration becomes essentially impossible as a result of the technical character of their task and their near-monopoly of experts. They become self-governing bodies whose proposals are in the main rubber-stamped by Congress. The able and ambitious men who make their careers in them are naturally anxious to expand the scope of their agencies and it is exceedingly difficult to prevent them from doing so. If the expert says yea, who is there competent to say nay? So we have seen an increasing fraction of the population drawn into the social security system, and now that there remain few possibilities of expansion in that direction, we are seeing a move toward the addition of new programs, such as medical care.

I conclude that the case against the nationalization of the provision of annuities is exceedingly strong, not only in terms of liberal principles but even in terms of the values expressed by proponents of the welfare state. If they believe that the government can provide the service better than the market, they should favor a government concern to issue annuities in open competition with other concerns. If they are right, the government concern will prosper. If they are wrong, the welfare of the people will be advanced by having a private alternative. Only the doctrinaire socialist, or the believer in centralized control for its own sake, can, so far as I can see, take a stand on principle in favor of nationalization of the provision of annuities.

3. *Compulsory purchase of annuities.* Having cleared away the underbrush, we are now ready to face the key issue: compelling individuals to use some of their current income to purchase annuities to provide for their old age.

One possible justification for such compulsion is strictly paternalistic. People could if they wished decide to do individually what the law requires them to do as a group. But they are separately shortsighted and improvident. "We" know better than "they" that it is in their own good to provide for their old age to a greater extent than they would voluntarily; we cannot persuade them individually; but we can persuade 51 per cent or more to compel all to do what is in their own good. This paternalism is for responsible people, hence does not even have the excuse of concern for children or madmen.

This position is internally consistent and logical. A thoroughgoing paternalist who holds it cannot be dissuaded by being shown that he is making a mistake in logic. He is our mortal enemy on grounds of principle, not simply a well-meaning but misguided friend. Basically, he believes in dictatorship, benevolent and maybe majoritarian, but dictatorship none the less.

Those of us who believe in freedom must believe also in the freedom of individuals to make their own mistakes. If a man knowingly prefers to live for today, to use his resources for current enjoyment, deliberately choosing a penurious old age, by what right do we prevent him from doing so? We may argue with him, seek to persuade him that he is wrong, but are we entitled to use coercion to prevent him from doing what he chooses to do? Is there not always the possibility that he is right and that we are wrong? Humility is the distinguishing virtue of the believer in freedom; arrogance, of the paternalist.

Few people are thoroughgoing paternalists. It is a position that is most unattractive if examined in the cold light of the day. Yet the paternalistic argument has played so large a role in measures like social security that it seems worth making it explicit.

A possible justification on liberal principles for compulsory purchase of annuities is that the improvident will not suffer the consequence of their own action but will impose costs on others. We shall not, it is said, be willing to see the indigent aged suffer in dire poverty. We shall assist them by private and public charity. Hence the man who does not provide for his old age will become a public charge. Compelling him to buy an annuity is justified not for his own good but for the good of the rest of us.

The weight of this argument clearly depends on fact. If 90 per cent of the population would become charges on the public at age 65 in the absence of compulsory purchase of annuities, the argument would have great weight. If only 1 per cent would, the argument has none. Why restrict the freedom of 99 per cent to avoid the costs that the other 1 per cent would impose on the community?

The belief that a large fraction of the community would become public charges if not compelled to purchase annuities owed its plausibility, at the time OASI was enacted, to the Great Depression. In every year from 1931 through 1940, more than one-seventh of the labor force was unemployed. And unemployment was proportionately heavier among the older workers. This experience was unprecedented and has not been repeated since. It did not arise because people were improvident and failed to provide for their old age. It was a consequence, as we have seen, of government mismanagement. OASI is a cure, if cure it be at all, for a very different malady and one of which we have had no experience.

The unemployed of the 1930's certainly created a serious problem of the relief of distress, of many people becoming public charges. But old-age was by no means the most serious problem. Many people in productive ages were on the relief or assistance rolls. And the steady spread of OASI, until today more than sixteen million persons receive benefits, has not prevented a continued growth in the number receiving public assistance.

Private arrangements for the care of the aged have altered greatly over time. Children were at one time the major means whereby people provided for their own old age. As the community became more affluent, the mores changed. The responsibilities imposed on children to care for their parents declined and more and more people came to make provision for old age in the form of accumulating property or acquiring private pension rights. More recently, the development of pension plans over and above OASI has accelerated. Indeed, some students believe that a continuation of present trends points to a society in which a large fraction of the public scrimps in their productive years to provide themselves with a higher standard of life in old age than they ever enjoyed in the prime of life. Some of us may think such a trend perverse, but if it reflects the tastes of the community, so be it.

Compulsory purchase of annuities has therefore imposed large costs for little gain. It has deprived all of us of control over a sizable fraction of our income, requiring us to devote it to a particular purpose, purchase of a retirement annuity, in a particular way, by buying it from a government concern. It has inhibited competition in the sale of annuities and the development of retirement arrangements. It has given birth to a large bureaucracy that shows tendencies of growing by what it feeds on, of extending its scope from one area of our life to another. And all this, to avoid the danger that a few people might become charges on the public.

Charles E. Silberman
Critics of Welfare Programs: Welfare Colonialism

The rate of expenditure for public assistance has been rising rapidly in every large city, without making a dent in any of the problems they are supposed to solve. Indeed, a good many of these expenditures seem to have been a waste of money at best, and at worst a positive disservice to the people they are supposed to help. Relatively few disinterested students would agree with the social worker-turned-novelist Julius Horwitz, that the whole welfare system is an "ugly, diseased social growth that must be removed from American life." But few can argue with the studied judgment of Professor S. M. Miller of Syracuse University: "Welfare assistance in its present form tends to encourage dependence, withdrawal, diffused hostility, indifference, ennui."

A growing number of social scientists and government officials, in fact, have acquired a growing sense of disenchantment with the entire

From *Crisis in Black and White* by Charles E. Silberman (New York: Random House, Inc., 1964), pp. 309–313. Copyright © 1964 by Random House, Inc. Reprinted by permission.

Charles E. Silberman is a member of the Board of Editors of *Fortune* and a frequent contributor to that magazine.

welfare-social worker-settlement house approach. These are not reactionaries anxious to cut taxes by forcing relief clients to move somewhere else, but men genuinely concerned with solving the day-to-day problems of the poor. And they are troubled by the evidence that the present welfare system is self-perpetuating—that far from relieving dependency, it *encourages* dependency. Thus, a study of public assistance in New York State, made by the management consulting firm of Greenleigh Associates for the Moreland Commission, reported that existing policies and procedures lead to *increased* dependency. And a national study of the Federal Aid to Dependent Children Program, made by M. Elaine Burgess and Daniel O. Price of the University of North Carolina for the American Public Welfare Association, called for major changes to reduce long-term dependency and prevent the continued development of second-generation dependents.

Nor does the answer lie in expanding the number of social workers, settlement houses, mental health clinics, and the like. In New York City, for example, the *Directory of Social and Health Agencies* contains 721 pages; social work is one of the city's major industries. In the Harlem-Upper Manhattan area alone, according to a study by the Protestant Council of the City of New York, there are some 156 separate agencies serving an estimated 240,000 people—roughly 40 per cent of the total population of the area. Without question, there are gaps here and there in the services offered, and many existing services are grossly inadequate. But it seems clear that the solution to Harlem's problems does not lie in any expansion of social agencies.

There is no dearth of agencies and programs elsewhere in the city, either. Municipal expenditures for youth services, for example, have approximately tripled since the beginning of the postwar period, to some $800 million a year, exclusive of expenditures by private agencies. As a recent survey, made at the city's request by the Institute of Public Administration, reported, "this enormous effort has not abated the major social problems affecting children and youth." On the contrary, the Institute argued, many programs "tend to perpetuate the conditions they are intended to alleviate." For example, the Aid for Dependent Children (ADC) Program "tends to produce female-centered households, with increased rates of illegitimacy and other undesirable results." Other programs, by concentrating on symptoms rather than causes, may simply substitute a new set of symptoms for the old. For example, herculean efforts by the city's Youth Board, the police, the courts, and a host of voluntary agencies, succeeded in taming the fighting gangs that had erupted in the early 1950s. But if ever there was a Phyrric victory, this was it; "bopping" has now been replaced by alcoholism and drug addiction, which are much harder to combat, and far more crippling in their long-run effects. And so it goes.

New York City probably is exceptional in the number and variety of its welfare programs, but the fact remains that virtually every large city has increased its welfare budget at least in proportion to, and more often than not faster than, the growth in the number of people being served. No honest man can suggest that the accomplishments have been remotely commensurate with the effort. On the contrary, one sometimes has the feeling that welfare agencies almost welcome failure, for failure if repeated frequently enough only demonstrates the need to expand their services still more. In appealing for governmental or private support, these agencies remind one of J. Edgar Hoover's requests for more financial aid to fight communism: his agency is the only "bulwark against the communist threat"; but that threat seems somehow to grow rather than diminish, in spite of all the work of his agency. So with the social agencies in the fight against delinquency, family disorganization, drug addiction, and so on.

What has gone wrong? Why the failure? These questions must be answered before we can propose an alternative course of action.

What has gone wrong, primarily, is that social agencies and social workers have concentrated far too much on symptoms rather than on causes—and on symptoms seen and treated individually rather than in connection with other symptoms. This concern with symptoms has been a reflection, in good measure, of the preoccupation of the social work profession with case work and the study and treatment of individual maladjustment. The goal, that is to say, has been to teach maladjusted individuals how to adapt themselves to society as it is, rather than to change those aspects of society that make the individuals what they are.

Unlike the early sociologists who were reformers, contemporary sociologists and social workers, as Professer Lewis Coser has commented, have focused attention "predominantly upon problems of adjustment rather than upon conflict; upon social statics rather than dynamics"; they have been concerned largely with "the maintenance of existing structures and the ways and means of insuring their smooth functioning." Social workers, in particular, have made Freud their God when they should have been worshiping at the shrine of the sociologist Emile Durkheim. For the problems of the slum stem far less from individual neuroses (though certainly there are plenty of those) than from an objective lack of opportunity, from a social system that denies the individual dignity and status.

The result, as *West Side Story* suggested with some wit, is that slum youngsters regard social workers with a good deal of scorn; more to the point, they see them as "con men" sent to hypnotize them into accepting a society they loathe—a society which denies them (or seems to deny them, which amounts to the same thing) the means to achieve the goals to which they are exhorted to aspire. To a degree, at least, the gang members, the delinquents, the dropouts, the ordinary slum dwellers are justified in their cynicism: Americans have used welfare programs and social work agencies the way the Romans used bread and circuses—to keep the poor happy and non-threatening.

The obsession with "case work" and individual pathology has had another extremely unfortunate effect: the great bulk of resources, financial and professional, have been concentrated on a very small proportion of slum dwellers, the so-called "multi-problem families." There is a growing mass of evidence that those receiving the greatest assistance are the ones least likely to benefit from it. Dr. Thomas Gladwin, for example, has suggested that there may be considerable merit in reviving the old distinction between "the deserving poor" and "the undeserving poor." The great majority of slum dwellers, that is to say, work hard for very little material reward; they try their best to raise themselves, and their children, out of the morass in which they find themselves. Their problem is not any lack of good intent, but simply that their best is not good enough. These are the "deserving poor." The "undeserving poor"— those who, for whatever reasons of individual or social pathology, are truly antisocial in their behavior, destroy other peoples' lives or property, trade in narcotics, pimping, or whoring—in fact represent a small proportion of slum society. The fact that the deserving and the undeserving poor live in the same neighborhood and in much the same way reflects a common state rather than a common interest, and limited social welfare resources might be far more effective if directed at the deserving rather than at the undeserving poor.

In the last analysis, however, the failure of the enormous American social welfare effort stems from the same factor that has produced the political strain between Negroes and white liberals: the social workers' preoccupation with doing *for* people instead of doing *with* them— a preoccupation that destroys the dignity and arouses the hostility of the people who are supposed to be helped. All too often, social services are motivated by a sense of superiority, a patronizing "white man's burden" attitude that would offend the most thick-skinned slum dweller.

Michael Harrington
The Role of Public Housing

... the 1960 census (these are preliminary figures) reported that 15.6 million of the 58,000,000 occupied dwelling units in the United States were substandard. This represented 27 per cent of the nation's total housing supply. Of these, some 3,000,000 were shacks, hovels, and tenements. Another 8.3 million units were "deteriorating," and 4.3 million units were structurally sound but lacking some or all of the essential plumbing facilities. In addition, these figures do not take account of "sound" housing that is terribly overcrowded.

As the AFL-CIO Civil Rights Department put it, "It seems, therefore, certain that 30 per cent of American families are living in substandard homes today." For those interested in historical echoes, that amounts to one third of a nation that is ill housed.

Perhaps a more dramatic statement of the problem was made by Charles L. Farris, the president of the National Association of Housing Officials: at the end of the fifties there were more Americans living in slums than on farms.

These figures apply only to the "old" slums, the obvious tenements and the broken-down houses. But the new public housing projects themselves have become a major problem. Many of them have become income ghettos, centers for juvenile gangs, modern poor farms where social disintegration is institutionalized. In addition, the destruction of old slum neighborhoods for public housing or Title I programs has resulted in mass evictions. The new public housing did not provide enough units for those who had been driven out to make way for improvement. The projects thus created new slums and intensified the pressures within the old slums, particularly for minority groups.

This grim inventory could be continued indefinitely, yet that would be to miss a major point about America's slums. The problem of housing is not simply a physical matter. In 1950, for instance, the Census defined "dilapidation" as occurring when "a dwelling unit is run down or neglected, or is of inadequate original construction so that it does not provide adequate shelter or protection against the elements or it endangers the safety of the occupants." Such a definition has a bureau-

Reprinted with permission of The Macmillan Company from *The Other America* by Michael Harrington, pp. 139–157. © Michael Harrington 1962.
Michael Harrington is a member of the editorial board of *Dissent*.

cratic neatness to it, but it misses the very essence of what a slum is.

A slum is not merely an area of decrepit buildings. It is a social fact. There are neighborhoods in which housing is run-down, yet the people do not exhibit the hopelessness of the other Americans. Usually, these places have a vital community life around a national culture or a religion. In New York City, Chinatown is an obvious example. Where the slum becomes truly pernicious is when it becomes the environment of the culture of poverty, a spiritual and personal reality for its inhabitants as well as an area of dilapidation. This is when the slum becomes the breeding ground of crime, of vice, the creator of people who are lost to themselves and to society.

Thus, there are in the United States old slums where the buildings are miserable and decayed; and there are new slums in which the culture of poverty has been imported into modern housing projects. Both are parts of the other America.

I

First, take the obvious slum of tenements and hovels. The most important fact about these places in the sixties is that they are the environment of pessimism and of hopelessness.

Indeed, there is a sense in which the "old" slums are new. There once was a slum in American society that was a melting pot, a way station, a goad to talent. It was the result of the massive European immigration in the late nineteenth and early twentieth centuries. That flood of human vitality came to an end after World War I when the nation established quota systems, but the tradition of the ethnic groups survived for a generation. Symbolically, the tenements in which these newcomers lived had been built for them and had not been trickled down after the middle class found them inadequate. The neighborhoods were dense and the housing was inadequate, yet the people were not defeated by their environment. There was community; there was aspiration.

In most cities in the United States, it is still possible to take a bus or subway into this part of the American past. The Kerry Patch, the Ghetto, Little Italy, and other ethnic slums remain. Yet, like archaeological remnants of some dead culture, they are being buried under the new metropolis. Yet, even today, there is still a unique feeling of life in the remains of the old ethnic slums. The crowding gives rise to a lusty richness of existence. The children swarm on the streets throughout the day and into the early evening, but they rarely form themselves into violent gangs. If the neighborhood is strident, it is vital, too; if it is dotted with the signs of the Old Country, it is a way station to the new land as well. . . .

Where the ethnic slum once stood, in the "old" slum neighborhood, there is a new type of slum. Its citizens are the internal migrants, the Negroes, the poor whites from the farms, the Puerto Ricans. They join the failures from the old ethnic culture and form an entirely different kind of neighborhood. For many of them, the crucial problem is color, and this makes the ghetto walls higher than they have ever been. All of them arrive at a time of housing shortage (when the public housing program was first proposed in the thirties, around a quarter of the slum units were vacant), and thus it is harder to escape even when income rises. But, above all, these people do not participate in the culture of aspiration that was the vitality of the ethnic slum. . . .

II

The current American answer to the problem of the slum is the low-cost housing project. The theory behind this approach contains at least the beginnings of an attack upon the culture of poverty: a public commitment to create a new environment for human beings.

But the practice has lagged far behind the intention. The concerned citizen sees that tenement eyesores have been torn down, and he is satisfied. He does not understand that the number of units that have been built do not equal the number that have been destroyed in clearing the project sites. In New York in 1954, for instance, there was one unit for every 7.1 eligible new families; in 1956, one for every 10.4 eligible new families. And these figures are roughly typical of the nation as a whole.

In some areas people who have priority for getting low-cost housing do not take advantage of it. Some refuse to go in because of their reputation for violence or because of their interracial character. Some are on the fly and fear any contact with the public authorities— and not necessarily because of crime; perhaps because of marriage irregularities, for instance. Still another group, according to Tom Wolfe of New York's Hudson Guild, simply do not know about the opportunity. Long-time citizens of the other America, they assume that there is no real hope, that no one is going to help them, and they vanish. That is one reason why over half of the people displaced by projects in the United States are listed on the records as "address unknown."

So, first of all, there is not enough public housing to go around. But there are some hundreds of thousands of people who have gone into projects recently, and their experience is perhaps even more significant than that of those who were simply displaced. . . .

Most public housing, even at its best, fails to solve the problem of the slum and, above all, the problem of slum psychology. In some cases the gains appear minimal, for one must balance the physical improvement (and, hopefully, the consequent improvement in health) against the new forms of alienation and, at the extreme, of violence. But, perhaps most crucial, the housing policy of America has sought the integration of the poor with the poor—which is to say, the segregation of the other Americans from the society at large.

III

For some people the failures of public housing are cited as an argument against national involvement in this problem. This is a disastrous and wrongheaded deduction.

With all that has been said about the inadequacies of the housing projects, it is clear that only one agency in America is capable of eradicating both the slum and slum psychology from this land: the Federal Government. Time and time again, private builders have demonstrated that they are utterly incapable of doing anything. If the Federal Government deserts the field, that would be tantamount to a decision to enlarge the slums of America. A new determination and imagination are needed, not a retreat.

The cost of an all-out attack upon the slums is measurable. In 1955 Joseph P. McMurray, then State Housing Commissioner of New York (and now chairman of the Federal Home Loan Bank), testified before the House Subcommittee on Housing. He estimated that it would take $125,000,000,000 of public and private investment to end slums within twenty-five years. This, he said, would require a combined program five times larger than the current Government commitment. Clearly, this is an expensive business; clearly it is not beyond the bounds of possibility.

In 1961, Leon Keyserling, former chairman of the President's Council of Economic Advisers, calculated that a serious attack upon the problem would require about two million units a year for the next four years. Of these, 1.2 million would be privately financed housing for upper-middle-income families; about 500,000 would be provided for lower-middle-income families (with some kind of Government subsidies); and about 300,000 homes a year would be brought into the reach of low-income families, including the aging, through joint Federal and local contributions.

Predictably, the plans put forward by Washington as the sixties began fell far short of these appraisals. The Kennedy Administration proposed funds for 100,000 new low-income public-housing units (this would mean that the United States would still be short of the goals projected in 1949 for a four-year period!), and subsidies that would provide for about 75,000 middle-income housing units.

Second, under the present setup, it is the poor who are victimized by urban renewal. In 1959 Charles Abrams told a Senate Committee that the public housing program had become "tattered, perverted and shrunk... little more than an adjunct of the publicly subsidized private urban renewal program. This urban renewal program too, while it does help the cities to get rid of slums, has developed into a device for displacing the poor from their footholds to make way for higher rental dwellings which those displaced cannot afford. Thus, the lowest-income family remains the forgotten family, though it is still the most home-needy in the American family circle."

If these problems of financing are not solved, if America does not have the will to eradicate the slum in its midst, then no amount of imagination will deal with the situation. But if the will were there, if the money were appropriated, then there is a crying need for new directions in public housing.

Public housing must be conceived of as something more than improved physical shelter with heat and plumbing. It must be seen as an important organism for the creation of community life in the cities. First and foremost, public housing should avoid segregating the poor off in some corner of the metropolis. That is the "modern poor-farm mentality," as one critic described it. The projects and subsidized homes should be located as parts of neighborhoods, so that income groups, races, and cultures will mingle.

Many housing experts have already laid down some fairly obvious principles for accomplishing these ends (The vision is not lacking; only the will.) For example, Charles L. Farris of St. Louis has proposed specific steps: low-cost and middle-income units should be interspersed, and there should be an attempt to integrate public housing with existing and vital neighborhoods. There should be a limit on building size (Farris suggests eight families) so as to avoid the creation of an impersonal, bureaucratic environment. And the private individual housing that still exists should become the focus of a campaign for rehabilitation.

Private ownership is one of the great myths of American life— for more than half the people do not, and cannot, own their homes. In 1959 Charles Abrams estimated that an annual income of over $6,000 was required before an American family could seriously think of buying a home. In 1957, for instance, less than 6 percent of the families who purchased new homes under the FHA had incomes under $4,200. In other words, the upper half of the population benefited from this program to the extent of 94 per cent of the housing, while those who most desperately needed it shared 6 per cent of the total.

It would be magnificent if America were to make home ownership a goal of national policy. As it is today, the poor are completely excluded from this possibility, and even the great middle third of the income pyramid have considerable difficulties.

Where projects are undertaken (and it must be emphasized that the reference is not to huge high-rise ghettos, but to a new kind of public housing) there must be an adequate budget for social work. You cannot take people out of an old-fashioned slum, where reality has been giving them a grim, distorted education for years, place them in a project, and expect them to exhibit all kinds of gentle, middle-class virtues. This transition is a crucial moment. If the people are left to themselves, then the chances are that they will import the culture of poverty into the public housing. If they are helped, if there is real effort to forge neighborhood communites, this need not happen.

Many of the public-housing administrators are sincere and imaginative public servants, but they have been frustrated at every turn by the inadequacy of funds and by the fact that the nation has yet to make a real commitment to build a human environment.

And the cost? The point has already been made, but it deserves repeating: we already pay an inordinately high price for poverty in the United States. Misery generates social chaos, and it takes money just to police it, just to keep it from becoming so explosive that it will disturb the tranquillity of the better off. In cold cash-and-carry terms, there would be a long-range pay-off if slums were abolished in the United States. In human terms, such an action would mean that millions of people would be returned to the society and enabled to make their personal contribution.

At this writing, one must sadly report that it does not seem likely that there will be an adequate crusade to end the misery of the millions of Americans who live in substandard housing. The figures have all been tabulated; the reports are in; and the direction of human advance is clear. But, as the sixties open, there is not yet the political will to get at the root of the problem.

So the new form of the old slums will continue; the inadequacies and tragedies of our past public housing policy will remain with us; and that tenacious organism, the culture of poverty, will settle down comfortably in our urban rot.

Theodore W. Schultz
The Welfare of Farm People

...Long before the New Deal and McNary-Haugenism, farmers in the United States had had a large hand politically in developing our welfare state. The earlier agrarian movements protested strongly against the doctrine of laissez faire, not because farm leaders had been schooled in European socialism or in Marxian thought. Their protests were a direct, indigenous response to the raw industrialism of the decades after the Civil War and to the long decline in the general level of prices. More recently, mainly after World War I, farmers turned to the federal government to intervene on their behalf in adjusting agricultural production and in supporting particular farm prices in what J. D. Black called "Assisted Laissez Faire." But, despite the strong political influence they have had in the development of the welfare state, farmers have not acquired many of the social services that it renders to others. The puzzle is, Why?

My aims here are, first, to recount briefly the objectives of the agrarian movements of the 1880's and 1890's; second, to list several social services that specifically benefit farm people and, last, to give reasons for the government's neglect of social services for farm people.

Early Political Objectives

The agrarian protest movements that appeared soon after the Civil War repeatedly challenged the nineteenth-century doctrine of laissez faire. In practice, laissez faire, so it seemed to many farm people, sheltered all manner of monopolies. The agrarian movements demanded that trusts be "busted," and they eventually won the enactment of far-reaching antitrust legislation. They were also convinced that private banks, with an eye to profits, had all too free a hand in determining the supply of money and thus the general level of prices, regardless of what happened to the economy and to farmers as debtors. Bryan electrified a political convention by espousing the agrarian cause in his "Cross

Reprinted from "Our Welfare State and the Welfare of Farm People" by Theodore W. Schultz, *The Social Service Review* (June 1964), pp. 123–129 by permission of The University of Chicago Press. Copyright © 1964 by the University of Chicago.

Theodore W. Schultz is Charles L. Hutchinson Distinguished Service Professor of Economics, University of Chicago, and past president of the American Economics Association.

ɔf Gold" speech. Then, as a response, although after a long lag, the
Federal Reserve System was established.

In retrospect, it is noteworthy that these early farm leaders anticipated what has since become a major purpose of modern monetary-
fiscal policy. They also protested the then extreme inequalities in the
distribution of personal income and wealth. The response came during
the first term of the Wilson administration, when a constitutional amendment was finally approved; progressive taxation was then enacted to
begin to redress the existing inequalities in personal income and wealth.
But, for all these important modifications of the doctrine of laissez faire,
farm people have not acquired for themselves many of the major social
services of the United States welfare state.

Distribution of Social Services

Farmers did acquire, among others, the following: rural free
delivery of the mail (RFD); improved farm roads often better, at least
until recently, than the roads in our cities; co-operatives to provide electricity and telephone services to farmers; and some credit to improve
farm homes. The land-grant colleges and universities began mainly as
an agricultural venture. They are undoubtedly one of our outstanding
institutional innovations. While they have contributed to the dignity of
farming and to its modernization and productivity, the economic benefits
have become widely diffused among consumers who are predominantly
non-farm people. These are all welfare services for which farm people
have taken political action.

But there are other important services now provided by the
welfare state that farm people have been reluctant to share in or that
they have opposed strongly enough to have been by-passed. Farm people generally are opposed to extending to hired farm labor the unemployment and related benefits available to non-farm laborers. There is
virtually no concern on the part of farm people about the social deprivation of migratory farm workers or about the social costs of cheap imported farm labor. For years there appeared to be widespread uneasiness
among farm people in having old age and survivors' insurance extended
to farmers, although it has become in less than a decade a major source
of benefits, more important in terms of welfare than much of the farm
legislation enacted on behalf of agriculture. Except for agricultural vocational training and for land-grant teaching, research, and extension work,
there is strong opposition to any and all federal aid to education. There
is also objection to public measures for medical care and health facilities.
The puzzle with which I began is not resolved by this review of the
role that farm people have had in the development of our welfare

state, although their reluctance in having some of the major services come to them provides a clue. . . .

Reasons for Neglect

. . . As I interpret our political and economic history, there are four major reasons for governmental neglect of the social aspects of welfare of farm people.

1. Influence of the southern tradition.   Lest we forget, the South is a key, critical part of agriculture. It accounted for over 45 per cent of all farms when the 1959 agricultural census was taken. Jefferson's agricultural views are often featured. But what is not emphasized is the political influence of the southern tradition long supported by an undemocratic political structure. The weakness of this tradition with respect to social responsibility is evident in an indifference and an antagonism to public schools. William H. Nicholls' study leaves no room for doubt on this matter. The social services of the United States welfare state, with few exceptions, are an anathema to the South politically, although these services are used heavily once they become available.

2. Conflicts of interest.   Who represents whom with respect to the interests of farm people? Or, more narrowly, which classes of farmers are represented? Precisely, which particular interests of particular farmers? The conflicts among farm-commodity groups, though well known, have little direct bearing on the welfare issues under consideration. What is relevant here is the conflict in interest between imported farm laborers and the farmers who want cheap labor. Migratory farm laborers of domestic origin are situated somewhat like hired farm workers generally. There is also the long-standing animosity of poor whites toward Negroes. Another conflict exists when one considers national sharing of some of the costs of schooling, with its implied tax burden on the North and West, to assist the South, where taxes on farm land to support local schools are often less relative to the value of farm land than in the rest of the country. Patently, the poorest whose needs are the greatest have the least political influence, which is necessary to gain access to the social services of the welfare state.

3. Lack of knowledge.   Farm people and their leaders are not in general conversant with the ideas, the philosophical basis, and the historical processes inherent in the urbanization and industrialization of which modern agriculture is an integral part. The scientific and technological knowledge underlying modern agriculture is well understood by farm people, but the changing social and economic framework is still largely in the realm of myth. If blame we must, we must look at our land-grant colleges and universities. Where are the county agents who can hold forth competently on these cultural, economic, and historical issues? They are not to blame, for where is the instruction to prepare them for this task?... In the area of cultural and historical analysis, there is a great void in research and instruction.

4. *Price-production programs.* This brings us to the principal reason for the neglect by government of the welfare of farm people. These price supports, acreage restrictions, and subsidies hold top priority in United States farm policy. Virtually all of the time and thought of the United States Department of Agriculture, the agricultural committees of Congress, and the farm organizations is spent on them. They exhaust the political influence of farm people. But these programs do not improve the schooling of farm children; they do not reduce the inequalities in personal distribution of wealth and income; they do not remove or alleviate poverty in agriculture. On the contrary, they worsen the distribution of income within agriculture.

But is this summary of their income effects not a flat contradiction of what really happens? Surely, it will be said, high price supports, with or without large government payments, must mean that farm income is larger than it would otherwise be, and hence farm people must be able to afford the consumption underlying welfare. Faith in this false proposition has lasted unbelievably long. Ever since the McNary-Haugen period, parity prices, parity income, acreage allotments, government payments, and then an expensive round of supply management have held the center of the United States farm-policy stage. Who benefits most? Landowners. Who least? The poorest farm families. By any meaningful welfare test, helping least those who need help most is absurd.

There are signs that some farm people have lost faith in these acreage restrictions, marketing quotas, and price-support programs. Nevertheless, alternative programs designed to reduce the real poverty in agriculture, to raise the level of consumption of those who are very poor, and to provide first-class primary and secondary schooling for farm children are not welcomed by the agricultural committees of Congress or demanded politically by the strongest farm organization....

The combination of the political influence of southern tradition, the conflicts of interests among farm families, the fact that farm leaders are not conversant with the ideas, the philosophical basis, and the historical process of which modern agriculture is an integral part, and the extraordinary commitment to having the government enact and administer production-price programs—all these create a formidable barrier to welfare. It is a high wall against the social services of the welfare state, but this wall will come tumbling down.

7
The Great Society's Program: Breaking the Chain

The overtones of much of the discussion [about poverty] and its sudden eruption create the impression that we are in the throes of another emotional jag.
—Professor Margaret G. Reid

The ineffectiveness of existing welfare programs in reducing poverty has led to a search for new remedies. Traditional welfare programs focus on income maintenance; they attempt to reduce the inequalities that result from the competitive economic struggle, but they do little to change the underlying causes. At best, therefore, income-maintenance programs merely alleviate the circumstances of the poor. These programs do not increase the productivity, change the behavior, or in any way improve the effectiveness of the poor in coping with their environment. Nor do income-maintenance measures increase the likelihood that children of the poor will be more successful than their parents.

If income maintenance was the hallmark of the war on poverty in the 1930's, "opportunity" and "involvement" have become key words in the sixties. It is no accident that the new federal agency which leads and coordinates the anti-poverty drive is called the Office of Economic Opportunity. This name symbolizes a new effort, designed to halt the inevitable transmission of poverty from one generation to the next.

Much of the new program focuses on the provision of education, work, and training for the children and youth of low-income families. The Job Corps, the Neighborhood Youth Corps, Head Start, and the work-study programs are all in this category. Although several of these programs provide some income to poor families, their primary aim is to prevent poverty in the future by providing the youngsters in low-income families with the training they need.

More controversial is the Community Action Program, which utilizes about half of the funds that have been allotted to the new agency. In this program each local community is expected to mobilize its resources and develop an integrated plan of action for combating poverty. This plan may then be submitted to the Office of Economic Opportunity, where it is considered for funding—with the federal government paying 90 percent of the total cost. Fundamental to this part of the program is the concept that the residents of low-income areas must become involved in the solution of their own problems—that the poor themselves must play a major role in planning and operating their community anti-poverty programs.

In the articles that follow, the Presidential Message on Poverty and the analysis of the Economic Opportunity Act by Sargent Shriver convey the philosophy that underlies this new approach to poverty. The statements by Professor Reid and by the Republican minority on the Senate Committee on Labor and Public Welfare contain most of the major arguments that have been leveled against the program. Knoll and Witcover discuss the problems associated with the attempt to activate the poor under the Community Action Program, and the article from *Newsweek* summarizes the progress made under the Economic Opportunity Act after one year of operation.

Lyndon B. Johnson
Presidential Message on Poverty

We are citizens of the richest and most fortunate nation in the history of the world.

One hundred and eighty years ago we were a small country struggling for survival on the margin of a hostile land.

Today we have established a civilization of free men which spans an entire continent.

From Message to the Congress of the United States on the Economic Opportunity Act of 1964 by President Lyndon B. Johnson, March 16, 1964.

With the growth of our country has come opportunity for our people—opportunity to educate our children, to use our energies in productive work, to increase our leisure—opportunity for almost every American to hope that through work and talent he could create a better life for himself and his family.

The path forward has not been an easy one.

But we have never lost sight of our goal—an America in which every citizen shares all the opportunities of his society, in which every man has a chance to advance his welfare to the limit of his capacities.

We have come a long way toward this goal.

We still have a long way to go.

The distance which remains is the measure of the great unfinished work of our society.

To finish that work I have called for a national war on poverty. Our objective—total victory.

There are millions of Americans—one fifth of our people—who have not shared in the abundance which has been granted to most of us, and on whom the gates of opportunity have been closed.

What does this poverty mean to those who endure it?

It means a daily struggle to secure the necessities for even a meager existence. It means that the abundance, the comforts, the opportunities they see all around them are beyond their grasp.

Worst of all, it means hopelessness for the young.

The young man or woman who grows up without a decent education, in a broken home, in a hostile and squalid environment, in ill health or in the face of racial injustice—that young man or woman is often trapped in a life of poverty.

He does not have the skills demanded by a complex society. He does not know how to acquire those skills. He faces a mounting sense of despair which drains initiative and ambition and energy.

Our tax cut will create millions of new jobs—new exits from poverty.

But we must also strike down all the barriers which keep many from using those exits.

The war on poverty is not a struggle simply to support people, to make them dependent on the generosity of others.

It is a struggle to give people a chance.

It is an effort to allow them to develop and use their capacities, as we have been allowed to develop and use ours, so that they can share, as others share, in the promise of this Nation.

We do this, first of all, because it is right that we should.

From the establishment of public education and land-grant colleges through agricultural extension and encouragement to industry, we have pursued the goal of a nation with full and increasing opportunities for all its citizens. The war on poverty is a further step in that pursuit.

We do it also because helping some will increase the prosperity of all.

Our fight against poverty will be an investment in the most valuable of our resources—the skills and strength of our people.

And in the future, as in the past, this investment will return its cost manyfold to our entire economy.

If we can raise the annual earnings of 10 million among the poor by only $1,000 we will have added $14 billion a year to our national output. In addition we can make important reductions in public assistance payments which now cost us $4 billion a year, and in the large costs of fighting crime and delinquency, disease and hunger.

This is only part of the story.

Our history has proved that each time we broaden the base of abundance, giving more people the chance to produce and consume, we create new industry, higher production, increased earnings, and better income for all.

Giving new opportunity to those who have little will enrich the lives of all the rest.

Because it is right, because it is wise, and because, for the first time in our history, it is possible to conquer poverty, I submit, for the consideration of the Congress and the country, the Economic Opportunity Act of 1964.

The act does not merely expand old programs or improve what is already being done. It charts a new course. It strikes at the causes, not just the consequences of poverty. It can be a milestone in our 180-year search for a better life for our people.

This act provides five basic opportunities:

It will give almost half a million underprivileged young Americans the opportunity to develop skills, continue education, and find useful work.

It will give every American community the opportunity to develop a comprehensive plan to fight its own poverty—and help them to carry out their plans.

It will give dedicated Americans the opportunity to enlist as volunteers in the war against poverty.

It will give many workers and farmers the opportunity to break through particular barriers which bar their escape from poverty.

It will give the entire Nation the opportunity for a concerted attack on poverty through the establishment, under my direction, of the Office of Economic Opportunity, a national headquarters for the war against poverty.

This is how we propose to create these opportunities.

First, we will give high priority to helping young American who lack skills, who have not completed their education or who canno complete it because they are too poor.

The years of high school and college age are the most critica stage of a young person's life. If they are not helped then, many wil be condemned to a life of poverty which they, in turn, will pass on to their children.

I, therefore, recommend the creation of a Job Corps, a work training program, and a work-study program.

A new national Job Corps will build toward an enlistment o: 100,000 young men. They will be drawn from those whose background health, and education make them least fit for useful work.

Those who volunteer will enter more than 100 camps and centers around the country.

Half of these young men will work, in the first year, on specia conservation projects to give them education, useful work experience and to enrich the natural resources of the country.

Half of these young men will receive, in the first year, a blend of training, basic education and work experience in job training centers

These are not simply camps for the underprivileged. They are new educational institutions, comparable in innovation to the land-grant colleges. Those who enter them will emerge better qualified to play a productive role in American society.

A new national work-training program operated by the Department of Labor will provide work and training for 200,000 American men and women between the ages of 16 and 21. This will be developed through State and local governments and nonprofit agencies.

Hundreds of thousands of young Americans badly need the experience, the income, and the sense of purpose which useful full or part-time work can bring. For them such work may mean the difference between finishing school or dropping out. Vital community activities from hospitals and playgrounds to libraries and settlement houses are suffering because there are not enough people to staff them.

We are simply bringing these needs together.

A new national work-study program operated by the Department of Health, Education, and Welfare will provide Federal funds for part-time jobs for 140,000 young Americans who do not go to college because they cannot afford it.

There is no more senseless waste than the waste of the brain-power and skill of those who are kept from college by economic circumstance. Under this program they will, in a great American tradition, be able to work their way through school.

They and the country will be richer for it.

Second, through a new community action program we intend to trike at poverty at its source—in the streets of our cities and on the farms of our countryside among the very young and the impoverished old.

This program asks men and women throughout the country to prepare long-range plans for the attack on poverty in their own local communities.

These are not plans prepared in Washington and imposed upon hundreds of different situations.

They are based on the fact that local citizens best understand their own problems, and know best how to deal with those problems.

These plans will be local plans striking at the many unfilled needs which underlie poverty in each community, not just one or two. Their components and emphasis will differ as needs differ.

These plans will be local plans calling upon all the resources available to the community—Federal and State, local and private, human and material.

And when these plans are approved by the Office of Economic Opportunity, the Federal Government will finance up to 90 percent of the additional cost for the first 2 years.

The most enduring strength of our Nation is the huge reservoir of talent, initiative, and leadership which exists at every level of our society.

Through the community action program we call upon this, our greatest strength, to overcome our greatest weakness.

Third, I ask for the authority to recruit and train skilled volunteers for the war against poverty.

Thousands of Americans have volunteered to serve the needs of other lands.

Thousands more want the chance to serve the needs of their own land.

They should have that chance.

Among older people who have retired, as well as among the young, among women as well as men, there are many Americans who are ready to enlist in our war against poverty.

They have skills and dedication. They are badly needed.

If the State requests them, if the community needs and will use them, we will recruit and train them and give them the chance to serve.

Fourth, we intend to create new opportunities for certain hard-hit groups to break out of the pattern of poverty.

Through a new program of loans and guarantees we can provide incentives to those who will employ the unemployed.

Through programs of work and retraining for unemployed fa thers and mothers we can help them support their families in dignity while preparing themselves for new work.

Through funds to purchase needed land, organize cooperatives and create new and adequate family farms we can help those whose life on the land has been a struggle without hope.

Fifth, I do not intend that the war against poverty becomes a series of uncoordinated and unrelated efforts—that it perish for lack of leadership and direction.

Therefore this bill creates, in the Executive Office of the President, a new Office of Economic Opportunity. Its Director will be my personal chief of staff for the war against poverty. I intend to appoint Sargent Shriver to this post.

He will be directly responsible for these new programs. He will work with and through existing agencies of the Government.

This program—the Economic Opportunity Act—is the foundation of our war against poverty. But it does not stand alone.

For the past 3 years this Government has advanced a number of new proposals which strike at important areas of need and distress.

I ask the Congress to extend those which are already in action, and to establish those which have already been proposed.

There are programs to help badly distressed areas such as the Area Redevelopment Act, and the legislation now being prepared to help Appalachia.

There are programs to help those without training find a place in today's complex society—such as the Manpower Development Training Act and the Vocational Education Act for youth.

There are programs to protect those who are specially vulnerable to the ravages of poverty—hospital insurance for the elderly, protection for migrant farmworkers, a food stamp program for the needy, coverage for millions not now protected by a minimum wage, new and expanded unemployment benefits for men out of work, a housing and community development bill for those seeking decent homes.

Finally there are programs which help the entire country, such as aid to education which, by raising the quality of schooling available to every American child, will give a new chance for knowledge to the children of the poor.

I ask immediate action on all these programs.

What you are being asked to consider is not a simple or an easy program. But poverty is not a simple or an easy enemy.

It cannot be driven from the land by a single attack on a single front. Were this so, we would have conquered poverty long ago.

Nor can it be conquered by government alone.

For decades American labor and American business, private institutions and private individuals have been engaged in strengthening our economy and offering new opportunity to those in need.

We need their help, their support, and their full participation.

Through this program we offer new incentives and new opportunities for cooperation, so that all the energy of our Nation, not merely the efforts of Government, can be brought to bear on our common enemy.

Today, for the first time in our history, we have the power to strike away the barriers to full participation in our society. Having the power, we have the duty.

The Congress is charged by the Constitution to "provide . . . for the general welfare of the United States." Our present abundance is a measure of its success in fulfilling that duty. Now Congress is being asked to extend that welfare to all our people.

The President of the United States is President of all the people in every section of the country. But this office also holds a special responsibility to the distressed and disinherited, the hungry and the hopeless of this abundant Nation.

It is in pursuit of that special responsibility that I submit this message to you today.

The new program I propose is within our means. Its cost of $970 million is 1 percent of our national budget—and every dollar I am requesting for this program is already included in the budget I sent to Congress in January.

But we cannot measure its importance by its cost.

For it charts an entirely new course of hope for our people.

We are fully aware that this program will not eliminate all the poverty in America in a few months or a few years. Poverty is deeply rooted and its causes are many.

But this program will show the way to new opportunities for millions of our fellow citizens.

It will provide a lever with which we can begin to open the door to our prosperity for those who have been kept outside.

It will also give us the chance to test our weapons, to try our energy and ideas and imagination for the many battles yet to come. As conditions change, and as experience illuminates our difficulties, we will be prepared to modify our strategy.

And this program is much more than a beginning.

Rather it is a commitment. It is a total commitment by this President, and this Congress, and this Nation, to pursue victory over the most ancient of mankind's enemies.

On many historic occasions the President has requested from

Congress the authority to move against forces which were endangering the well-being of our country.

This is such an occasion.

On similar occasions in the past we have often been called upon to wage war against foreign enemies which threatened our freedom. Today we are asked to declare war on a domestic enemy which threatens the strength of our Nation and the welfare of our people.

If we now move forward against this enemy—if we can bring to the challenges of peace the same determination and strength which has brought us victory in war—then this day and this Congress will have won a secure and honorable place in the history of the Nation, and the enduring gratitude of generations of Americans yet to come.

Sargent Shriver
An Annotated Summary of the Economic Opportunity Act of 1964

The Economic Opportunity Act of 1964 would establish an Office of Economic Opportunity in the Executive Office of the President. The OEO would be headed by a Director who would have a planning and coordinating staff. This staff would be responsible for coordinating the poverty-related programs of all Government agencies.

Within the OEO, staff personnel would operate a Job Corps, a program for Volunteers In Service To America (VISTA), a community action program, and special programs for migrant workers. In addition, the OEO would distribute funds to existing agencies to operate a variety of programs authorized under the bill: work-training programs would be administered through the Labor Department; work-study programs through HEW; adult basic education through HEW; special rural antipoverty programs through Agriculture; small business loans through the Small Business Administration; and community work and training projects for welfare recipients through HEW.

From a summary of the act by U. S. Congress, Senate Committee on Labor and Public Welfare. Economic Opportunity Act of 1964, S. Rept. 1218, 88th Cong., 2nd sess., pp. 1–45; Sargent Shriver's comments are from *The War on Poverty*, issued by the above Committee as Senate Document #86, July 23, 1964, pp. 43–69.
Sargent Shriver is Director, Office of Economic Opportunity.

A summary of the programs proposed under the Economic Opportunity Act of 1964 follows in *italics*. The comments after each section of the act are from a congressional presentation by Sargent Shriver on March 17, 1964.

Title I.   *Youth Programs*

Part A—Establishes a Job Corps to provide education, work experience, and vocational training in conservation camps and residential training centers; would enroll 40,000 young men and women, aged 16 to 21, this year, 100,000 next year. Administered by Office of Economic Opportunity.

Job Corps

The Job Corps will consist of conservation camps and training centers. The most important aspect of the experience for the enrollees will be their development as self-respecting individuals who are ready for a job or for more intensive education and skill development. In conservation camps, young men with problems of attitude and resistance to learning will be given basic skills training, as well as reading, writing, and arithmetic. The training centers will offer more intensive and advanced education and training to young men who are ready for this experience. In the long run, it is anticipated that many youths will be coming to the training centers as conservation camp "graduates." Enrollment in both types of camp will be strictly voluntary. It will normally be limited to a period of less than 2 years. Although the details of operation require further study, the following reflects current thinking on the subject:

A. Conservation camps.   It is the task of the conservation camps to do far more than provide basic education, skill training, and work experience; they must change indifference to interest, ignorance to awareness, resignation to ambition, and an attitude of withdrawal to one of participation. In order to achieve this, the camps must provide a series of living, working, training, counseling, and recreational experiences, and a sense of belonging which the homes and neighborhoods rarely supplied.

The work component.   Work in conservation camps will be undertaken in small supervised groups with an adult supervisor, and will be designed to give enrollees a sense of participation, self-confidence, and pride of accomplishment, as well as to give them certain basic skills. They will work under experienced members of Federal conservation agencies—such as forest and park rangers, or members of the Bureau of Indian Affairs, Land Management, Reclamation, or Sports Fisheries and Wildlife—in projects which can accomplish long-needed conservation work and recreation development on public lands.

The young men who are members of conservation camps will work in carpentry and masonry; with bulldozers, axes, and shovels; and in the kitchens, offices, and maintenance shops of the camps. They will learn to use basic tools, to plan and organize work, to follow instructions, to lead and to follow. . . .

The education component.   The education program in conservation camps will be designed to meet the needs of young men who are so lacking in basic academic skills that they cannot undertake vocational training. (A fifth- to sixth-grade literacy equivalency is considered necessary to profit from vocational training. An analysis of Selective Service System rejectees indicates that over half of those who fail to meet mental achievement requirements will be below this level.) Reading, writing, arithmetic, and speech will be taught . . . new instructional materials designed especially for the purpose will be developed. But the education component of the program cannot wait. The availability of current materials will be reviewed by the Office of Education, and those determined to be best suited will be used. . . .

. . . camp life will also be designed to improve the attitudes of the young men involved. A typical camp might have some 5 to 10 cabins of 20 young men each, with 1 adult resident and 2 youth assistants in every cabin. This responsibility will be rotated regularly, so that each may have a chance to lead. In addition, each cabin group will elect one representative to a camp council, designed to instill an appreciation of democratic principles.

The unifying force in the life of the camp will be a counseling program, dealing with every aspect of the experience—living, work, education, and recreation. At the end of each young man's tour, the counselors will have the major responsibility for guiding him to placement opportunities or further vocational training through the U.S. Employment Service. . . .

B. Training centers.   Life in the training centers will be similar in many ways to life in the conservation camps, with several important differences. The centers themselves will be considerably larger, ranging in size from 500 to 5,000 enrollees, which will call for different plans for handling groups. The major emphasis of the training centers can be on vocational training and basic educational improvement in preparation for permanent employment. Although high skill levels in particular vocations will not be achieved in most cases, the program will develop work habits and an attitude toward learning which will enable the young men involved to profit from more advanced education or work experience outside the centers.

The training component.   Vocational training and basic education will consume most of the day in a training center. The courses to be taught are those for which the occupational outlook is good, for which the entering skills are within the capability of the young men in the program, and which can be taught within the framework of the existing facilities.

The skills to be taught may vary from center to center, and within each occupational group, trades requiring several levels of ability may be taught. For example, in a single center some young men might be trained as calculating machine operators, others as appliance repairmen, still others as clerks ...

Basic education courses will also be given in the training centers, since the academic achievement level of many of the young men involved will not be adequate for them to get and keep jobs. The goals of the basic education component in the training centers will be the same as those in the conservation camps, but less time—about 2 hours a day—will be alloted for daily instruction.

Other components.   Health training, recreation, and counseling will also play an important role in the life of the training center. The young men will be housed in barracks of approximately 200 each, under the direction of an adult leader, with 1 youth assistant for every 25 youths. Physical fitness and recreation programs will be organized by barracks groups. . . .

> *Part B—Establishes a work-training program under which the Director of the Office of Economic Opportunity would enter into agreements with State and local governments or nonprofit organizations to pay part of the cost of full- or part-time employment to enable young men and women, 16 to 21, to continue or resume their education or to increase their employability; would directly involve 200,000 young adults. Administered by Labor Department.*

Work-Training Program

. . . The work-training program . . . will provide productive full- or part-time work experience and training in State and community public service jobs to these young people. It will thus increase their employability, and, whenever possible, it will encourage them to continue or resume their education. Unlike the Job Corps, it will be open to women as well as to men.

The cornerstone of the work-training program is local initiative and control. Any agency of a State or local government, including Indian tribal groups, or an approved private nonprofit organization may develop and conduct work projects. Such projects might place young people in work assignments in hospitals, settlement houses, school libraries, courts, children's homes, parks, playgrounds, public and private welfare agencies, and so on. . . .

The possibilities for projects and jobs are limited only by local resourcefulness and imagination, and by several basic criteria established in the act. These require that—

(1) Projects must increase the employability of the young men and women involved by providing work experience and training in jobs in which there is a reasonable expectation of employment or by enabling students to continue or resume their education.

(2) Projects must contribute to an undertaking in the public interest which will not otherwise be provided or which will contribute to conservation of State or local natural resources or the protection of recreation areas.

(3) The work done by enrollees in the program must not result in the displacement of employed workers or impair existing contracts for services.

(4) The rates of pay and other conditions of employment of the young people involved must be appropriate in view of such factors as the type of work performed, the level of skill involved, and the locality where the project is situated.

(5) Projects must be coordinated, as far as possible, with vocational training and educational services so that the special needs of the enrollees may be met by State or local school authorities.

(6) Projects must include standards and procedures for the selection of applicants which will include assurances that they are encouraged to continue or resume school attendance, if that is appropriate to their needs. . . .

Part C—Establishes a work-study program under which the Director of OEO would enter into agreements with institutions of higher learning to pay part of the cost of part-time employment for undergraduate or graduate students from low-income families to permit them to enter upon or continue college level education; would involve 140,000 youths the first year. Administered by Department of Health, Education, and Welfare.

Work-Study Program

Under the standards of financial need most commonly used by this country's colleges, families with incomes of $3,000 or less cannot be expected to make any contribution for the college education of their children. In fact, even at the $4,000 bracket, the contribution expected from a family with two or more children is extremely small. Students coming from such families must be self-supporting while in college. And the need of these students is so great relative to their capacity to pay that institutions of higher learning are usually able to provide only for the extremely bright student, the boy or girl in the top 2 or 3 percent of a high school graduating class. . . .

The proposed college work-study program . . . will provide a financial base for the able, but extremely needy, student to which can be added a loan or a limited scholarship grant. As a result of this program, the present levels of student employment are expected to be increased by 140,000 to 150,000 a year or over 30 percent. In addition to enabling a wider range of students to attend college through financial assistance, the program will sharply reduce the heavy debt load that often weighs on the student who is least able to bear it.

In order to avoid a program which will be detrimental to a student's academic work, however, the legislation provides that no student may be employed under the work-study program for more than 15 hours a week while classes in which he is enrolled are in session. . . .

On-campus work under this program will include both the service-type job which requires no specialized training—such as dormitory and plant maintenance, food service, clerical and stenographic work, and the like—and jobs in somewhat more sophisticated areas which do require some degree of training or skill development—such as work with a university press, computer programing, materials cataloguing, and library work. . . .

There are a number of off-campus jobs in health, welfare, recreation, and similar social service work which hold immediate promise of job expansion through a college or university work-study arrangement. A case in point are teacher aid and tutorial assistant jobs, in which students work either directly as teacher assistants, or as tutors with small groups of students having difficulty in a specific subject area. . . . In this way, the college or university can help meet the financial needs of the student; the student can gain valuable work experience; and the community can gain a talented and highly motivated group of students for a variety of service jobs. . . .

Title II.   Community Action Programs
>   *Part A—Authorizes the Director of OEO to pay up to 90 percent of the total costs of financing antipoverty programs planned and carried out at the community level. Programs will be administered by the communities and will mobilize all available resources and facilities in a coordinated attack on poverty.*

Across the Nation there are countless . . . examples of imaginative community programing to expand opportunity and break the cycle of poverty. Many are created locally. Some received impetus from State agencies, private foundations, industry, or labor unions. Others were initiated with the help of creative Federal programs, such as those undertaken by the President's Committee on Juvenile Delinquency. But nearly all share a common handicap—their scope is sharply limited by shortages of local and State resources. . . .

The most successful community action . . . usually includes the political, business, labor, and religious leaders, the school board, the employment service, the public welfare department, private social welfare agencies, and neighborhood houses in a coordinated attack on local poverty. Above all it includes the poor people of the community whose first opportunity must be the opportunity to help themselves.

. . . Federal support of community efforts has generally involved insufficient coordination among the various Federal agencies. The programs are administered by different agencies under different terms and conditions with different objectives in mind. Nowhere in the Federal Government can a community find broad support for a concentrated program to attack poverty. . . .

Two steps are needed to change this situation. The first . . . demands a focal point within our Government for marshaling Federal programs to support communities ready to do battle with poverty. The creation of the Office of Economic Opportunity will achieve this.

But community action also encompasses many activities for which existing Federal programs can provide no support. The existence of special funds clearly designated for community action support is critical to spurring communities with existing programs to direct more resources into this area. The community action fund is therefore necessary.

The local organization applying for a community action program grant must satisfy only one basic criterion: it must be broadly representative of the interests of the community. It may be a public agency which seeks to build into its programs the advice and expertise of business, labor, and other elements of the private sector. Or it may be a private nonprofit agency which has the support of the relevant elements of community government. It may be an already existing organization, or it may be newly created for the specific purpose of fighting poverty. The community may be a city or a town, a metropolitan area, a county or a multicounty unit, or a combination of rural and urban areas. But above all, it must provide a means whereby the residents of the program areas will have a voice in planning and a role in action. . . .

Communities will have wide discretion in determining what program activities should be undertaken, for the needs will vary throughout the Nation. In keeping with the focus upon opportunity and with the emphasis upon improving human performance, motivation, and productivity, and the conditions under which people live and work, it is likely

hat community action programs will include activities such as the following, all focused on the problems of poor people:

1. Services and activities to develop new employment opportunities;
2. Strengthening the teaching of basic education skills, especially
   reading, writing, and mathematics
3. Providing comprehensive academic counseling and guidance services and school social work services
4. Providing after-school study centers, after-school tutoring, and
   summer, weekend, and after-school academic classes
5. Establishing programs for the benefit of preschool children;
6. Reducing adult illiteracy
7. Developing and carrying out special education or other programs
   for migrant or transient families
8. Improving the living conditions of the elderly
9. Arranging for or providing health examinations and health education for school children
10. Rehabilitation and retraining of physically or mentally handicapped
    persons
11. Providing health, rehabilitation, employment, educational, and re-
    lated services to young men not qualified for military service
12. Providing community child-care centers and youth activity centers
13. Improving housing and living facilities and home management
    skills;
14. Providing services to enable families from rural areas to meet prob-
    lems of urban living; or
15. Providing recreation and physical fitness services and facilities

*Part B—Authorizes the OEO Director to make grants to States to
provide basic education and literacy training to adults. Administered
by the Department of Health, Education, and Welfare.*

Title III.   Programs To Combat Poverty in Rural Areas

*Part A—Authorizes grants up to $1,500 to very low-income rural
families where such grants are likely to produce a permanent increase
in the income of such families, and loans up to $2,500 to finance non-
agricultural, income-producing enterprises for the same purpose. The
Director of OEO also may provide assistance to nonprofit corporations
to acquire lands to be reconstituted into family farms, and may make
loans to low-income family cooperatives. Administered by Department
of Agriculture.*

Farm Investment: Strength in the Marketplace

A keystone of the assault on rural poverty, therefore, is what
might be termed a "package" of loan and grant programs and advisory
services designed to get these poor farm families off dead center, to get
their output up, and to give them some strength in the marketplace.

The rural economic opportunity program will make grants to
farm operators with meager earnings who have the character and ability

to improve the earning capacity of their farms thereby. The grant would be made individually or in conjunction with a loan. The grant would be made with the specific purpose of moving the farmer to a position where he could finance continued improvements and developments through loans from public or private sources. At present, many small poverty-stricken farmers either have no debt-paying ability or they are unable to amortize a large enough loan out of anticipated earnings to give them a new start. To gain a position where they can obtain conventional loan financing, they first have to expand their operations. However, they can't expand their operations without financing, for which they now are not eligible. The program will break this cycle by extending carefully managed grants.

Regardless of the financing available for farming expansion, however, some poor families will not benefit. They may not be able to obtain additional resources for farming because the resources—land in particular—simply aren't available. The rural opportunity program would, therefore, provide loans and grants to finance small items of machinery for nonagricultural enterprises on farms. Examples of such items might be a chain saw for felling trees, woodworking tools, a sewing machine, a small electric feed mixing mill, or similar capital equipment that can be operated easily and will significantly increase the productivity of family labor. . . .

A direct assault is also proposed on what is probably the single most serious cause of poverty among low-income farm families: Their inability to pay the high costs of farmland coming on the market and thereby obtain the basic resource of agriculture. The value of farm land has been rising at the rate of 3 percent each year, a rise stimulated in part by speculative forces and the fierce competition among large agricultural operators for land to meet the requirements of modern farm technology. It is extremely difficult—indeed, almost impossible—for the Nation's poorest farm families to buy good land at a price they can pay. . . .

The rural opportunity plan thus includes a program of loans and grants to State and local nonprofit corporations which will enable them to purchase at the going price farm land coming on the market and resell this land to individual small family farmers at its appraised value. The Department of Agriculture, through its regular farm lending activities, would help the individual families to buy the land from the corporation. Any loss the corporation might sustain in the transaction would be made up by a grant from the funds appropriated for the antipoverty program. In the initial period of the program, an estimated 2,500 carefully selected families would be assisted in getting the land resources they must have to earn an adequate income.

Finally, the rural effort provides a credit program to finance co-operatives made up wholly or partly of low-income farm and other rural families. Such cooperatives would provide services, supplies, and facilities not now available to low-income families, and would serve as a market place for their products. . . .

The proposals to combat farm poverty must be viewed as a single package. Major items of the package complement and reinforce each other. They have a single, unified objective: To raise the income-producing capacities of families by giving them access to capital, land resources and management aids on the farm and by opening up new opportunities for them to obtain economic strength in the community.

Part B—Sets up a program of assistance to establish and operate housing, sanitation, education, and child day-care programs for migrant farmworkers and their families.

Title IV.   Employment and Investment Incentives

The OEO would be authorized to make, participate in, or guarantee loans to small business of up to $25,000 on more liberal terms than is possible under the regular loan provisions of the Small Business Act; administered by the Small Business Administration.

Employment and Investment Incentives

. . . title IV would establish a new program of business loans for poverty areas or pockets beyond the reach of the regular ARA [Area Redevelopment Administration] program, either because the poverty pockets are too small for designation as redevelopment areas or because capital resources in the other areas are so lacking that it is impossible to comply with the local participation requirements of an ARA loan. It is expected that most of the loan requests will come from business enterprises based on local natural resources, local markets, and local labor. These industries probably will predominantly include the lighter types of manufacturing enterprises rather than large, national concerns requiring highly skilled labor. Also included will be businesses catering to tourist income such as handicraft and gift industries, and other service and commercial establishments which will help to install a viable economic base in the poverty areas.

The Director of the Office of Economic Opportunity would be authorized to establish a program of direct loans, participations with banks, and loan guarantees, to provide funds for the establishment, preservation, and expansion of promising business ventures which will hire the long-term or hard-core unemployed. . . . Most of these funds would be used for direct loans, since banks in the poverty areas often lack the resources to make large or long-term loans. . . .

At least half of the employment openings created by the investment must be recruited from among the long-term unemployed, or from members of low-income families. No financial assistance will be extended to relocate businesses from one area to another, and assistance will be limited to areas undertaking an approved community action program. In order to assure that assistance extended under this program creates a significant number of new employment opportunities, loans will be made primarily in labor-intensive industries, or in industries in which the investment cost per employee is relatively low. In no case will any loan be made for which loan-cost-per-job exceeds $10,000; the average cost-per-job created will be substantially lower. . . .

The Small Business Administration has made more than 40,000 loans to small business concerns totaling more than $2 billion over the past 10 years. However, there remain many small businessmen who have been unable to meet normal credit eligibility requirements under existing law. More often than not, these are the very small retailer or serviceman, the business with one, two, or perhaps five employees. . . .

. . . title IV would [also] establish a broader lending program designed to meet the needs of the small proprietor. Such a program—

[1] Will help put a new or incipient business on its feet.

[2] Will enable an existing business to grow where there is a need for growth and provide small loans for longer terms than existing SBA programs will permit.

[3] Will enable small firms to ready themselves for the higher levels of economic activity which the tax reductions in 1964 and 1965 will produce; and for firms in areas where the ARA or other development programs have spurred economic growth, to share in the improved conditions which such development yields.

[4] Will hold out the promise of increased employment by every firm which can with the help of a modest loan from the SBA expand its labor force.

[5] Will provide for these small businessmen an opportunity to learn by making available a program of management training in connection with which both the business community and the educational institutions will be encouraged to share their knowledge and their experience.

Title V.   Work-experience programs

Authorizes the Director of OEO to transfer funds to HEW to pay costs of experimental, pilot, or demonstration projects designed to stimulate the adoption by the States of programs providing constructive work experience or training for unemployed fathers and needy persons.

Family Unity through Jobs

For the unskilled and the semiskilled, loss of a job may mean far more than the loss of income. It is likely to mean eventual exhaustion of unemployment benefits, loss of dignity, loss of hope. And the long period of enforced idleness, with nothing to do and nothing to contribute, may result in the disintegration of the family.

What is needed is a program that will give even the least qualified of those low-skilled workers a chance to avoid this descent into hopelessness. The way for such a program has already been cleared.

In 1961, the Social Security Act was amended to authorize Federal financial participation in assistance to families with an unemployed, but employable, parent living at home. The following year the act was again amended to permit this assistance to be paid in the form of wages for work or training in special programs.

Thirteen of the eighteen States which have expanded their aid to families of dependent children (AFDC) program to include unemployed parents (AFDC-UP) have undertaken or are completing plans for such work and training programs. . . .

Accordingly, the family-unity-through-jobs program has been designed to encourage the expansion of existing programs, the establishment of new AFDC-UP programs, and the inclusion of work and training programs on a pilot basis where they do not now exist. It is estimated that approximately 80,000 unemployed fathers who are not now receiving public assistance can be reached during the first year of an expanded program. Since the average family receiving AFDC-UP contains 5.7 people, this part of the program alone will directly affect some 456,000 people.

An estimated 35,000 able-bodied fathers are now receiving public assistance while what skills they have wither from disuse, while technological change renders even those skills obsolete, and while pride and self-respect become luxuries which can no longer be afforded.

In order to avoid the perpetuation of this waste, the Department of Health, Education, and Welfare would also underwrite pilot efforts to stimulate the adoption of work and training programs in connection with public assistance. It is estimated that approximately 20,000 families or a total of 114,000 people at an average family size of 5.7, could be reached during the first year in an expanded program.

A majority of the families in the AFDC program are headed by women. The father is absent, dead, or incapacitated. Of the over 700,000 women heading families receiving AFDC, about 14 percent are now employed and another 13 percent, or approximately 100,000 could work if employment were available. Many more would seek employment if adequate day-care facilities were available. Moreover, less than one-third of the AFDC mothers have more than an elementary school education, and their children will almost inevitably suffer from such a home environment. These mothers (primarily those with older children for whom day care arrangements can be made) would benefit both themselves and their children if they were to receive basic education and training. . . .

It is estimated that during the first year of this program, about 30,000 of the 100,000 mothers seeking employment could be given basic literacy education and vocational training. Since the average size of an AFDC family headed by a female is 3.9 people, this would affect some 117,000 people.

Title VI.   Treatment of unemployment compensation and income for public assistance purposes

> *A policy declaration that an individual's opportunity to participate in certain programs under this act should neither jeopardize, nor be jeopardized by, his receipt of unemployment compensation or public assistance.*

Volunteers for America—The Opportunity to Help

The response throughout America to the Peace Corps has demonstrated with dramatic clarity the intensity of the spirit of service in this country. It is proposed to tap this vital source for domestic service through a volunteers for America program within the Office of Economic Opportunity. . . .

Volunteers will participate not only in the programs proposed in the Economic Opportunity Act of 1964. They will also work in existing Federal programs related to poverty problems, and in State and local activities. A volunteer may teach in a Job Corps training center, or he may work on an Indian reservation on projects administered by the Bureau of Indian Affairs. He may work in a community undertaking a community action program, or he may, on request of a State or municipality, be assigned to projects which are supported wholly by local resources. In each case, the aim of the Office of Economic Opportunity will be simply to bring together a Volunteer willing to serve and an opportunity for service.

The term of service in the volunteers for America program will normally be 1 year, including training. To be eligible, applicants must be at least 18 years of age. Specific standards of selection—including physical condition and level of education and experience required—will vary depending on the job to be done, but a high degree of motivation and stability will be required in every case. . . .

Title VII.   Administration and coordination

Authorizes the Director of OEO to recruit and train VISTA volunteers to serve in specified mental health, migrant, Indian, and other federally related programs including the Job Corps, as well as in State and community antipoverty programs.

Margaret G. Reid
A Critic of the Act

I am very happy to be here to comment on some aspects of the discussion and the bill that relates to the employment opportunity.

It seems to me, in view of what I have to say, it might be appropriate first to comment on my work. I am a professor of economics at the University of Chicago, and my research and teaching deals directly with consumption, income distribution, and the relationship of the economic system to the welfare of consumers.

Poverty and what can be done about it, are matters of very deep interest to me.

This bill has something to say about poverty, and a great deal of the discussion of it, both inside and outside the Government, has dealt with poverty.

As I read the discussion, I find an enormous amount of confusion; in fact, I would say that the discussion is full of confusion. Some speakers and writers seem to say that the great upsurge of productivity that has come in the past few decades has bypassed many people. Undoubtedly, all groups in the population have not shared equally in the increases.

In our dynamic society, sharing tends to change as the technology and choices of consumers change the demand for various skills. In spite of all this, workers on farms and in cities, white and Negro workers, young and elderly workers, have shared importantly in the secular rise in national income.

These are matters on which there are no questions.

For the population in general, there has been a decline in the frequency of inadequate diets, of housing without plumbing facilities, and

From the statement by Dr. Reid at Hearings before the Subcommittee on the War on Poverty Program of the Committee on Education and Labor, House of Representatives, 88th Congress, 2nd session, Part 3, April 24, 1964, pp. 1427–1430.
Margaret G. Reid is Professor Emeritus of Economics, University of Chicago.

of children who have had to drop out of school because of low income of parents. All of these trends have been very carefully measured and are generally accepted.

In addition, new products such as television sets have come quickly into universal use, testifying to the equality of sharing of consumption experiences. These and other trends indicate an ever-widening diffusion of welfare levels.

With the rise in income and its diffusion throughout the population, a marked decline has occurred in poverty, if one measures poverty in terms of consumer products and services. This decline has been documented in a recent report of the U.S. Bureau of the Census, and in some of my writings.

Poverty, in the basic sense of how well people live, has declined markedly in the United States. It will decline further as productivity rises. Why then, all this hullaballoo about poverty?

The overtones of much of the discussion and its sudden eruption create the impression that we are in the throes of another emotional jag. Not long ago there was an outpouring of books and articles in magazines and newspapers on affluence. We were pictured as satiated, but not very wise, consumers: Every household with an electric refrigerator stocked with soft drinks and every household with one or more TV sets to provide entertainment with a generous supplement of comics to further relieve the tedium of life.

I am sure many of you have had this brought to your attention. A dearth of consumption for our public needs, such as roads and schools, was stressed. Affluence is now being overshadowed. We are portrayed as a poverty-ridden society and urged to undertake a large-scale program for increasing economic opportunity.

Extravagant estimates of poverty have appeared, some indicating as much as two-fifths of the population poverty stricken.

The Council of Economic Advisers to the President has used $3,000 as the poverty point. There are many other estimates. We are, in fact, witnessing a veritable battle of the poverty yardsticks.

Who is going to win out and say what is poverty? And this battle is likely to continue because there is no definite way of resolving the arguments.

There is no scientific method for determining the income necessary to prevent poverty. The policymaker who needs a measure of poverty can choose one suitable for his purpose. Once he has chosen it, he is likely to say, along with Humpty Dumpty, that "when I use the word, it means what I choose it to mean, neither more or less."

A poverty yardstick suitable for his purpose would show the amount of poverty that serves the purpose of the policy. The claims must not appear absurd, but they must be impressive. The Council of Economic Advisers reached the conclusion that 33 to 35 million American people were living at or below the boundary of poverty in 1962, nearly one-fifth of the population. Such a judgment will of course be impressive to those people who are unaware of how it was reached.

There is no scientific method of defining poverty. Even so, something definite can be said about the meaning of any yardstick used.

For example, if a yardstick calls for money income of $3,000, then this test will overstate the number of people whose consumption is below $3,000. Current income of some families with incomes under $3,000 is less than usual, and their consumption is likely to be higher than their income. They are drawing on past assets, accumulated earlier, or they are borrowing on the basis of expected future income. Examples are easily found.

The ups and downs of annual incomes are experienced by many families and these changes get represented in the income data because the income data describes the situation for only a given year. Their presence cannot be readily seen except in consumption surveys.

These surveys more fully than income surveys indicate the conditions associated with incomes in any one year.

I would like to point out that all the estimates we have floating around in regard to poverty have used income distribution data, they have not used consumption data, and very few people are acquainted with the consumption studies in the policy field. I find this over and over again in my experience even with students who come to me on research problems. They do not know how to use the consumption data, and the volume is much smaller than the income data, so lots and lots of judgments based on the income data are quite unrealistic. So families reporting low income have consumption expenditures much in excess of income.

In order to give some examples of this, I pulled down some reports that are just now reaching my desk from the U.S. Bureau of Labor Statistics. They made a large scale consumption survey for the year 1960, and the reports are just coming out.

For example, a consumption survey of 1960 reported for Washington only two families with incomes under $1,000. Their average expenditure, including their income tax payments and personal instance, was $5,404. In other words, their outlays were more than five times their income. In fact, it was more than that. Their average income was about $600. They were almost 10 times above their income.

It seems highly unlikely that either of these families should be classed as important. These are not isolated examples.

For the large cities of the United States, in 1960 consumers with incomes under $1,000 were spending $224 for every $100 of income received, and those with incomes from $2,000 to $3,000 were spending $116. Many low current incomes reported in surveys understate ability to pay. This understatement that I have given these examples for come from the fact that in any one year you go to make a survey, you catch in it low-income group people who are below their normal income position, and in addition, it has been fully documented in the studies on incomes that a large number of the low-income people do not report their income. They are much more likely to underreport their income than to underreport their consumption expenditures. They are rather practiced in underreporting incomes in the way means tests are used for those seeking help.

However, there are other things that make the use of a $3,000 income meaningless in terms of what its relationship to welfare and consumption is. Money income alone understates the consumption of families because they have income in kind apart from the money income. Farm families provide a notable example. Much of their food and housing is in addition to money income. This is recognized clearly in consumption studies, but often overlooked by those who attempt to relate the distribution of money income to welfare.

Poverty, judged in terms of money income, greatly exaggerates the proportion of the poor that live on farms.

That is only looking within the entire structure of the group that someone decides to call poor because they have decided to use a certain money income as the test. In that particular kind of testing, you get an exaggerated notion of the poverty of the farm people.

Extravagant claims as to the number of poor may influence the reception accorded this bill. The measures proposed, however, have very little to do with the families whose normal incomes, that is income year after year, including their income in kind, is less than $3,000.

The provisions of the bill deal, however, with enlarging the economic opportunity of some persons through education and training and thus enhancing their ability to earn and work. The great bulk of the really poor are going to be untouched by these programs.

The programs proposed would undoubtedly result in some persons having higher incomes than they would otherwise achieve. That the programs would add to general productivity and welfare is by no means so clear. It is in such terms that the merits of the bill should be appraised. There are many questions to debate—how many people would benefit by the programs?

To what extent might they be served by existing programs?

To what extent are the programs proposed geared to modern technology?

To what extent was the development of the program influenced by the experience of the great depression?

Surely we have come a long way since then in terms of the type of training needed and the initiation of workers to jobs appropriate to 1933. There is also the matter of how the costs of the program bear on other uses of resources, including a reduction of the income tax imposed on them who are reported to be poverty ridden.

If you look at the consumption data, which includes the full outlay of consumers, you can see where the income tax falls where you have a judgment such as has been rendered.

The bill only marginally relates to poverty. To sell it as a poverty bill is misleading advertising. Alas, sellers of the bill are not subject to our truth-in-advertising laws, legislation that I am currently discussing in my class. . . .

Senators Barry Goldwater and John Tower
Minority Views

The undersigned members of the committee oppose the enactment of this bill. We consider it an attempt to reap political rewards from the American people's natural and human desire to improve the lot of our less fortunate citizens. The poverty program and the claims and justification which have accompanied it constitute a curious combination of the techniques made famous by the phrases "Madison Avenue" and "The Wizard of Oz."

This bill, with its generous use of programs tried during the depression-ridden thirties, is illusory in leaving untouched the difficulties which prevent some Americans from sharing in our general prosperity. At best, the hodgepodge of programs which make up S. 2642, treat only the results, not the causes of poverty. In short, the bill, whatever its professed purposes, seems designed to achieve the single objective of securing votes; the problems of the truly destitute will not be solved by this legislation.

The War on Poverty

On March 16, 1964, President Lyndon B. Johnson, launched his much heralded "War on Poverty." In his message to the Congress that

From the minority views which accompanied S. 2642, the Economic Opportunity Act of 1964, in U. S. Congress. Senate. Committee on Labor and Public Welfare, Report 1218, 88th Cong., 2d sess., pp. 69–85.

day, he proclaimed no less an objective than "total victory." It is ironic to note that "victory" is a policy which the administration is congenitally unable to propose in the realm of foreign affairs; yet this great objective is dangled misleadingly before America's poor without the slightest hesitation.

Prof. Emeritus Harley L. Lutz, of Princeton University, recently described the problems surrounding both the real and the illusory wars on poverty as follows:

> " 'War on Poverty' is a slogan that can reasonably be expected to yield considerable political mileage. No one is in favor of poverty and criticism of a program purporting to deal with it is as risky, politically as being in favor of sin or against motherhood.
>
> "Yet the odds are heavily against complete elimination of poverty by any kind or degree of Government action. The dramatic announcement of the slogan may carry for some the implication that theretofore poverty had been tolerated but that little serious thought or effort had been given to its amelioration.
>
> "The fact is that the whole history of economic progress is a record of the struggle against poverty in the sense of a scarcity or deficiency of goods in relation to needs. Everything that has been done to increase production, from the most primitive tools and implements to today's enormous complex of machines, materials, technology, and skills has broadened and strengthened the drive to minimize scarcity."

The essentially specious nature of the Johnson "war" is illustrated by the confusing and misleading descriptions of those who are supposed to be helped by this bill. It was necessary, of course, to define poverty before a public relations offensive could be launched against it.

The President, in his "Message on Poverty," conjured up the following bleak portrait of destitution in America.

"What does this poverty mean to those who endure it?"

"It means a daily struggle to secure the necessities for even a meager existence."

Remarks such as these have led the American people to believe that a large number of our people are virtually starving, and parenthetically, that they would be saved by the Johnson poverty program. This compelling and emotionally explosive picture is, in fact, the key to the political impact and value of the bill.

A vastly different picture emerges, however, when the administration goes beyond this "Grapes of Wrath" imagery and attempts to describe in detail what poverty really is in the America of today. Walter Heller, the Chairman of the President's Council of Economic Advisers outlined what he called the dimensions of poverty as follows:

"* * * a series of standards converge on a $3,000 annual family income, or roughly $60 a week—and a $1,500 single-person income, or roughly $30 a week—as the statistical dividing line which sets off the poor in America today.

"By this widely accepted benchmark, one-fifth of America's families live in poverty: 9.3 million families, or 35 million persons."

The misleading and inconsistent nature of this benchmark can be shown by one or two examples of its practical application:

Defense Department figures indicate that 1,049,248 members of the U.S. Armed Forces had less than a $3,000 annual income, including all allowances for food, clothing, shelter, plus the value of Federal income tax exemptions. Are we to believe that a substantial proportion of our servicemen are among those who Mr. Johnson claims are engaged in a daily struggle to barely exist?

Another interesting insight into the validity of the administration's poverty yardstick is that the average individual, retired on social security benefits supplemented by part-time wages, loses all social security benefits before he can reach a total annual income of $3,000.

Sargent Shriver, the administration's chief antipoverty advocate, has conceded, moreover, that the Johnson-Heller yardstick is fallacious. He stated, in the hearings before our Select Committee on Poverty, that:

"The definition or the cutoff point that the Council of Economic Advisers has used, of the $3,000, is the subject of criticism, because there is no question about the fact that some people who have an income of more than $3,000 in a particular year are poor, and some people who have less than an income of $3,000 in a particular year are not poor."

There is an obvious conflict between a poverty definition which includes servicemen, farmers, and retired persons within its 35-million-person reach and another definition which describes abject destitution. Despite this obvious conflict, the two concepts have been used interchangeably by the Johnson administration in a desperate attempt to sell this program. This, we submit, is political slight of hand of the very worst sort.

High Pressure Tactics Result in the Bill
Receiving Inadequate Consideration

The "war on poverty" if we are to believe President Johnson, is one of the three major legislative objectives of his administration. The President and his supporters have been blowing the publicity trumpets for months and apparently intend to make poverty a prime campaign issue. It would seem only logical then, that the administration's supporters within the U.S. Senate generally, and within the Labor Committee in particular, would devote an equal amount of attention to the bill as it was moved through the legislative process.

Instead, however, of developing a massive and thoroughly reasoned case for the program, the administration and its followers within
the committee rushed the bill through with such haste that its record is
practically nonexistent. Consider, for a moment, the following facts re
garding the consideration and attention devoted to the 70-odd pages o
S. 2642 by the Select Subcommittee on Poverty and the Committee on
Labor and Public Welfare itself:

(1) The bill includes some seven titles, nine separate programs, and
establishes a new bureaucratic apparatus; its scope is so vast that i
could affect virtually every section, community, and person in the
country.

(2) Despite the scope of the bill's programs and its length, only two
witnesses were presented by the administration to make its case.

(3) R. Sargent Shriver, the proposed "poverty czar," read a statement
one page long as his presentation in behalf of the bill; he then spent
portions of 3 different days answering questions. This exercise, which
barely scratches the surface of the problems and implications contained
in the proposal, was reported in 91 pages of the hearing, only a few
more than the bill itself.

(4) Secretary of Labor W. Willard Wirtz, the other administration
witness, was able to conclude his testimony within approximately 13
minutes.

(5) The hearings on the bill lasted only 4 days.

(6) The Select Subcommittee on Poverty met once in executive session
and reported the bill to the full committee within 2 hours; the full
committee also held a single executive session which resulted in the
bill being hurried on to the Senate Calendar. Thus, from the close of
the hearings on June 24, 1964, to the full committee's action on July 7,
1964, less than 12 days were allowed the committee members for
study of this long and complex bill. . . .

. . . a flagrant perversion of the functions of the committee system
can be observed in the bill's inclusion of Title III: Special Programs To
Combat Poverty in Rural Areas. The proposals included within this title
infringe upon important Federal agricultural programs and would affect
our entire agricultural economy. The Agriculture Committee, whose members are knowledgeable in this complex and specialized area, should, if
any rational procedure was followed, have considered this title. That the
proper committee was bypassed and our committee, whose members
do not include a single Agriculture Committee member, undertook to
legislate a farm prgoram is symptomatic of the errors which can infect
those who act in haste. In short, this legislative bungle illustrates that
almost "anything goes" where President Johnson's "war on poverty" is
concerned.

The Basic Cause of Poverty Today

An elementary first step in any effort to eradicate poverty would seem to be that of determining its causes. President Johnson gave tacit recognition to this when, in his message to Congress, he declared that his program "strikes at the causes, not just the consequences of poverty."

A recent study published by the American Council on Education, written by Dr. Grant Venn, pointed out that the United States is confronted by the paradox of between 4 and 5 million persons unemployed, while there are job openings for some 4 million skilled workers constantly available. The study went on to state that "young people are entering a technological world of work unequipped with tools they need for survival."

The cause of poverty, the condition which results from an inadequate income, is the inability on the part of a large number of Americans to qualify for the millions of adequately paying jobs which are going begging. A majority of the people who constitute America's poor by whatever definition is used, are in that predicament because they do not possess the needed skills. It is patently obvious that providing these people with skills is the only possible means of getting at the cause rather than the consequences of poverty.

It seems plain, therefore, that any program which does not provide our young and, for that matter, our older citizens with necessary "tools" is doomed to failure.

This incontrovertible fact of life is, however, seemingly lost on the present administration. The advocates of S. 2642 do not even contend that its variety of programs will give our poorer citizens the skilled training they need if they are to increase their incomes.

A graphic admission of this bill's worthlessness was made by Secretary of Labor Wirtz, when, referring to 1963's youth employment bill which is contained, substantially, in S. 2642 as the "Job Corps," said that "there is no suggestion that this training program will qualify one of the enrollees for a skilled occupation. That we should dismiss completely."

The Poverty Package—A Throwback to the Thirties

A logical explanation for the administration's failure to develop a program which comes to grips with the basic cause of today's poverty is that its thinking is geared to the problems and the nostrums of a bygone era, the 1930's. Several of the proposals contained within the bill are, in fact, almost exact replicas of programs that were tried by the New Deal during the depression.

The Job Corps, the work-study program, and the rural area title found in this bill all trace their lineage directly from the Civilian Conservation Corps (CCC), the National Youth Administration (NYA), and the farm resettlement programs of the thirties. In addition, title II of the bill, the community action portions, is a sort of retread WPA. These and other measures authorized by this bill will attempt to apply desperation procedures that may have been appropriate in the emergency conditions of the 1930's to the challenges that we face today in a completely different domestic and world economic environment.

These New Deal programs were designed to afford make-work relief employment at a time when more than 20 percent of the labor force was jobless. Today, as we have indicated, the unemployment problem is much less severe in total impact and is largely related to the rising but unsatisfied demand for workers possessing new skills.

The Job Corps—A New CCC

Although the proponents of the Job Corps have made a to-do about the program's alleged value in making youths "more employable" the best, and incidentally the only, justification for this claim that they have been able to come up with is that better work habits will be developed. The Corps, we are told, will prepare these young people to take and complete the training they actually need.

The specific accomplishments which the Corps is to inculcate into its members include improved physical health, increased weight, cheerfulness, self-confidence, and a feeling of security. These benefits, mainly psychological or esthetic in nature, are not to be deprecated. When they are combined with the conservation aspects of the Corps, the program has obvious appeal as a force for "good."

We do not dispute the possible esthetic or psychological values of this program. We submit, however, that the fact that the Corps would be "nice" or "good" is not enough to justify the expenditure of millions of the taxpayers' dollars. For the underlying purpose of the program is claimed to be the improvement of the employment prospects of our youth. Supplying them with suntans and an appreciation for outdoor living clearly won't help them find jobs.

One further aspect of the proposed resurrection of the CCC deserves some attention even in this necessarily brief critique.

We contend that this legislation, in addition to failing to meet the problems of our young people, would do positive harm. Several provisions of the bill consciously weaken the family relationship which has been the backbone of our free society for hundreds of years.

The tie between parent and child is severed by some of the bill's provisions. For example, young men and women, some as young as 16 years of age, may join the Corps without the permission of their parents.

Once in the Corps, the child will be given whatever money he or she earns without reference to the parents or legal guardian, with the single exception that the Director may decide, in his wisdom, to pay portion of the earnings to a member of the enrollee's family.

These aspects of the Job Corps constitute a further development in the erosion of the institution of the American family which has been such an ominous and expanding characteristic of American life during the past generation. Ignoring the family and treating children as if they were wards of the state were common to Soviet Russia, Nazi Germany, and Fascist Italy, and were in fact important devices for building and strengthening the totalitarian state.

Other Depression Era Revivals

It is truly remarkable to contemplate the inclusion within this bill of two of the New Deal years' most ill-fated innovations. The revivals of the National Youth Administration and the farm resettlement programs of that bygone era are notable even for this poorly conceived legislation. These programs were generally accepted as ignominious failures even back in the depressed 1930's.

The rural area program title III contains two particularly dubious provisions. The first is the section which permits the "poverty czar" to give grants and loans totaling up to $4,000 to low-income-farmers whose operations are so marginal and unpromising as to disqualify them for FHA loans. This program, the American Farm Bureau has pointed out, would operate to perpetuate subsistence farming and rural slums.

Existing FHA loan programs for farmers are designed to help those who have some reasonable chance of creating a going agricultural concern. The inevitable result of this title will be to keep some farmers in poverty.

The second aspect of the bill's rural aid provisions which requires some comment is the family farm development corporations section. This land reform proposal is taken directly from the unsuccessful resettlement program which was run by the Farm Security Administration back in the 1930's. The provision authorizes the Director to organize public or private corporations and to finance their purchase of farmland which would then be reconstituted into family-sized farms and resold to "poor" farmers at a loss borne by the taxpayer.

This, as the American Farm Bureau has stated, "is an old and reactionary idea. The result would be stabilized Government-directed and subsidized poverty." The farm resettlement program, it should be noted, was abandoned after a few years' trial during the Roosevelt administration.

The reason for its abandonment can be made clear through a brief reference to a House committee's investigation of the program. A select committee of the House Agriculture Committee completed its study of the resettlement program in 1944. Among its highly critical findings was the following:

"The investigation disclosed that, beginning with the administration of Rexford G. Tugwell and continuing throughout the administration of C. B. Baldwin, the Farm Security Administration was financing communistic resettlement projects, where the families could never own homes or be paid for all that they made or for all the time they worked, and was supervising its borrowers to the extent of telling the borrower how to raise his children, how to plan his homelife, and, it is strongly suspected in some cases, how to vote. Some families were 'kept on the Government' indefinitely, while other families that were willing to work just as hard and do their best to pay their debts, would not get any help from the Government at all."

It is not at all surprising that such a program, based upon a philosophy which is alien to the best traditions of our country, was discontinued. It is, however, shocking that this reactionary concept, found unsuitable even in the social experiment and emergency days of the depression, has been exhumed from the decent burial it was given years ago, and included in the proposed poverty program.

The current situation which involves a lack of needed skills among our poorer citizens is in marked contrast to the conditions that prevailed in the thirties. Then the 13 million unemployed included men and women possessing all degrees of education and skilled training. During this era skilled jobs were not going begging by the millions. In short, we were in the midst of an overpowering depression which required all kinds of desperate measures.

The problems of the sixties will not be solved by adopting the panic programs of another era. What is necessary, obviously, are reasoned answers to the problems of today, not yesterday. . . .

The Poverty Czar

Perhaps the most alarming of the many ominous facets of this disastrous bill is the virtually unlimited grant of power which it hands to the Director of Economic Opportunity. The proposed Director will be the general in command of the poverty war; as such, the bill (referred o as the Landrum-Powell bill in the House of Representatives) would make him the head of a new bureaucracy called the Office of Economic Opportunity.

The all-encompassing powers which the administration seeks to confer on the Director can be most clearly shown by referring to the language of the bill itself. The authority of the Director is most specifically spelled out in the administration and coordination title (title VI) of the bill.

For example, the Director is exempted from the laws and regulations which govern other executive departments regarding the printing and binding of various kinds of material. The need for such an exemption arises, it has been explained, because otherwise the Government Printing Office and Government Services Administration procedures might slow up the Director's issuance of "comic books" and other propaganda. The GPO and GSA regulations, which this bill bypasses, were written, it should be noted, to prevent the bureaucrats from wasting even more money than they ordinarily would by turning out mountains of unnecessary printed matter.

Whatever the inadequate reasons which might be offered in behalf of this section, it is impossible to justify another exemption from the laws of the United States contained in this title. Section 602(i) allows the Director to "disseminate, without regard to the provisions of section 4154 of title 39, United States Code, data and information, in such form *as he shall deem appropriate,* to public agencies, private organizations, and the general public." [Emphasis added.]

Section 4154 of the United States Code to which this language refers lists the restrictions on the use of the "free" mailing privilege by the executive departments and others. These limitations on the use of the U.S. mail are designed, simply, to prevent anything but material with some reasonable connection with Government business from being disseminated throughout the country at the taxpayers' expense. One portion of this statute states that officers, executive departments, and independent agencies are not prohibited from mailing "enclosures reasonably related to the subject matter of official correspondence."

Certainly these restrictions, which are similar to those placed upon the congressional franking privilege, are designed to prohibit the distribution of self-serving propaganda; it cannot be considered too onerous for an agency of the Government which is conducting its business in a reasonable and prudent manner. Why then is it deemed necessary to exempt the Director of Economic Opportunity from the rules? The answer is quite simple—the Johnson administration's nakedly political approach to the problems of our poor people sweeps away all obstacles. The printing and mailing of politically tinged materials, which would be a violation of the law if attempted by other agencies, is part and parcel of the opportunistic philosophy underlying the war on poverty.

The poverty czar would also be handed a blank check with which to dispose of Federal funds and property if other provisions in this incredible bill are left intact. He would be exempt from all provisions of the law regarding the "acquisition, handling, or disposal of real or personal property by the United States"; he could, moreover, "deal with complete, rent, renovate, modernize, or sell for cash or credit *at his discretion* any property acquired by him in connection with loans, participations, and guarantees made by him pursuant to titles III and IV of this act." [Emphasis added.]

It is interesting to note, in this connection, that such phrases as "in his discretion" and "as he may deem necessary or appropriate," are found throughout this bill. Legislative guidelines and criteria are almost completely absent from S. 2642. Inevitably the result will be, if this legislation is passed, to create a new and more dangerous bureaucratic monster. The implications contained in the use of the term "czar" do not exaggerate in the least the powers to be given to the Director.

One further aspect of the czar's powers deserves some attention. The administration has made a great deal of noise about the fact that the Director would primarily "coordinate" the programs to combat poverty. This, like so much else in this bill, is not what it appears to be—it is just another "gimmick."

Every authorization listed in the bill, except one which permits the President to shuffle the entire poverty agency about within the executive branch, goes to the Director. His function as a "coordinator" is a deceptive one. Consider two examples:

First, the various powers to lend money and assist organizations and individuals which are contained within title III (special programs to combat poverty in rural areas) are not, as might be expected, delegated to the Agriculture Department and other agencies which have experience in this area. The authority to operate this program is held *exclusively* by the czar or Director.

Second, the employment and investment incentives program (title IV) which is merely an expansion of the current activities of the Small Business Administration is not to be bossed by that agency. Once again administrative logic has been tossed aside in the open attempt at political empire building being engaged in in behalf of the proposed Director Sargent Shriver, and his mentor, the President.

The bill gives the poverty czar the power to *direct, not* to work with, members of the President's Cabinet and various agency heads. The creation of a superbureaucracy to be headed by a superbureaucrat sets a precedent that is both unique and dangerous. . . .

A Few of the "Sleepers" in the Bill

The Landrum-Powell poverty package is a hastily conceived and poorly planned collection of programs having little or no logical connection with each other. It should not be surprising, therefore, that in addition to its most blatant and highly publicized defects, it contains a number of hidden but no less significant elements.

A statement of Mr. Donald B. Straus, the chairman of an organization called Planned Parenthood World Population, which was submitted to this committee, illustrates one of these hidden problems. Mr. Straus' organization feels very strongly that any antipoverty program worthy of the name should promote and assist programs of birth control. He argues—

"* * * that neither a 'basic knowledge of the facts' nor of the 'real causes of poverty' can ignore the grave problem of the gap between children wanted and children born. This gap can only be closed when public health and welfare agencies make available to low-income Americans the same effective voluntary family planning techniques that are now available to—and extensively used by—the rest of the Nation."

No less an authority than Mr. Sargent Shriver himself admitted, in testimony to the House Committee on Education and Labor, that if a birth control project was included within a community action program that was otherwise qualified, he would approve it. Without arguing the merits or demerits of birth control programs, we submit that the fact that such projects could be aided or promoted by the Federal Government regardless of local mores or feelings pinpoints the basic danger inherent in this bill.

Another sensitive problem which has arisen because of the all-encompassing nature of this legislation is the legal and political controversy over Federal aid to church-related activities. The bill which the committee originally began work on permitted the Director to provide assistance to church-related facilities under the work-study and work-training programs of title I so long as they were not to be used solely for religious activities. The majority of the committee promptly voted to amend these provisions by striking out the word "solely." The net effect of this amendment would have been to prevent a local church-related organization or parochial school from receiving aid to assist the poor.

In one of the few attempts to improve this bill that was permitted to succeed by the majority, Senator Goldwater moved to correct this inequitable situation. His amendment limited the prohibition against aid to church-related institutions or activities to "so much of * * * any facility used or to be used for sectarian instruction or as a place for religious worship."

The Goldwater amendment would now permit the nonreligious portions of church-owned or supported buildings and other facilities to be used as a part of the antipoverty program. Direct aid to churches is in accordance with the spirit and the letter of the Constitution, still prohibited.

Conclusion

It has been suggested, by some of the more demagogic supporters of the committee bill, that those who oppose it are in favor of perpetuating poverty. This, of course, is arrant nonsense; it does, however, illustrate the political and emotional aura surrounding the poverty war.

The Johnson administration's ruthless campaign in behalf of this legislation will not work. We will not be silenced by these intolerant appeals and easy answers to complex and difficult problems. We oppose this poorly constructed and misbegotten legislation.

We fully agree with the criticism of the administration program set forth in the platform adopted by the Republican Party at its recent presidential convention in San Francisco.

"The administration has proposed a so-called war on poverty which characteristically overlaps and often contradicts, the 42 existing Federal poverty programs. It would dangerously centralize Federal controls and bypass effective State, local, and private programs."

The views we have outlined here do not begin to deal with all of the varied aspects of the bill. We have attempted, however, to uncover and discuss a few of the poverty war's most glaring defects, defects which render the entire program unacceptable. Our counterparts on the House Education and Labor Committee have written a comprehensive set of minority views on the companion to S. 2642, the Landrum-Powell bill: we urge that this excellent document be read in conjunction with the views expressed here.

This bill does not address itself to the primary cause of poverty. It does nothing to provide our poorer citizens with the skills necessary to gain regular employment in this modern age. Instead, it resurrects the tired slogans and applies the ineffectual poultices of a bygone era.

Barry Goldwater (Arizona)
John G. Tower (Texas)

:rwin Knoll and Jules Witcover
Organizing the Poor

Should the Federal Government finance mass social protest? Should it, as part of the war on poverty, help the poor fight city hall?

These questions have been raised as a result of a $314,000 Federal grant to Syracuse University to help organize the community's poor into a pressure group.

The Federal Office of Economic Opportunity (OEO) regards the university program as a significant test of the theory that poverty can be fought most effectively when the poor are directly involved in community programs.

Congress, in passing the antipoverty act last year, demanded 'maximum feasible participation" of the poor in local planning and administration. The university experiment, a national pilot study, proposes to meet the goal in an unorthodox and potentially explosive way.

It calls for mobilizing the poor into an aggressive and powerful group that can win a voice in community decisions affecting their welfare. Low-income neighborhood organizations will be set up and will elect leaders.

Syracuse has another antipoverty agency, designated as official by the city and county governments. The university program is an effort to work with the poor outside the official structure, rather than within it.

The officially backed program, called Crusade for Opportunity, also has a Federal grant of $483,000. Most of the traditional social welfare agencies in Syracuse are represented in the crusade. "Representatives of the poor," as required by the Federal law, also are included, but they have been selected by the crusade.

The main target of both programs is a deteriorated downtown area that includes most of the city's poor—and 80 percent of its Negro population. Syracuse, with a total population of 200,000, has about 12,000 Negroes. According to 1960 census data, 13 percent of the white population and 30 percent of the nonwhites had family incomes of less than $3,000 a year.

Frictions between the two federally supported programs have

From "Fighting Poverty and City Hall," Syracuse *Herald-Journal* (May 12, 1965). Copyright © 1965 by Newhouse National News Service. Reprinted by permission.

Erwin Knoll and Jules Witcover are Washington correspondents for the Newhouse National News Service.

produced a jurisdictional civil war among Syracuse's antipoverty warriors' fought over the questions of how the poor shall participate and who shall speak for them.

To the average citizen of Syracuse, it has been an invisible civil war so far. The cab driver who is asked what he thinks about the controversy—or about the war on poverty generally—shrugs and says: "I don't know nothing about it. I mind my own business."

But to the participants, and to the antipoverty agency in Washington, where "involving the poor" is a major issue, the controversy looms as a basic conflict over social philosophy.

Ben Zimmerman, executive director of the crusade, says:

"They (the university's social action planners) are looking at poor people as a class—poor people rising as a class. We're thinking about making opportunities for individuals.

"This makes all the difference. If you're talking about a mass program, you're saying, 'How do you galvanize the poor to break down the walls of the city?'

"Anger and frustration can bring a program together. But you have to keep fanning the flames if that's what keeps the program going. Also, this is the kind of program that really demands an outside 'enemy.'

"They're out organizing on one level and we're organizing on another, and so the chance of collision is great. The worst thing that could happen is for a fight to develop over who 'owns' the poor."

Prof. Warren Haggstrom of the Syracuse University School of Social Work, who is directing the social action program, says:

"Ours is a philosophy of self-help—help the neighborhoods develop strong democratic organizations with as wide a base as possible that will achieve an additional level of power; enough power to enable those individuals excluded from the community to enter it.

"The poor are outsiders. The problem is: how can they enter the community? If you just give them services, it doesn't pull them in. The failure of past welfare programs proves that."

The poor can become a part of the community, Haggstrom argues, "only in a process where people are in charge of their own lives. And in order to be self-responsible, you have to have a certain level of power."

Though they head the two programs involved, neither Zimmerman nor Haggstrom is the central figure in the controversy. The tempest really revolves around Saul D. Alinsky, a Chicagoan who has been hired by the university as a consultant and visiting lecturer.

Alinsky is executive director of the Industrial Areas Foundation, a private organization that specializes in setting up urban neighborhood power blocs through the same mobilization of the poor that is being used now in Syracuse.

He comes to Syracuse 4 days a month to lecture to the program's trainees and to advise Haggstrom and Fred W. Ross, the university project's field director and former west coast director for Alinsky's foundation.

Alinsky is paid directly by the university and avoids any direct contact with the community and the low-income citizens his plan seeks to organize. But his reputation as a "revolutionary" in the field of social work has unnerved community leaders.

A veteran of labor battles in the early days of the CIO and of decades of community organization work in Chicago, Alinsky speaks bluntly of making the poor "powerful enough to help themselves." He contemptuously dismisses much of the conventional welfare approach as "sentimental slop."

"Unless the poor are organized," he said in an interview, "it is impossible for them to get effective representation in policymaking."

Syracuse is not the only city in which Alinsky is involved in anti-poverty projects. He is, or is about to become, a consultant to community efforts in Rochester, Buffalo, and Kansas City, Mo. In these cities, as in Syracuse, his program of organizing the poor to fight city hall has stirred debate over the proper limitations on the nationwide war on poverty.

"This is part of a ferment that is developing throughout the country now," Alinsky says.

The alarmed responses of Syracuse community leaders has been stirred not only by Alinsky's tough attitude but also by a brochure issued to describe the university project.

"This program," the booklet declares, "differs from most in being solely concerned with the creation of powerful self-directed democratic organizations in areas of poverty."

Applicants for the training program, the brochure adds, "should have a controlled but intense anger about continued injustice and should be committed to hard work for people who are grappling with apparently overwhelming problems."

A number of young civil rights veterans have been recruited as trainees, including several members of the Congress of Racial Equality (CORE) and a Catholic priest.

The Syracuse University project is divided into two parts—training under Haggstrom and field demonstration under Ross. Six master's degree students and eight non-degree students without formal social work training, with two trainee organizers in campus seminars and in actual fieldwork.

The fieldwork sends the student organizers into six selected low-income areas in Syracuse. In teams of two—usually one Negro and one white student—they conduct house meetings and, later, neighborhood citizens' sessions to air and press complaints. Actions committees are formed to investigate charges of insufficient garbage disposal, excessive rents and gas bills, unjustified evictions, lack of recreational facilities and other grievances.

Also, a voter registration committee starts at once to put as many low-income citizens on the rolls as possible. This step is the basic under-pinning of the program. "Register for Power" is one of the slogans dis-played in mimeographed neighborhood newspapers.

The program calls for eventual election of permanent officers and the linking of all the neighborhood groups into one organization of organizations that can claim to be the actual representative of the poor in Syracuse.

Elected officers then would take up grievances with city hall or whatever agency might be involved.

Alinksy and Ross contend that this approach, if successfully car-ried out, could mean less open strife in the community than would occur if the poor were frustrated in pressing their complaints. The poor's power as a pressure group would win redress of grievances, they say, and make open demonstrations unnecessary.

This confidence among the social-action planners that their efforts will not precipitate violence has apparently not been bought very widely among Syracuse civil leaders. They worry about the fact that Alinsky's programs in Chicago included rent strikes and sit-ins even before such tactics were used in the civil rights movement.

Some community leaders also are disturbed about participation in the university project of several active members of CORE, which is conducting a controversial hiring practices drive against the Niagara-Mohawk Power Corp. One of the university trainees is Bruce Thomas, former chairman of the city's CORE chapter.

In this atmosphere of conflict, prominent members of the com-munity see a considerable potential for trouble in the Alinsky approach.

"They try to pit the poor against everyone else in the commu-nity," says Mayor William F. Walsh. "Such talk as 'guerrilla warfare' and 'agitation to the point of contact' is certainly not in keeping with social work techniques, because the purpose of social work is to help people help themselves."

Walsh, a Republican, says the Alinsky approach can spell po-litical trouble for him. He is likely to be a candidate for reelection this fall and the voter registration drive of the university project is expected to favor the Democrats. In fact, Democratic voter rolls are rising already in the low-income areas where organizers are active.

"These people go into a housing project and talk about setting up a 'democratic' organization—small 'd'—but it sounds just the same as

)emocratic—big 'D,' " Walsh says. "In a close election, it could be decisive."

Reverberations from the Syracuse controversy have already
eached the White House. A month ago Charles A. Walker, a commisioner of the Syracuse Housing Authority, wrote to President Johnson
o protest that the federal antipoverty grant was being used to finance
activities which do no good and will ultimately cause serious trouble in
ur community if allowed to continue."

Walker complained to the President that university-trained organizers "are claiming that all kinds of benefits will accrue to the tenants
f our housing projects if they will join these 'action committees.'

"One of the promised benefits," he continued, "is the improvement
f conditions in the housing project known as Pioneer Homes. Conditions
n Pioneer Homes are as good as the tenants will permit them to be."

Walker enclosed a memorandum from William L. McGarry,
xecutive director of the Syracuse Housing Authority, who charged that
this social action program follows all of the old patterns of class distinction and hate, so easily identified with Marxism."

Dean Clifford Winters of University College issued a statement
ıranding the charges as "false." The complaint to the White House
ırought an OEO investigator to Syracuse for 3 days of intensive discusions with parties to the dispute. He has written a report, which has not
ıeen made public.

The housing authority's letter to President Johnson has only compounded the difficult position of the university. Mayor Walsh met recently
vith Chancellor William P. Tolley to attempt to smooth over the dispute,
ut the university has been obliged to take some of the heat off itself.

To this end, a new nine-member board is being established under
he Reverend Thomas Costello, superintendent of schools of the Catholic
liocese. The controversial action phase of the Federal grant to the uniersity will be subcontracted to this board, which in turn will seek to
aise funds of its own.

The object is to leave to the university only the training portion
ıf the program, which is regarded as clearly a proper educational function. The board, made up of community leaders, would then provide a
ıridge to the crusade, of which Father Costello is also a member.

But while this device may give the university some technical
elief and may placate some community leaders, it is not likely to remove
he basic alarm about the organizing the poor project itself.

Some principals in the controversy, including Zimmerman of the
rusade, say community pressure could force the university to kill the
ocial action project, thus triggering a campus revolt. But the consensus

among a number of faculty members and students is that a "Berkeley" at Syracuse is quite unlikely.

McGarry and the operations of the housing authority have been sharply criticized at tenants' meetings organized by the university trainees. One leaflet circulated among public housing tenants contrasted a photograph of a littered lot in the public housing area with a picture of McGarry's handsome suburban home.

In an interview, McGarry was bitterly critical of the university program and the social trends that brought it into being. He stressed that he was not opposed to organizations of public housing tenants provided they are constructive.

If, for example, the tenants were to organize garden clubs, Mc Garry said, he would be glad to help them by providing grass seed. But the university's social action program, he declared, "is simply not conducive to focusing the efforts of the people in the right direction.

"To fail to include the established institutions in this community is completely wrong," he said.

Mayor Walsh, caught between the university and community leaders alarmed by Alinsky blames his dilemma on Washington.

"I feel that the responsibility for this rests with OEO in Washington," he said in an interview. "It was our feeling that nothing should be done in this community without being cleared with the crusade."

Neither the crusade nor the university program has formally ruled out the possibility of getting together, but parties to the controversy say privately that a joint effort in the present atmosphere is highly unlikely.

The crusade is making its own effort to involve the poor in running its programs by setting up neighborhood boards that, according to Zimmerman, will play a genuine role in policymaking. Federal antipoverty officials have made several efforts to promote cooperation between the two projects. A showdown may come when the university's 9-month Federal grant comes up for renewal later this year.

As of now, the Federal antipoverty agency is caught in the middle. Congress has ordered "maximum feasible participation" by the poor, and the university project seeks to achieve it. Congress has also recommended local "umbrella" antipoverty agencies to coordinate all fronts of the war on poverty, and that is what the crusade is.

To date, the Federal agency has shown a disinclination to get involved in local jurisdictional or philosophical disputes. Still, it has been aggressive in demanding genuine involvement of the poor in local programs. Accordingly, it is possible to hazard an educated guess about how Washington will answer the questions posed at the start of this account.

Should the Federal Government finance mass social protest? Should it, as part of the war on poverty, help the poor fight city hall?

Given the prevalent attitude at the Office of Economic Opportunity, Washington's answer very probably will be "yes"—unless more local eruptions and congressional criticism force a reappraisal.

Newsweek
The War on Poverty after One Year

In the drab brown headquarters in Washington and in outposts from New York's Harlem to Yell County, Ark., to San Francisco's Chinatown, the war is being waged with an eclectic energy that recalls the early days of the New Deal. And it is being fought with a fervent conviction that scorns all the scriptural fatalism about the poor.

One top general has lost 22 pounds in the eleven months since joining the fight. He can't sleep at night. "I don't just wake up," he says. "When I wake, I'm bolt upright ready to go again." If the reason for nights of insomnia and days of activity in a cause almost as old as the hills of Appalachia—or Galilee—was not apparent from the start, it became suddenly illuminated last month by the flames of Watts. "The clock is ticking," President Johnson warned afterward—and the cause assumed a measure of unmistakable national urgency.

The war on poverty at last came to Watts as a result of the bitter uprising there. Elsewhere, it was already being waged on a broadening front—750 cities and counties formed the scattered battle line. And everywhere, this novel thrust of government had met doubts, suspicions, some outright condemnation.

"Administrative bungling, haphazard haste and costly waste," charged a Senate minority report. Republican leader Everett McKinley Dirksen pirouetted in sarcasm on the Senate floor over a program to show slum children choreographers, among others, at work. "I think there is trouble everywhere in the land," snorted poverty-war critic Adam Clayton Powell, chairman of the House Education and Labor Committee and overseer of a special anti-poverty fiefdom in Harlem. He announced last week that he was sending investigators to the poverty war's "problem areas."

Militant Negro leaders have scorned the whole Federal effort as a sop in the struggle for racial equality. Rightist groups have condemned the program as "a blueprint for revolution." And many of the poor themselves feel that what's happening, maybe, is nothing at all. "It's exactly the same as it was," says Mrs. Phyllis Jackson, secretary of the Cleveland Citizens United for Adequate Welfare. "It's even the same people who are doing it."

The war on poverty has just turned one year old, to date in from Congress's passage of the Economic Opportunity Act.

Its origins and purposes—almost obscured by its actions and reactions—were recalled last week by Walter Heller, chairman of the Council of Economic Advisers under Presidents Kennedy and Johnson, and a chief strategist of the opening assault. John F. Kennedy, the rich young senator from Massachusetts, who had hardly noticed Boston's slums, had been appalled by the squalor of West Virginia during his primary campaigning there and later as President was shocked to learn that 50 per cent of draftees who reported for induction were unqualified to serve, half of them for "mental reasons." During his year-end economic review in December 1962, Mr. Kennedy asked his chief economist: "What about the poverty problem in the United States?" The President asked Heller to get him a copy of Michael Harrington's "The Other America" and a study of poverty by economists Leon Keyserling and Robert Lampman. Together these works documented a grim statistic: in the midst of abundance, one out of every five Americans was poor—37 million in all.

Heller and his Council of Economic Advisers first explored the possibility of reducing poverty with a tax cut: "We concluded that even though the tax cut would create between 2 and 3 million new jobs, even though it would open up exits from poverty, the difficulty is that there are millions of people who can't use those exits, who can't move into new jobs." For Heller, that was the key conclusion. "These millions are caught in the web of poverty through illiteracy, lack of skills, racial discrimination, broken homes, ill health. These are conditions that are hardly touched by prosperity and growth. These are conditions which call for a specially focused and specially designed program."

At about 7:30 P.M. on the evening of Nov. 19, 1963, Heller went to see Kennedy. "When I got there, John-John followed me into the President's office. After we shooed him out, I asked the President whether he wanted our work to go forward on the assumption that the antipoverty measure would be part of his 1964 legislative program. His answer was an unhesitating, 'Yes.'"

President Kennedy was dead three days later. And the following day, recalled Heller, "the very first matter I took up with President

ohnson was the poverty program. His immediate response was, "That's
ny kind of program ... I want to move full speed ahead."

The program has been gathering momentum ever since ...

But just where is the poverty war running? Total spending on
he poor in the U.S.—private and public—amounts to roughly $35 billion
nnually. The bulk of the outlay—some $20 billion—comes from tradi-
ional Federal sources. Shriver's share of $1.8 billion for the coming year
mounts to a tiny fraction of the whole. But on its controversial contents
ide new hopes of remedying a national ill that previous billions have
eft uncured.

Shriver's war is moving forward on two major fronts. The main
hrust of the war, the program with the biggest outlay ($667 million)
nd the most profoundly disruptive approach to attacking the poverty
rogram is the so-called community-action program (523 already in ac-
ion). Sample undertakings: summer day camps for poor children in
Detroit, fencing classes for poor kids in Harlem, a university-run health
enter in Boston. The contents are hardly revolutionary. The form, how-
ver, may be just that.

Evolving out of cooperative community efforts to fight juvenile
lelinquency (pilot project: Mobilization for Youth in Manhattan's Lower
ast Side, once accused of being staffed with Communists), the CAP
s in effect an escalation of that specific battle into a general war on
overty. In theory, a CAP is jointly formulated by existing public and
rivate organizations in an impoverished area. Its purpose: to coordinate
xisting schemes and initiate and run new Federally financed ones in a
rontal attack on poverty. "Up to now, social agencies have been splinter-
ng the individual, each agency getting a piece of him," explains Richard
immons Jr., the bull-necked director of Detroit's central community-
ction agency. "We're trying to put him back together."

In fact, however, existing social agencies have widely bogged
lown into bureaucratic inefficiency, indifference and misguided pater-
alism. They have lost contact with their impoverished constituency. "Our
ocial workers are entangled in bureaucracy," lamented Los Angeles
County Supervisor Kenneth Hahn after the Watts outbreak. "They simply
an't get into poverty-stricken areas because of all the red tape ... We
ave to wade through state welfare laws that weigh 104 pounds and
tand 5 feet 2 inches high ..."

So from the outset, many of Washington's new breed of poverty
warriors concluded that the best bet for helping the poor was to sidestep
regular welfare channels wherever possible. The men from OEO similarly
oped to set up the community action programs without the interference
of city halls and state houses. It was an ambitious aspiration.

The State Houses were finally technically removed from the picture when the OEO, with President Johnson's personal assistance, managed to convince Congress last month to water down a governor's power to veto poverty projects in his state—a veto that was written into the original Economic Opportunity Act. After some strategic telephoning by LBJ, the Senate refused to restore the full veto by a parliamentary stand-off—a 45-to-45 vote.

But the mayors ye have ever with you, as the poor and poverty warriors can attest. Control of welfare is one of the cherished corner-stones of City Hall's economic and political strength. The prospect of relinquishing this control is distasteful in any case—and unthinkable when a fresh flood of Federal funds is on the way. Thus the Mayors' Conference in June barely restrained itself from accusing the OEO of "undermining the integrity of local government."

More than that, the OEO was also "fostering class struggle," said a resolution proposed to the conference. As much as competition from Washington, the mayors feared challenges to their control from their own grimy backyards—challenges being financed by Federal funds. Just how literally, the city chieftains began to ask, would the Washington warriors take the wording of the Economic Opportunity Act requiring "maximum feasible participation" of the poor in community poverty pro-grams?

This phrase is at the crux of the smoldering conflict and contro-versy in the poverty war.

The OEO itself is not quite sure what it means. When the words were put into the act—by the task force that helped draw up the legisla-tion—they signified a fond hope: to give the poor a say in their own salvation and to break the hammerlock hold of the traditional welfare agencies.

This hope is still nourished in Washington. But a rising rank of self-styled poor leaders have seized the wording and made it a rallying cry in a political struggle for control over local poverty programs. Logi-cally and literally applied, the phrase meant that the Federal government could be in the business of underwriting politically explosive agitation such as rent strikes and economic boycotts. Naturally, the mayors pro-tested.

Walking gingerly between City Hall and slum, the OEO has pressed the former to give some voice to the latter. The working compro-mise: an unofficial, but widely heeded, guideline that representatives of the poor be allotted one-third of the seats on community-action policy committees. The OEO has also tried to see that the poor representatives on such bodies are not simply swamped by City Hall's people. "Here's a telephone number," an OEO staff member told a New York poor leader the other day. "Give me a ring if there's any interference from the city fathers."

The idea of a Federally financed, bloodless uprising of the down-trodden is enough to make most free-lance activists sneer, but there are already a few small indications that the war on poverty, through the community-action programs, could become just that.

OEO-financed poor organizers in Syracuse, N.Y. (slogan: "Register for Power"), have led the poor in protests against city agencies. Philadelphia's poor used OEO funds to travel to Harrisburg last month and demonstrate against Gov. William Scranton's planned veto of several welfare measures. And members of the East New York–Brownsville anti-poverty council had hardly been elected before they were talking about demanding improved public services from the city—better garbage collection and rigorous housing inspection. Says lean, articulate Frank Espada, a charter member of the council: "I don't think the power structure really understands what's going on."

OEO deputy director Conway thinks he does, however. "There will be accommodation," he said recently, "but first there'll be a lot of creaks, bends and groans." The question remains where the accommodations will come. Indications are that they will not all be by the "power structures." Shriver indicated recently that he would be happy to de-emphasize community-action programs. "Everybody thinks of them as the cure-all, the Hadacol that's going to cure falling arches and baldness." He pointed out that when the poverty war was first being considered, there were thoughts of spending $500 million on community action programs alone, but that he cut the figure back to $200 million and "went around shopping to decide what to do with the $300 million." The White House itself, unquestionably sensitive to the political explosiveness of the CAP's, indicated recently that it, too, thought more stress should be placed on some of the other programs Shriver turned up.

The alluring second front in the poverty war: nationwide programs—more directly controllable from Washington and with far fewer political implications. Most of these programs are aimed at the young.

Head Start. "You feel he thinks he can lick this thing overnight with Head Start," says one top Washington warrior, speaking of his commanding officer. "It was Shriver who really pushed the program." And indeed Head Start above all bears the mark of Shriver's salesmanship—from its beginning with Lady Bird Johnson as honorary chairman to its summer session conclusion with the Walt Disney-designed "diplomas."

An eight-week course designed to give pre-school poor children (ages 4 through 6) some of the cultural enrichment they lack in impoverished homes, Head Start was conceived the 19th of January. Shriver recalls: "They said, 'You're crazy. You can't do it in six months.' But we went ahead anyway." Full speed ahead. Announced as a modest $17 million program for 100,000 children in 300 communities, Head Start's

dimensions doubled and redoubled. Final count: 561,031 children in 13,
337 communities. Cost: $82,704,513.

There was grumbling about Head Start's headlong start. Ye
Head Start's own report card is generally favorable. It got highest mark
from President Johnson. It "has been battle-tested," he said last week
"and it has been proven worthy."

Job Corps. "Don't promise more than you can deliver," says the
title on a drawing in Job Corps director Otis Singletary's paper-strew
office. Underneath, a hand-drawn slip of paper says in red ink, "Opera
tion 20,000." Together the messages stand as a poignant reminder of over
estimated goals and underestimated problems for the Job Corps. Origina
plans called for 40,000 corpsmen in the first year. This was cut to 20,000
As of last week only 12,000 youths had been assigned to 60 Job Corps
centers, in 30 states.

The stated goal of the Job Corps is to give remedial education
and vocational training to boy and girl dropouts (ages 16 through 21)
in healthy environments away from the slums and shanties of their child
hood. An unstated, but at least as fundamental a purpose is to get the
kids off the streets so they don't start trouble.

A major trouble for the corps, however, has been that many communities around the centers or planned centers don't want the kids or
their streets either, and these fears haven't been eased by a spate of
heavily headlined incidents involving the Job Corpsmen. Two weeks ago,
some 80 corpsmen in Camp Breckinridge, near Morganfield, Ky., rioted
and injured thirteen persons before state troopers were sent in to keep
order. (Uncovered in FBI investigations of the outbreak: an extortion
racket in which some corpsmen were shaking down others for as much
as $13.50 a month for "life insurance.") Arrests of seven boys at Camp
Atterbury, Ind., for sexually assaulting an eighth, also made national
headlines. So did a city-council protest against a St. Petersburg, Fla.,
girls' center; citizens had complained that motorcycling boys were dis-
turbing the town's serenity. And in San Antonio, five Job Corps youths
allegedly shot two airmen.

"People are dwelling on isolated incidents to attack the program,"
broods corps commander Singletary, who will return this winter to the
calm of the University of North Carolina campus where he was chancellor
before Shriver asked him to come to Washington.

Singletary would prefer that everybody looked at the pride of
the Job Corps, Camp Kilmer, N.J., one of the centers being operated
under contract to industry. Shriver himself did so the other week, beginning in a former regimental kitchen on the abandoned Army post—
the Cook's Course—where kids in traditional white garb gaped at the

nan from Washington. Next stop was a huge hangar-like building in
vhich a dozen boys in blue overalls worked on old Army cars. Then
hriver popped into the refrigerator-air conditioning repair section, where
nore kids in dark coveralls and goggles peered up from soldering irons.
'What can we do to make this camp better?" he asked each group of
oys. The universal answers: more cigarettes, more money, better food.

Kilmer has an 8 per cent dropout rate compared to 10.6 per cent
nationally. Its record, Shriver feels, supports his decision to enlist corpora-
ions to run some Jobs Corps centers. Federal Electric (a branch of
T&T) operates Kilmer, and now has its eyes on the whole Job Corps.
'We are going to run the best camp," says its president, "and get the

The $20-Billion Poverty War

Shriver's Share	Millions
Community Action	$ 667
Head Start	150
Job Corps	281
VISTA	20
Neighborhood Youth Corps	300
College Work Study	84
Adult Basic Education	33
Rural Loans, Migrant Aid	55
Work Experience	150
Other	45
Total	$1,785

Other Federal Programs

Cash Payments	
Social Security	6,700
Old Age Assistance	1,400
Unemployment Insurance	2,800
Dependent Children	1,600
Kerr-Mills	447
Relief	952
Food	
Stamps	33
Distribution	235
Education	
Aid to Slum Schools	1,060
Teacher Corps	36
Aid to Impacted Schools	400
Federal Scholarships	70
Manpower Training	400
Housing	
Rent Subsidy	30
Public Housing	80
Regional	
Economic Development	665
Appalachia	1,100
Total	$18,008

best job-placement results and then submit a proposal in eighteen month:
to take over the whole program."

Neighborhood Youth Corps. While the Job Corps has gainec
most of the headlines, bad and good, the Neighborhood Youth Corp.
has quietly put to work 27 times the number of poor boys and girl:
on hometown streets performing such tasks as park maintenance, traffic
control, painting, even cleaning parking meters. And it has suffered only
one major flap—over recruits' salaries. The Labor Department, which
runs the Youth Corps for the OEO, decreed originally that the kid:
everywhere be paid the Federal minimum wage of $1.25 an hour. Toc
high, many communities yelled. The kids are earning more than thei
fathers, Gov. John Connally of Texas publicly lamented. As a result,
the Labor Department reluctantly agreed to allow adjustments.

VISTA. Least publicized of the major programs under Shrive
has been VISTA (Volunteers in Service to America), which sends lowly
paid, highly motivated people into poor areas. Like the Job Corps, it
has suffered from too-great expectations. The original goal for the program's first year was 4,000 VISTA volunteers. ("A VISTA Volunteer,"
decrees an OEO guide sheet, tackling the redundancy head on, "shall be
known as a 'VISTA Volunteer'.") As of last week, only 1,110 volunteers
were in the field (in 150 projects in 38 states); 370 more were in training. The 4,000 goal, deputy director Jack Conway now bluntly declares,
"was unrealistic." But, he adds, VISTA is ahead of the Peace Corps at
the same stage, and should reach 2,000 by Christmas.

Other OEO experiments include funds to employ poor college
students (115,000 are expected to benefit this fall). An adult basic-edu-
cation program has reached 43,372 men and women so far. Rural loans
to poor farmers, small business loans to poor businessmen have totaled
almost $23 million. And with hardly a notice, some 91,400 participants
have taken part in a $114,500,000 placement program designed primarily
for jobless parents.

Beyond these main prongs in the assault, some smaller pincer
movements can also be glimpsed that may well develop into major
thrusts:

Birth Control. "There's no possibility the bill would allow any
such thing," promised the Economic Opportunity Act's floor manager in
the House last year. Yet to date, seven birth-control projects have been
approved by the OEO under community-action grants; another fifteen
to twenty have received local approval and are awaiting clearance in
Washington. (One project that hasn't incubated in nine months since its
submission comes from Milwaukee, where a 40 per cent Catholic popula-

on joined protest against Federal "sexmobiles.") A top OEO staffer considers birth control as potentially the most important single program that can be developed. Polls, he says, show the poor want just as few children as the affluent. "If all the poor had the same number, we would have 5 to 20 per cent of the poverty licked right there."

Negative Income Tax. One of several proposals to boost the incomes of the poor is an idea long considered revolutionary but now under serious consideration by the OEO and the President himself. It is based on the fact that many of the poor, because of large families and disabilities, are entitled to income-tax exemptions that exceed their incomes. The idea: give them money for unused exemptions.

Legal assistance. So far, twelve projects to provide free legal advice to the impoverished have been approved. Youthful law groups such as the Law Students' Civil Rights Research Association have proven eager to help; they see such assistance as a major way of empowering the poor against bureaucracies, landlords, merchants. Under the OEO's encouragement communities are beginning to open up neighborhood legal clinics.

Aid to the aged. Two weeks ago, the President announced a $41 million program for the 5.5 million elderly poor—the "most invisible of the invisible poor." A major ingredient is to be the Foster Grandparent program whereby some 4,000 persons over 65 will be paid to care for some 7,000 children living in institutions. And the OEO is foraging for more such programs, acknowledging that the poverty war's emphasis on the young has neglected the aged.

All told an immensely varied—and highly experimental—arsenal. Who can possibly look at it and say that it contains the best combination of weapons to fight poverty? Shriver, the pragmatic warrior, posed the question himself last year.

At the beginning of World War II, he argued, if you had asked Admiral Nimitz if submarines or destroyers were going to be the most effective, well, he couldn't say ... Since Secretary McNamara has been in [the Defense Department], there has been much analysis of relative effectiveness so that when they decide whether to spend $2 billion for a Skybolt or a TFX they have a sound basis for judgment. But this has never been done in the social sciences. I don't think you could find anybody who would know whether it would be better to spend $5 billion on pre-school children or teen-agers. Nobody can tell that."

But Shriver, the energetic administrator, aimed to find out. He already had somebody in mind to help him—Dr. Joseph A. Kershaw, provost of Williams College and formerly head of the economics division of the Rand Corp., honing grounds of many of the Defense Department's best analytical minds. "I was sitting on a veranda last September at Martha's Vineyard," Kershaw recalls, "when the phone rang. 'My name i Sargent Shriver,' a voice said. 'We're going to spend a lot of money...'"

Kershaw arrived two and a half months ago to figure out how the poverty war could achieve maximum feasible effectiveness for it dollars. An IBM 1410 computer arrived soon after—Kershaw's persona side arm. His aim: to devise the best "mix" for OEO's own program and also for the vast array of poverty-war programs run by other gov- ernment agencies (in line with the Economic Opportunity Act's mandate that the OEO coordinate all Federal spending in the fight). As a crude indication of what's involved, Kershaw lugs out a 3-inch-thick book his department has just finished assembling at a cost of $75,000. Unless he has overlooked an agency or two, the book for the first time names all Federal programs to aid the poor.

Cost-conscious President Johnson is intrigued by the compilation and by Kershaw's cost-effectiveness approach to poverty spending, and if OEO efforts can bring logarithms and logic to bear on Federal bud- gets, provost and computer may prove to have the biggest impact on poverty of all.

In fact, without such a sophisticated, broad-gauge attack, the war on poverty may flounder hopelessly. Many skeptics doubt that Shriv- er's modest array of programs by itself could ever break the sinewy web that grips the poor. Loudest doubter: Leon Keyserling, onetime head of President Truman's Council of Economic Advisers. "The generals," he says, "have fallen short in their analysis of the causes of poverty and... consequently their entire strategy is not only inadequate in size and scope ... but also substantially misdirected." The real answer, argues big- spender Keyserling, is a truly massive increase in Federal spending. Ten people could be lifted out of poverty by basic changes in economic and social policies, Keyserling claims, for every one helped up by specialized programs to help the poor.

The same argument has been stated in another way—that the war on poverty is not against poverty, but against the poor, that the government is trying to change them rather than change the institutional flaws (a weak educational system, for instance) that allow them to exist. What good is Head Start, it is asked, if Head Starters end up in dilapi- dated, understaffed slum schools? As for the Job Corps—"Is this diploma," a corpsman at Kilmer asked NEWSWEEK's Eleanor Clift, "going to get me a job when I get out of here?" The answer is that the Job Corps does not create jobs.

Shriver is just beginning to worry about this last, largest hurdle —finding the jobs—as his corps camps approach the point when they will e discharging 2,500 youths a month. Recent jobless figures underscore ust how high that hurdle is. While over-all unemployment fell in August to the lowest rate in eight years (4.5 per cent), the jobless rate or teen-agers was still 12.4 per cent and non-white unemployment, while alling, was 7.6 per cent. It is at the stubborn special situations, the Vattses of America—and at the young—that the war on poverty is specifically directed.

The new assault in an age-old crusade has just been launched. Last week, Congress authorized a second-year appropriation of $1.8 billion to underwrite the vanguard of the attack. The sniping from the ear mounts even before the first reports from the front are in. Yet, Sargent Shriver, the commandant of the war on poverty, imperturbably predicts total victory. How long will it take to win? A decade, predicts one top OEO general. A generation, says another. Forever, says a third with an uncertain smile. You just continue to upgrade the definition of poverty.

8
Other Solutions:
A Peek into the Poverty Toolbag

I cannot help believing that before
this generation has passed away, we
shall have advanced a great step toward that good time when poverty
and the degradation which always
follow in its camp, will be as remote
to the people of this country as the
wolves which once infested its forests
—David Lloyd George

There's a great day a comin'
And its not far off,
Been long, long, long on the way
—American Folk Song

The outstanding features of current discussions about poverty are
the wide range of programs, policies, and issues that are being discussed
In the past, major emphasis was placed on (1) social security, public
assistance, and other types of welfare payments that provide help for
the nonworking poor, and (2) on unemployment compensation, minimum
wage laws, labor market services, and similar programs designed to help
the working poor. Many of these programs, and some newer ones, are
reviewed in Levitan's articles in the present chapter and in chapter 6
General economists, who did not participate much in earlier discussions of poverty, are making important contributions to the debate
today. The article by Milton Friedman, for example, has led to serious
consideration at the highest levels in government of the use of a negative
income tax as a method of providing incomes for needy families. Reagan's
article on the guaranteed annual income is representative of a vast literature that has emerged during the past few years on the separation of
income from work. Minsky's article, set in the framework of aggregative

·conomic analysis, suggests the changes in monetary and fiscal policy that are required to obtain tight, full employment, which he regards as a necessary condition for the elimination of poverty for the working poor. His highly imaginative paper shows the close interrelationships between the attack on poverty and all other major aspects of our economic life.

Although we are still uncertain about the underlying causes of poverty, there seems to be general agreement that impressive inroads on economic poverty can and will be made. The real challenge is to find the right combination of programs to achieve the desired goal—the elimination of poverty for those now entrapped by it, the creation of new opportunities for children of the poor and the reduction of their anti-social behavior.

Milton Friedman
The Negative Income Tax

The extraordinary economic growth experienced by Western countries during the past two centuries and the wide distribution of the benefits of free enterprise have enormously reduced the extent of poverty in any absolute sense in the capitalistic countries of the West. But poverty is in part a relative matter, and even in these countries, there are clearly many people living under conditions that the rest of us label as poverty.

One recourse, and in many ways the most desirable, is private charity. It is noteworthy that the heyday of laissez-faire, the middle and late nineteenth century in Britain and the United States, saw an extraordinary proliferation of private eleemosynary organizations and institutions. One of the major costs of the extension of governmental welfare activities has been the corresponding decline in private charitable activities.

It can be argued that private charity is insufficient because the benefits from it accrue to people other than those who make the gifts—again, a neighborhood effect. I am distressed by the sight of poverty; I am benefited by its alleviation; but I am benefited equally whether I or someone else pays for its alleviation; the benefits of other people's charity therefore partly accrue to me. To put it differently, we might all of us

Reprinted from *Capitalism and Freedom* (pp. 190–195) by Milton Friedman by permission of The University of Chicago Press. Copyright © 1962 by the University of Chicago.

be willing to contribute to the relief of poverty, *provided* everyone else
did. We might not be willing to contribute the same amount without
such assurance. In small communities, public pressure can suffice to
realize the proviso even with private charity. In the large impersonal
communities that are increasingly coming to dominate our society, it is
much more difficult for it to do so.

Suppose one accepts, as I do, this line of reasoning as justifying
governmental action to alleviate poverty; to set, as it were, a floor under
the standard of life of every person in the community. There remain
the questions, how much and how. I see no way of deciding "how
much" except in terms of the amount of taxes we—by which I mean
the great bulk of us—are willing to impose on ourselves for the purpose.
The question, "how," affords more room for speculation.

Two things seem clear. First, if the objective is to alleviate poverty, we should have a program directed at helping the poor. There is
every reason to help the poor man who happens to be a farmer, not
because he is a farmer but because he is poor. The program, that is,
should be designed to help people as people not as members of particular occupational groups or age groups or wage-rate groups or labor
organizations or industries. This is a defect of farm programs, general
old-age benefits, minimum-wage laws, pro-union legislation, tariffs, li-
censing provisions of crafts or professions, and so on in seemingly endless profusion. Second, so far as possible the program should, while
operating through the market, not distort the market or impede its functioning. This is a defect of price supports, minimum-wage laws, tariffs
and the like.

The arrangement that recommends itself on purely mechanical
grounds is a negative income tax. We now have an exemption of $600
per person under the federal income tax (plus a minimum 10 per cent
flat deduction). If an individual receives $100 taxable income, i.e., an
income of $100 in excess of the exemption and deductions, he pays tax.
Under the proposal, if his taxable income minus $100, i.e., $100 less
than the exemption plus deductions, he would pay a negative tax, i.e.,
receive a subsidy. If the rate of subsidy were, say, 50 per cent, he would
receive $50. If he had no income at all, and, for simplicity, no deduc-
tions, and the rate were constant, he would receive $300. He might
receive more than this if he had deductions, for example, for medical
expenses, so that his income less deductions, was negative even before
subtracting the exemption. The rates of subsidy could, of course, be
graduated just as the rates of tax above the exemption are. In this way,
it would be possible to set a floor below which no man's net income
(defined now to include the subsidy) could fall—in the simple example
$300 per person. The precise floor set would depend on what the com-
munity could afford.

The advantages of this arrangement are clear. It is directed ecifically at the problem of poverty. It gives help in the form most eful to the individual, namely, cash. It is general and could be substited for the host of special measures now in effect. It makes explicit e cost borne by society. It operates outside the market. Like any her measures to alleviate poverty, it reduces the incentives of those lped to help themselves, but it does not eliminate that incentive enely, as a system of supplementing incomes up to some fixed minimum ould. An extra dollar earned always means more money available for penditure.

No doubt there would be problems of administration, but these em to me a minor disadvantage, if they be a disadvantage at all. The stem would fit directly into our current income tax system and could administered along with it. The present tax system covers the bulk income recipients and the necessity of covering all would have the y-product of improving the operation of the present income tax. More portant, if enacted as a substitute for the present rag bag of measures rected at the same end, the total administrative burden would surely reduced.

A few brief calculations suggest also that this proposal could far less costly in money, let alone in the degree of governmental intervention involved, than our present collection of welfare measures. Alnatively, these calculations can be regarded as showing how wasteful ir present measures are, judged as measures for helping the poor.

In 1961, government spending amounted to something like $33 llion (federal, state, and local) on direct welfare payments and proams of all kinds: old age assistance, social security benefit payments, d to dependent children, general assistance, farm price support proams, public housing, etc. I have excluded veterans' benefits in making is calculation. I have also made no allowance for the direct and indirect sts of such measures as minimum-wage laws, tariffs, licensing provisions, and so on, or for the costs of public health activities, state and cal expenditures on hospitals, mental institutions, and the like.

There are approximately 57 million consumer units (unattached dividuals and families) in the United States. The 1961 expenditures $33 billion would have financed outright cash grants of nearly $6,000 er consumer unit to the 10 per cent with the lowest incomes. Such ants would have raised their incomes above the average for all units the United States. Alternatively, these expenditures would have finced grants of nearly $3,000 per consumer unit to the 20 per cent with le lowest incomes. Even if one went so far as that one-third whom ew Dealers were fond of calling ill-fed, ill-housed, and ill-clothed, 961 expenditures would have financed grants of nearly $2,000 per conmer unit, roughly the sum which, after allowing for the change in

the level of prices, was the income which separated the lower one-thir
in the middle 1930's from the upper two-thirds. Today, fewer than on
eighth of consumer units have an income, adjusted for the change i
the level of prices, as low as that of the lowest third in the middle 1930'

Clearly, these are all far more extravagant programs than ca
be justified to "alleviate poverty" even by a rather generous interpret;
tion of that term. A program which *supplemented* the incomes of th
20 per cent of the consumer units with the lowest incomes so as t
raise them to the lowest income of the rest would cost less than ha
of what we are now spending.

The major disadvantage of the proposed negative income tax
its political implications. It establishes a system under which taxes a
imposed on some to pay subsidies to others. And presumably, thes
others have a vote. There is always the danger that instead of bein
an arrangement under which the great majority tax themselves willing
to help an unfortunate minority, it will be converted into one und
which a majority imposes taxes for its own benefit on an unwilling m
nority. Because this proposal makes the process so explicit, the dang
is perhaps greater than with other measures. I see no solution to th
problem except to rely on the self-restraint and good will of the electo
ate.

Writing about a corresponding problem—British old-age pensior
—in 1914, Dicey said, "Surely a sensible and a benevolent man ma
well ask himself whether England as a whole will gain by enactin
that the receipt of poor relief, in the shape of a pension, shall be cor
sistent with the pensioner's retaining the right to join in the election
a Member of Parliament."

The verdict of experience in Britain on Dicey's question mu
as yet be regarded as mixed. England did move to universal suffrag
without the disfranchisement of either pensioners or other recipients
state aid. And there has been an enormous expansion of taxation
some for the benefit of others, which must surely be regarded as havin
retarded Britain's growth, and so may not even have benefited most
those who regard themselves as on the receiving end. But these measur
have not destroyed, at least as yet, Britain's liberties or its predom
nantly capitalistic system. And, more important, there have been som
signs of a turning of the tide and of the exercise of self-restraint on th
part of the electorate.

Liberalism and Egalitarianism

The heart of the liberal philosophy is a belief in the dignity
the individual, in his freedom to make the most of his capacities an
opportunities according to his own lights, subject only to the provis

at he not interfere with the freedom of other individuals to do the
me. This implies a belief in the equality of men in one sense; in their
equality in another. Each man has an equal right to freedom. This is
important and fundamental right precisely because men are different,
cause one man will want to do different things with his freedom than
other, and in the process can contribute more than another to the
neral culture of the society in which many men live.

The liberal will therefore distinguish sharply between equality
rights and equality of opportunity, on the one hand, and material
uality or equality of outcome on the other. He may welcome the fact
at a free society in fact tends toward greater material equality than
y other yet tried. But he will regard this as a desirable by-product
a free society, not its major justification. He will welcome measures
at promote both freedom and equality—such as measures to eliminate
onopoly power and to improve the operation of the market. He will
gard private charity directed at helping the less fortunate as an ex-
nple of the proper use of freedom. And he may approve state action
ward ameliorating poverty as a more effective way in which the great
lk of the community can achieve a common objective. He will do so
ith regret, however, at having to substitute compulsory for voluntary
tion.

The egalitarian will go this far, too. But he will want to go
rther. He will defend taking from some to give to others, not as a
ore effective means whereby the "some" can achieve an objective they
ant to achieve, but on grounds of "justice." At this point, equality
mes sharply into conflict with freedom; one must choose. One cannot
 both an egalitarian, in this sense, and a liberal.

Michael D. Reagan
Guaranteed Income: Separate Income from Work

The contrast between America's ability to expand production
d her inability to expand employment to keep pace presents a serious
roblem of public policy, and this is now almost universally conceded.

From "For A Guaranteed Income," *The New York Times Magazine* (June 7,
64), pp. 20, 120–121. © 1964 by The New York Times Company. Reprinted by
rmission.

Michael D. Reagan is Professor of Political Science, University of California,
verside, and the author of *The Managed Economy* (Oxford, 1963).

But the solutions enacted and proposed to date—tax cuts, investme
incentives, manpower retraining programs, work-study aid for colleg
students, for example—all assume that it still makes sense to wo
toward the goal of full employment, and that government's major ta
is to help people prepare themselves for jobs in the private sector
the economy.

One group of publicists, economists and educators (a grou
which included this writer) has recently presented a more radical anal
sis, however. This group, calling itself the Ad Hoc Committee on th
Triple Revolution,* explicitly challenges the possibility of ever reachir
full employment in the face of automation's increasing ability to repla
human muscle and skills with machines.

Asserting that automation is creating the capacity to produ
all the goods and services our society can use without employing a
the men and women who will seek places in the labor force, the A
Hoc Committee (A.H.C.) fears that "the traditional link between jot
and income is being broken." Its prescription is therefore as radical
its analysis: it proposes that "society, through its appropriate legal an
governmental institutions, undertake an unqualified commitment
provide every individual and every family with an adequate incom
as a matter of right." In short, a guaranteed income.

Why is the A.H.C. so pessimistic about full employment. Th
first reason is the record of over 6 consecutive years in which the u
employment rate has not fallen below 5 per cent, despite greatly i
creased production. Worse still, among unskilled laborers the unemplo
ment rate has been above 12 per cent since 1957; among Negroe
above 10 per cent.

The unprecedented nature of the situation we face is reveale
in cold statistical terms in the President's 1964 Manpower Report:
the period 1957–63, 4.3 million new jobs were created—but of these onl
300,000 fulltime jobs were generated by private demand. Even mor
startling, for the five years prior to 1963 there was an actual net d
cline in the number of privately generated positions. Most new jot
were the result of increased governmental employment (especiall
teachers) and procurement (especially military).

The extent to which automation lies behind the present difficu
ties is a matter of dispute; that it adds considerably to the problem
cyclical unemployment is hardly debatable. Secretary of Labor Wirt
has characterized the automatic machinery that is being introduce
widely today as having, on the average, the skills of a high scho
graduate. The question is, will we ever be able to find jobs for humar
whose skills are less developed than those of machines.

---

* The revolutions: (1) cybernation, or automated machinery: (2) weapons
—the development of weapons capable of obliterating civilization: (3) civil right

How would the guaranteed-income proposal handle the prob-
ms? What are the arguments for and against it? Are there any prece-
nts?

The claim that the job-income link is being broken has two levels
meaning, for there are two types of jobs: those arising from produc-
n for the market and those—such as teaching, highway construction,
blic health protection, much of basic research—which are called forth
′ governmental rather than market demand. As Robert Theobald (in
me ways the "father" of the current proposal) says in his book, *Free
en and Free Markets:* "Our scarcity is one of market-supported jobs,
ot of work that needs to be done."

What Theobald and the A.H.C. mean by a guaranteed income
, in part, that we cannot rely upon privately generated demand to
eate jobs, but must use government to underwrite income-producing
ork: to guarantee that public services and public works will take up
me of the slack created by the march of automation in the traditional
ods-producing industries. This is not too far from the thinking of
esident Johnson, who said recently that if the tax cut proved to be
1 insufficient stimulant he would advocate increased public works.

In larger part, and this is the more radical and controversial
pect of the proposal, it is claimed that a guaranteed income—without
1y work—is needed for the aged, those of low skills and education,
ose discriminated against by race and those displaced too late in life
learn a new skill and find employment to utilize it—in short, for those
ho are permanently unemployable, whom the A.H.C. expects to be an
creasing number.

Suppose that every family were guaranteed $3,000 a year. What
ould it cost? A detailed answer cannot be given at this point, yet we
ave one related estimate that is worth considering. The President's
ouncil of Economic Advisers says that "about $11 billion a year would
ring all poor families up to the $3,000 income level ... The burden—
e-fifth of the annual defense budget, less than 2 per cent of Gross
ational product—would certainly not be intolerable."

The economic hope would be that the giving of income which
ould be spent by its recipients would, by increasing demand for the
ods produced in automated plants, elicit higher profits and market-
lated incomes from which tax returns would help pay the costs.
hether deficits in the national budget would be involved cannot be
retold at this time. What is known from the experience of recent years
that deficits are definite in the absence of a sufficient stimulus to the
ll use of resources.

Even if costs were not an obstacle, would anyone be willing to
ork at all, given the availability of nonwork income? How would the
cessary dirty jobs get done?

First of all, loosely following Theobald's suggestions, guarantee income would be used by the permanently unemployable—the co miner automated out of the only work he knows at age 45, the cle replaced by an inventory computer, and others for whom there is choice because they lack jobs in any case.

Second, there would be some who simply prefer not to work perhaps chiefly those already categorized as welfare chiselers. Als some would use the guaranteed income by preference because th would rather be relatively poor but free to do what they wished tha better off financially in jobs alien to their interests. Many creative you people—artists, writers, actors, poets—might make this choice, for o society does little today to provide market or governmental jobs f them.

Third, there would be those workers who earned less than $3,0(a year and whose wages would need to be supplemented to bring the income up to that level.

The unpleasant jobs—the dirty ones that still require huma muscle power or dull routine—would, of course, still have to be dor Because one could have an income above the poverty level witho doing them, they would have to carry much higher wages than present to attract workers. In the long run the higher costs would le toward further automation, further reducing the number of jobs. At t other end of the scale, jobs requiring extremely high skill levels carrying great burdens of managerial responsibility would continue attract talent because of their intrinsic interest and increasingly high incomes.

There would thus be a distribution between the job holders ar the workless partly by fate (those who lack the skills called for by a job); partly by economic incentives (most men who can earn $6,0(will not be satisfied with an income of $3,000-witness the extent moonlighting); and partly by choice (creative activity that society do not otherwise support, or work because of inner drives.)

The crux of the proposal is that jobless income would be abs lutely guaranteed: an Office of Guaranteed Income would stand read to provide the agreed minimum income without question to any joble applicant. Incentives to work would have to be revolutionized: t threats of poverty, starvation or even a means test would no longer available as goads. Employers would have to make work more attra tive; the bargaining position of employes—even as individuals—wou be much stronger. The economy would have a vast new "built-in st bilizer"—along with considerable disruption of the labor market.

The average man would face a unique choice when work b came voluntary; his largest problem might be to make satisfying use

ew-found leisure. Some would doubtless abandon leisure and return
to work after a brief fling. Some would find it an agreeable kind of
vegetative existence. Yet others might find liberation, independence and
an opportunity for self-development through "serious activity without
the pressure of necessity," which Paul Goodman reminds us was one
meaning of leisure in ancient Greece.

To set forth this description of the plan and its implications is
to raise a host of objections—economic, psychological and ethical.

The feeling that a man's character is destroyed if he does not
work is deeply ingrained. That man should live by the sweat of his
brow is an ancient thought, but one which accords with the experience
of many modern men who expire through boredom when retired.

Furthermore, there are strong links between work and self-respect. Ours is a society in which success counts, and it is largely measured by job status and income. The leaf-raking of Depression days was
no more popular with those who did it than with those whose taxes
paid for it. Is human dignity separable from work? Can leisure be respectable?

It may be that, as Robert Theobald has written, "the discovery
of the proper uses of freedom is the fundamental task of the remainder
of the twentieth century." But many are doubtful that we can make the
discovery. Those who will have the most leisure are those with the least
education, the most inadequate backgrounds for making effective use of
freedom.

Initially at least, it is hard to dispute the contention that most
of us are unfit for leisure. Nor is this view confined to economic conservatives. Norman Thomas said at a recent conference that "money without
the pressures most of us need to work will make us a poorer and not a
richer nation." (However, he is uncertain that we can provide the work.)

And what of those who would make no pretense of useful activity—those who are just plain lazy? The lazy we will always have with
us, we might say, and we do not allow them to starve. But does our
sense of social ethics require—or even permit—us to support them with
some degree of comfort and as a socially guaranteed *right*?

It takes little imagination to picture the response of the Senate
Finance Committee or of Congress generally to a bill calling for taxes
and expenditures to benefit *voluntary* joblessness with no strings attached.
And would the proportion of the population opting for a minimal living
without work remain constant, or would it jump so drastically that the
economy would come to a grinding halt. No one can answer with
certainty.

It could also be argued that the A.H.C. is counseling unwar-
ranted defeatism—gloom and doom. Many will fear that such a pro-

posal would become a self-fulfilling prophecy: that if we assume the cannot be enough jobs to go around, then we will bring about th situation by not trying hard enough to create more jobs.

Finally, would not the guaranteed-income plan lead to a goveri ment-created class of hereditary wards of the state? Would not childr in this class be condemned to fatalistic apathy? And would not the re of society too easily shrug off the needs of the poor once its conscien had been salved by having provided minimal income? There are, aft all, signs that these unwanted outcomes are already present among least some second-generation welfare families.

Despite the finality that these objections will have for son readers, there are counterarguments and precedents to be considere before the balance sheet is complete.

Jobless pay is not unknown to us—in the form of unemploymer compensation, disability insurance, and old age and survivors' benefi under the Social Security program that has been part of our syste since 1935. Aid to the blind, to dependent children, to the indigent n covered by insured employment—these, too, are forms of guarantee income without work.

Nor should we forget two important forms of private separatic of income from work: inheritance and property income. If a wealth relative leaves me $100,000, which I invest in tax-free municipal bond I can have a workless income of $4,000 a year. Or if I buy a swam in Louisiana and the Space Administration then builds a missile bas nearby, I can have a very substantial income—even capital gains—fror property ownership without lifting a finger to work.

These ways of breaking the income-job link are not universall admired—though perhaps universally envied—yet they are accepted b our society, especially by those likely to be least sympathetic to th A.H.C. proposal.

To the objection that work and self-respect are inseparable, th major reply is that the real necessity is not for a production job, bu for meaningful activity. This may or may not be related to incom Voluntary efforts to improve our communities, pursue the arts or pa ticipate in public affairs are meaningful—sometimes more so than o regular jobs. Ours might be a richer nation in human and estheti dimensions if more of us were free to direct our skills and energi toward projects not at present supported by the market.

As for the problem of the lazy, it is difficult to believe that society noted around the world for the frenetic quality even of its recre; tion would suddenly turn soporific on any large scale. And of cours the man with a family will continue to have both conscience and pre; sures to keep him seeking the higher incomes available through work where work is available.

One practical advantage of the guaranteed-income plan is that would greatly simplify the welfare pattern. A thousand administrative quirements and much overseeing expense could be eliminated if in-ome without work were distributed without needing proof of age, blind-ess, dependency, length of residence, etc. Also, it would be far more quitable, for existing social-insurance programs-retirement, minimum age, etc.—leave out many who are most in need simply because they 'e not in covered types of employment.

Some supplementary action programs would, of course, be re-uired—especially social work and special education to stimulate chil-ren of guaranteed-income families and steer them away from apathy, d to aid families in coping with the multiple problems that already eset the unemployed and are not solved simply by the provision of ush. What is necessary is to recognize the need for such programs and eir value, and to accord both higher prestige and higher salaries to e enlarged corps of professionals required. One would hope also that e change from grudging welfare to income guaranteed as a right ould be accompanied by changes in public attitudes, changes that ould lessen the obloquy which underlies the psychological listlessness some welfare recipients today.

If we learn to educate for life—not just to earn a living—there no reason, in principle, to assume that we, or at least our children, nnot make productive use of leisure. Let us hope it is possible, because will have to be. Even without a guaranteed-income plan our working me has on the average been cut to less than half of our waking time. xtended vacations for steelworkers and a 25-hour week for New York lectricians are but minimal symbols of the revolution already taking lace.

It may be easy to scoff at the A.H.C. proposal, but only if we re unwilling to face up to the problem of automation. How else can e handle it? Long continued unemployment makes it clear that we o not yet have an adequate alternative.

The particular ways by which we will provide income without bs in the traditional sense remain to be developed, and the plan dis-ussed here is doubtless not the only possibility. But it is clear now at radical revision of our thoughts, our economic institutions and our yle of life are the inescapable accompaniments of man's increasing ility to substitute machines for muscles and computers for clerks.

Sar A. Levitan
Alternative Income Support Programs

Public assistance is currently the prime vehicle for transmittin aid to the poor. . . . The income support provided is inadequate to me basic needs of recipients, and even this support tends to discourag initiative because benefits are based on a stringent means test. Exce for minor exemptions, earnings by relief recipients are normally d ducted from benefits they receive, thus creating an incentive for th beneficiaries to withdraw from the labor force. Moreover, the majori of needy persons do not receive any assistance, and nearly four of eve five poor persons do not receive public assistance. The federal goverr ment shares the cost of public assistance to selected groups—age blind, permanently disabled, and families with dependent childre States and local governments provide some assistance to needy perso outside these categories. But in many areas the destitute depend c private charity or have no support at all.

An additional problem of public assistance programs is that th have limited applicability to the working poor. Related programs ir tended to aid workers in the labor force, employed as well as unem ployed, tend to by-pass most of the poor, yet minimum wage legislatic has raised the level of income of many working poor. The result these inadequacies, as noted earlier, is that 2 million family heads (1963) having full-time, year-round jobs received earnings insufficient raise them above the poverty threshold.

Family Allowances

While the acceptance of the principle of equal pay for equ work is desirable as a means of eliminating discrimination based c color or sex, it ignores the needs of families with children and ten to deprive children of large families of basic needs. The underlyin justification for family allowances is that the well-being of childre should be the concern of society as a whole. Family allowances als recognize that the wage system alone is an inadequate basis for distrib tion of income.

Providing minimum family needs under the wage system is a

From *Programs in Aid of the Poor* (Kalamazoo, Michigan: The W. Upjohn Institute for Employment Research, 1965). Reprinted by permission of th author.

ge-old problem which has occupied policymakers since the early days f the industrial revolution. It was tried first on a modest basis in England 170 years ago and has spread widely during recent decades. It is ow practiced, under one form or another, by most industrial countries. 'amily allowances are given in all European countries and in about a hird of the nations outside Europe. In several countries these allowances ccount for a significant share of the total income received by families /hose heads are low-wage earners and by families without bread-/inners.

The family allowance programs of France and Canada illustrate wo diverse types of systems. In France it is estimated that for a family >f five, including three children, family allowances amount to about a quarter of total average wages paid in manufacturing; for a family with ive children the family allowances would add about two-thirds to the .verage wages earned in manufacturing. Family allowances in France .re financed by employers and amount to 13.5 percent of total payroll. n Canada, by contrast, family allowances are paid by the government rom the general revenue. The monthly allowance amounts to $6 (Caadian) for each child under 10 years of age and $8 for each child >etween the ages of 10 and 16. Thus, the Canadian family allowances upply an insignificant proportion of total family income.

Our wage system is not adapted to take account of the diverse leeds of workers: except for some adjustments in income taxes, for ·xample, the take-home pay from two identical jobs is the same for a >achelor as for the head of a family with dependents. Despite the wide ·cceptance of the family allowance principle in other countries, the idea ias never received active consideration in the United States—though it ias been advanced on numerous occasions. An exception has been made mder AFDC for most needy children. Expenditures under this program ·ccount for 0.3 percent of national income. A number of countries spend ·en times this percentage or more of their national income for family ·llowances. France, for example, allocates about 5.0 percent of national ncome to family allowances. And the trend in these countries has been ·o raise the proportion of national income devoted to family allowances.

Negative Income Tax

With the current commitment to wage war on poverty, various >roposals have been advanced to supply additional income for the poor. The ultimate goal of these proposals is to raise the income of the poor ind to eliminate poverty. The Social Security Administration has estimated that the addition of $11.5 billion would permit the 34.6 million >ersons designated as poor in 1963 to escape poverty.

The most widely discussed proposal is utilization of the incom tax machinery as a vehicle to supply income to the poor. The law providing now only for the collection of taxes, might be extended t include grants based on family or individual needs. Professor Robert Lampman of Wisconsin University has prepared the most careful an detailed cost estimates of different types of negative income tax pro posals. The cost estimates presented in this section are based on Lamp man's calculations.

In its simplest form, a negative income tax would allow nontax able individuals or families to claim the unused portion of their curren exemptions. Such a plan would tend to spread the benefits thinly amon most of the poor, but would still cost about $2 billion. If it wer limited to families with children, the cost would be reduced by abou one-half. A family of four with zero income would be entitled to "rebate" of $420. An "average" AFDC family—a mother with three chi dren—would receive somewhat more than $200 in addition to the near $1,500 of AFDC benefits, assuming that the states will continue curren levels of assistance.

At the other extreme, negative income tax proposals would over haul the present tax system to pay the poor enough income to close th poverty income gap which, as stated, amounted to $11.5 billion in 196: Poverty would thus be eliminated. However, such an income mainte nance level would rob any pecuniary incentives for millions of peopl to work since the guaranteed income would be equal or in excess o their earned wages. A workable plan would therefore permit low-wag earners to keep at least a portion of their earned income in order t provide them an incentive to continue working. This would, of cours increase the cost of the income maintenance program, by a larger amoun than the $11.5 billion poverty income gap. Lampman estimates that th cost of such a program would be double the present poverty incom gap, or about $23 billion. This appears to be a conservative estimate

A compromise between the above two plans would guarante income to cover 50 percent of the poverty income gap. Thus a famil of four would receive a guaranteed annual income of $1,565, based o the Social Security Administration estimates of basic needs. The cost o such a plan would be $8 billion. But this amount includes about $: billion which is now currently paid to public assistance recipients. Th net cost would therefore be about $5 billion. If the plan were limite to families with children, the cost would amount to $4.8 billion less th $1.3 billion now paid to public assistance recipients. As in the previou proposal, this scheme would also have to provide for continued incentiv to work and allow low-income earners to keep all or part of their earn ings. The cost would therefore be raised appreciably above the esti mated $5 billion.

The three variations of negative income tax schemes suggest the ost magnitude of any negative income tax plan. The costs of the three roposals listed above range from an annual cost of $2 billion per year ɔ $23 billion or higher. Different variations of these plans would involve a cost anywhere between these two extremes. Huge as these sums night appear, an addition of $5 to $23 billion to the income of the oor—ignoring the first scheme which would distribute the limited funds roadly—might be an attainable goal, given our society's present commitment to combat poverty. However, providing the poor with added ncome is only one aspect of combating poverty. The poor also need ietter schools, housing, training, and diverse services to improve their bility to compete for jobs in the labor market. Any adequate public velfare system, whose goal is to reduce poverty, must therefore aim t a judicious distribution of resources, both for raising the income level ɩf the poor and for providing them needed services. . . .

Competing Goals

The goal of eliminating poverty is only one of many aspirations ɩf our society which involve substantial financial resources. . . . The National Planning Association has recently attempted to calculate the cost ɩf realizing the major goals of our society. Along with the 15 major ɡoals, including education, health, urban development, social welfare, ɩnd defense, outlined by President Eisenhower's Commission on National Goals, the NPA added space exploration as a 16th major program vhich has developed during the 1960s. Assuming an annual growth in ɔNP of 4 percent, the NPA estimated that the cost of achieving the najor goals of society by 1975 would exceed the projected GNP for hat year by $150 billion, or 15 percent. Leonard A. Lecht, director of he NPA study, concluded:

> We could well afford the cost of any single goal at levels reflecting current aspirations, and we could probably afford the cost for any group of goals over the next decade. We could rebuild our cities, or abolish poverty, or replace all the obsolete plant and equipment in private industry, or we could begin to develop the hardware to get us to Mars and back before the year 2000. We could make some progress on all the goals, perhaps substantial progress on many, but we cannot accomplish all our aspirations at the same time.

It is not likely that society will decide in the foreseeable future to allocate the resources needed to win total victory over poverty, nor vould excessive reliance upon transfer payments appear to constitute ɔound public policy. While allocation of additional income for the poor is an essential element in the war on poverty, simply raising income to

fill even their minimum requirements would result in economic disloca
tions by eroding incentives to work. It may also be preferable in many
cases to stress income in kind rather than in cash. . . .

It is apparent that the waging of a successful war on poverty
is a complex and costly undertaking. Even the 89th Congress, which i
generally acknowledged as being the most welfare conscious Congres
in more than a generation, has not shown any inclination to commit th
necessary resources to eliminate poverty in the immediate years ahead
As shown earlier, it has been particularly parsimonious in allocating
additional income to the poor. Only about 2 per cent ($150 million) c
the multibillion-dollar 1965 amendments to the Social Security Act wer
allocated to raising federal contributions to public assistance. Nor ha
the Administration, which is committed to a total war on poverty, urge
Congress to adopt programs which would raise the income level of th
poor in the immediate years ahead. Whatever may be the merits of th
varied income maintenance programs discussed above, there does no
appear to be any wide consensus supporting their adoption. Althoug
such a plan might receive serious consideration at some indeterminat
future, to improve the lot of the poor in the short-run we must realis
tically turn to more modest programs.

Short-Run Priorities

The programs in aid of the poor reviewed [above] carry an
annual price tag of about $13 to $15 billion. The exact cost of these
programs cannot be determined since many of the programs in aid o
the poor are closely interwoven with general government activity, bu
rough estimates can be made about the portion which is allocated to
the poor on the basis of need. Other programs not discussed in thi
summary—aid to Indians, workmen's compensation, farm aid measure
and business loans, as they pertain to the poor, and other programs—
would add another billion to the total cost. Private philanthropic effort
on behalf of the poor raise the total funds allocated in aid of the poo
by about another billion dollars. The total cost of programs is of littl
operational significance, since there exist no adequate criteria to sugges
what percentage of GNP, or even of governmental expenditures, shoulc
be allocated to the poor. The $11.5 billion poverty gap, noted earlie
is a poor measure, at best, since it ignores the costs of additional service
and goods that should be made available to the poor.

The above rough estimate of resources allocated to the poor or
the basis of need does, however, help to lend perspective to the recentl
much-heralded commitment for a war on poverty embodied in the Eco
nomic Opportunity Act of 1964. Assuming that all the funds appropri-

ted under this legislation actually reach the poor—a questionable as-
umption—the Economic Opportunity Act increased the anti-poverty
unds by about 5 percent during its first year of activity; this amount
vas doubled during the second year.

It would be misleading, however, to measure the war on poverty
olely in terms of direct expenditures. Minimum wage legislation, to
vhich no price tag can be attached, may be a more significant tool in
he war on poverty than the expenditures of billions under other programs, but its negative effect in causing disemployment cannot be measured. Some programs that may bring the greatest returns in the war on
poverty may require little or practically no financial resources. Chief
among these programs is an educational campaign to reduce, and pos-
ibly obliterate, discrimination practiced against minorities, particularly
Negroes. The Voting Rights Act of 1965 may turn out to be a more
mportant tool to secure equal rights for Negroes and thus to combat
discrimination and poverty than other legislation involving huge expenditures . . .

Yet the significant gaps in our understanding of the causes of
poverty and the best means for eradicating its roots are no valid reason
or inaction. We need not await returns from all the precincts to con-
inue a vigorous campaign to reduce poverty. Lacking comprehensive
knowledge for eliminating the roots of poverty, we can focus on specific
programs which would aid selected groups among the poor. This suggested emphasis upon helping specific groups is not intended to sup-
plant the generalized societal goal of eliminating all poverty. A free and
affluent society should aim at nothing less. But we should realize this
s an ultimate goal and only one of numerous and pressing demands
upon society's attentions and resources. For the time being, more modest
and specialized strategems should be selected with a view to achieving
he ultimate objective. Grand designs for the good society have been
avoided, not only because there is little evidence that society is ready
to allocate adequate resources to a speedy reduction of poverty and
because of the many pressing and competing goals faced by society,
but also because the road leading to the millenium of a poorless society
is not fully charted.

Even assuming that consensus can be reached on the amount
of additional resources that need to be allocated for the war on poverty, it is not at all clear how these resources should be distributed.
What share of any additional dollar should be allocated to raising the
cash income of the poor as compared with improving the quality and
quantity of services in kind that are offered to them? The poor are
not a homogeneous mass. Additional income will provide for the basic
needs of some; many others require services that will enable them to

enter the mainstream of our society. Until these special services an income in kind are adequate, it is premature to hope to achieve a r tional guaranteed level of acceptable minimum income—whether th is to be achieved through negative income tax or other simil schemes. . . .

A realistic program aimed at reducing poverty should therefo establish priorities and determine appropriate resources to be allocate Leaving aside rhetoric about the elimination of poverty, it is assum here that if society continues to increase resources allocated for alleviati poverty, say, at the cumulative rate of about 6 to 7 percent per year about half again as much as the anticipated growth of GNP—this wou increase the anti-poverty kitty by about $4 billion per year by the er of this decade. Given this modest, though far from negligible, short-ter goal, the immediate question is which existing or new programs shou claim priority for the additional resources.

Looking to the future, the most promising means of reducir poverty is to help the poor control the size of their families. This ca be achieved at negligible cost to the public. Primary emphasis shou be placed on helping the impoverished to plan parenthood and thr reduce the number of unwanted children. Measured in terms of add tional expenditures, the largest amount of expanded assistance wou go in aid of poor children, and to help create jobs for their parents.

It makes little sense to wage war on poverty without providin an adequate diet and other basic needs for millions of children wh are being reared with an insufficient income. To repeat the social wor er's slogan—"services do not fill an empty stomach." Most observe would, however, agree that it would be preferable to provide incom to impoverished families through the creation of jobs rather than throug providing cash assistance. This would suggest the desirability of creatin publicly subsidized jobs for parents of poor children, even though th creation of such employment may involve greater direct public outlay than mere cash assistance. Finally, in the area of providing goods t the poor, housing should claim top priority, not only because attainmer of adequate shelter is outside the reach of most poor families, but be cause outlays for subsidized housing would also help absorb genera economic slack.

Planned Parenthood

The first priority in the war on poverty should be given to dis semination of education about methods of birth control, and consisten with the religious beliefs of recipients, assistance should be made avail able to those who cannot afford private medical aid to plan parent hood. . . .

Broad support exists for dissemination of birth-control informa-
on. In reply to a recent Gallup Poll question: "Do you favor or oppose
e distribution of birth-control information" no less than 80 percent
Protestants, 60 percent of Catholics, and 84 percent of other religious
oups answered in the affirmative. . . .

One of the most tragic aspects of poverty is that many of the
ildren born to poor families are unwanted. The National Academy of
iences concluded that the poor have more children than affluent fam-
es because the poor "do not have the information or the resources to
an their families effectively according to their own desires." The same
udy found that 17 percent of white couples and 31 percent of non-
hite couples had unwanted children in 1960. But among couples with
e least education, and thus likely to be also poor, the comparative
ercentages were 32 percent for white couples and 43 percent for non-
hite couples. Medical science has developed effective birth-control
ethods that are within the means of poor families. Given the wide-
read desire on the part of poor parents to regulate the size of their
milies, birth control could be used as an effective tool to reduce
ature poverty . . .

With minor exceptions, federal agencies have thus far avoided
e funding of birth-control programs. Even the Office of Economic
pportunity has largely shunned this controversial area. Only about 1
ercent of the first 1,000 OEO-backed community action programs car-
ed specific budgets for birth-control programs. . . .

Potentially more effective support of birth-control programs
ame from President Johnson when he stated on June 25, 1965: "Let
s act on the fact that less than $5 invested in population control is
orth $100 invested in economic growth." The President did not specify
e basis on which he made his estimates, but ample evidence exists
 indicate the savings that accrue to the public as a result of family-
lanning services. For example, a birth-control program initiated in
1ecklenburg County, North Carolina, in 1960 was estimated to have
ived $250,000 in AFDC benefits within three years. Expenses involved
1 operating the program amounted to one-twentieth of the savings.
1any other examples could be cited. The arithmetic is simple. Even
onsidering the low cost of AFDC support, averaging just about a dollar
 day, the few dollars expended per case on birth-control saves the
overnment the support of an AFDC child for years to come, not to
1ention that it also reduces poverty.

Aiding Impoverished Children

If the current battle cry, "break the chains of poverty," is not to
ecome a hollow slogan, society must allocate additional resources to

prevent the rearing of children in abject poverty and deprivation. Tl child from an impoverished home is likely to become a school dropou an unemployable person, and a perpetual relief recipient when he gro into adulthood. Therefore, the next priority for any increased allocatic of funds should go to helping poor children.

Though in need of radical overhauling, the AFDC program pr vides a suitable vehicle for this purpose. The nearly one million far ilies, with about 3 million children, who are currently recipients AFDC are among the neediest and most impoverished families in tl United States; therefore, they deserve the most immediate attention. Tl average income paid by the government to AFDC recipients is abo $1.00 a day. Since the minimum cost of food for a balanced diet is ˀ cents per person per day and accounts for only a third of the bas needs, it is quite apparent that AFDC children exist on an inadequa diet, even if total food costs of young children are somewhat lower tha the 70 cent average.

Before AFDC can be adopted as the main instrument for decent relief system and as a tool for rehabilitation, the program w. have to be overhauled. Not only will the level of allowances paid recipients have to be increased, but the method of distribution will al: have to be changed. The Veterans Administration pension system . should be adopted as a model, since the VA experience has shown th. the government can offer assistance to needy persons without subjectir them to harrassment or degradation. And, unlike the AFDC prograr the VA does not discourage initiative of recipients. . . .

An effective AFDC program which does more than pay lip ser ice to the rehabilitation of clients must also raise payments made recipients. Even assuming that $600 per individual is the minimum i come needed—and for a family of four this is 23 percent below th Social Security poverty threshold level of income—it would be necessar to increase current benefits paid to AFDC recipients by about two-thirc in order to reach this income level. This suggested figure takes accoun of free food distribution available to many AFDC recipients. Such boost in the level of payments would also increase the number of eligibl recipients. The few states which meet or approach the level of benefi suggested above would not have to raise their AFDC outlays.

To meet the proposed standards, AFDC expenditures woul have to be raised by about a billion dollars. And expansion of coverag would possibly double the cost, though an effective birth-control prc gram would tend to reduce the number of children in impoverishe households and decrease future costs. The 1965 Social Security amenc ments raise the maximum amount of federal contributions to AFD(recipients by only $15 a year, and state action to match these benefi required before the increased federal grants can be paid to recipients. The miniscule increase in payments made possible by the 1965 federal action indicates the resistance that exists in Congress and elsewhere to higher AFDC payments. State and local resistance may be even more difficult to overcome. The federal share of contributions to AFDC will therefore have to be increased appreciably if an effective program is to materialize.

It makes little sense to spend $6,000 a year, and possibly more, to rehabilitate a Job Corps trainee while at the same time depriving children in impoverished homes of basic needs and thus assuring a supply of future Job Corps candidates. This is not to disparage the potential accomplishments of the Job Corps or other programs initiated under the Economic Opportunity Act, but it does suggest the serious gaps that now exist in the anti-poverty program.

Job Creation and Work Relief

Creation of jobs for which the poorly educated and unskilled would qualify is the third on our list of priorities. After almost complete neglect of work relief programs during the past two decades, the Economic Opportunity Act provided for job creation under its work-experience and youth employment programs. The continued high level of unemployment among the unskilled, particularly among Negroes, indicates the need for generating government-supported jobs for those who cannot qualify for gainful employment in private industry. This does not mean that the government should create make-work jobs.

Despite the gloomy forebodings of the prophets of cybernation, much of society's needed work is not being done; and the need for this work is going to increase rather than disappear. Many of these jobs can be performed by relatively unskilled and unemployed workers. And the work can be found in rural areas and urban centers. Stream clearance, reforestation, and park maintenance are some of the simple traditional work relief jobs. Many new ones can be added, for example: school aides, health aides, simple maintenance jobs in public buildings, and renovation of slum areas. Medicare, when it becomes effective, will not only expand the demand for services of physicians and technicians, but will also require the addition of many unskilled workers in hospitals and nursing homes.

The need for creating jobs for unskilled workers may become more pressing in the years ahead. Proposed congressional action boosting wages, if it materializes in 1966, is likely to cause additional disemployment of unskilled workers. If no new jobs are created for these worker relief will be the only method of providing income maintenance.

A major barrier to the creation of new public jobs for the un employed is the determination of appropriate wage rates. Unions nor mally oppose the allocation of work, even when unskilled jobs ar involved, at rates which undermine existing prevailing standards. Cre ation of these jobs is bound to be costly. A million dollars will bu no more than about 300 jobs, including some part-time jobs, payin modest wages and including cost of overhead and equipment. A pro gram which will create 300,000 jobs, not an overambitious goal, is thu going to cost about one billion dollars annually.

Housing

Housing for impoverished families is given high priority becaus it is evident that adequate shelter cannot be provided by private enter prise at a profit, considering the rent that they can pay. It thus meet the generally accepted maxim of Lincoln that "the legitimate objec of government is to do for the people what needs to be done, bu which they cannot, by individual effort, do at all, or do so well, fo themselves." The alternative to government subsidization of housing fo the poor is slums and dilapidated housing which, in turn, breed pov erty. Adequate housing is therefore a major instrument in "breakin; the chains of poverty."

A continuing vigorous program of public subsidized housin; would also act as an overall economic stimulant which would hel; decrease unemployment and expand job opportunities. Such a progran is therefore a multipurpose tool in fighting poverty.

The great shortage of adequate housing available to the poo: cannot be surmounted in the short-run. It would require, even unde; the most conservative estimates, an investment in excess of $30 billio; to eliminate substandard housing. The principle of housing subsidie: has already been accepted, as witnessed by congressional action i; 1965. The question now is how rapidly the program is to be imple mented. A constraining factor should be the extent to which under utilized resources, both human and physical, are available for the purpose of building housing. This is not to suggest that construction of housing for the poor is inherently of low priority compared with the supply of other consumer goods. Most consumer goods are produced in the free market and are not subject to government regulation. A vigorous imple mentation of public housing during a period of shortages would inten sify inflationary pressures, particularly in the field of housing construc tion where boosts in wage costs have tended to exceed increases in

roductivity. Since construction of subsidized housing is subject to gov-
nment control, the degree of priority assigned to this program is
iminished if it is to be undertaken at the risk of intensifying infla-
onary pressures.

Under the conditions that prevailed in the country between
958 and 1964, expansion of housing for the poor could have been
igorous and rapid. With developing labor shortages and increased
ommitments to expand defense activities, subsidized housing expan-
on must be more moderate and selective. However, the level of un-
mployment and the amount of unutilized plant resources still remain
igh in many areas where additional construction activity could absorb
ome of the existing economic slack.

Since the supply of adequate housing for the poor will remain
ecessarily far short of need, priority in allocating the limited supply
ould be given to the working poor. This judgment is not based
ecessarily on the assumption that the working poor are more deserving.
: is advanced because pragmatic considerations favor the working poor
or the allocation of subsidized housing. Public housing has been criti-
ized on the basis that it subsidizes the indolent, but this argument
ould be minimized if the bulk of subsidized housing were allocated
o the working poor. Even opponents of the welfare state find it difficult
o argue against helping the "deserving" poor. . . .

Leon H. Keyserling
Government Spending for Unmet Needs

. . . What are the insistent and unmet needs of the American na-
ion and its people?

What changes in national policies are required if these needs
re to be filled?

. . . Excessive unemployment is at the very heart of our economic
nd social problems. Although full-time unemployment was about 5.3
er cent of the civilian labor force (or close to twice as high as it should

From "Toward Bolder Action," *The Progressive* (December, 1964), pp.
3–16. Copyright © 1964 by The Progressive, Inc. Reprinted by permission of the
ublisher.

Leon H. Keyserling was chairman of President Truman's Council of Eco-
omic Advisers and is now president of the Conference on Economic Progress.

be) during the first half of 1964, the true level of unemployment (taking into account the full-time equivalent of part-time employment and the concealed unemployment resulting from potential workers not attempting to enter the labor force because of the scarcity of jobs) was 8.5 per cent.

Moreover, these monthly estimates of unemployment, when broken down, show that unemployment is about twice as high among nonwhites as among whites, and between three and four times as high among teen-agers as among adults; and that the number of people suffering serious unemployment within the course of a year is three to four times as high as the number unemployed when a particular survey is made. Beyond all this, persistently high unemployment, since it is an index of persistently poor overall economic performance, also affects the incomes and rate of advance of those employed. During the period from the beginning of 1953 through the middle of 1964, total private consumption was about 364 billion dollars lower (measured in 1963 dollars) and average family income for the period as a whole was about $8,500 lower, than if maximum employment and production had been sustained.

When all of these factors are taken into account, fully *forty per cent* of all the poor people in the United States are in consumer units (families or unattached individuals) whose heads suffer substantial unemployment during the course of the year. And the 550 billion dollars of additional national production which we would have enjoyed during the 1953–1964 period if maximum employment and production had been maintained would in itself have generated at least $135 billion of additional tax collections at all levels of government. Even a small portion of these additional revenues would have made immense contribution to the public aspects of a war against poverty.

Among the more than thirty-four million American poor today (those in families with total incomes less than $3,000 and unattached individuals with incomes less than $1,500), there are, of course, many who would not be employed no matter how well the economy performed. This is true of most of the more than thirteen million people aged sixty-five and older, for reasons of age alone. Because of the miserable inadequacies of old-age insurance benefits and many private pensions, nearly half of all families whose heads are aged sixty-five and older, and almost two-thirds of the unattached individuals aged sixty-five and older, live in poverty.

It is also true that the large numbers of people disqualified from employment by ill health or disability could not hold jobs even if the jobs were there. The irony here is that both the incidence of disease and its inadequate treatment are much more highly concentrated among the poor than in higher income groups because of the inability of the

)or to pay for adequate medical care. As for free, or low cost public
:alth services in the United States, they lag far behind those in most
ghly industrialized nations.

It is also true that many of the poor are in consumer units
:aded by women who because they are widows too old to work, moth-
s of young children, or for other reasons, are not eligible for employ-
ent.

But it does not follow at all that a nationwide program designed
) sustain maximum employment and production would not take care
f these many millions of the poor who are effectively outside the func-
oning economic system. For we can generate enough demand to main-
in maximum employment and production throughout the entire econ-
my only by elevating the purchasing power of these people enough
) enable them to play a substantial role in the effective demand for
oods and services. The essential lesson behind our burgeoning produc-
ve powers is that the American economy cannot perform at optimum
:vels until we cultivate the greatest underdeveloped market in the
/orld for our own products—the more than thirty-four million of our
wn poor, and the more than thirty-two million additional Americans
/ho live in deprivation—above the poverty level, but below the require-
ients for a minimum American standard of living.

The close relationship between the unemployment problem and
ie poverty problem is further revealed by re-examining the notion that
he poor are poor primarily because of their personal characteristics.
t is true that poverty is highly concentrated among Negroes and among
amilies headed by women, and even more among those who have had
ight years or fewer of education. Efforts to extirpate discrimination
ased upon color or sex are eminently desirable, and we do need vast
xpansion of educational and training efforts up and down the line.
3ut these achievements in themselves would change the *distribution* of
overty far more than they would change the *amount* of poverty, so
ong as the total number of jobs remained far too low, and the total
utput of the economy far too deficient, and so long as we avoided pro-
;rams designed to redistribute incomes. Similarly, although the poverty
n the depressed areas and in agriculture (which is in reality a chron-
cally depressed industry) do require programs aimed at relieving im-
nediate stress, these programs can be effective in the long run only in
he framework of an integrated nationwide effort to treat the larger
:conomic and social problems on a broad scale.

The challenge of the new technology and automation further
inderscores the fact that the economic problem of high unemployment
ind low economic growth, and the social problem of poverty, are inseparable. No matter how much we increase private consumer incomes

and expenditures, which indeed is essential to achieve a reduction
poverty, these increases in themselves cannot make a major contributi
toward the creation of the twenty-two to twenty-seven million add
tional jobs needed in the decade ahead. Output per man-hour in man
facturing and office work and in most of our conventional industri
as well as in agriculture, is advancing more rapidly than is any reaso
able expectation of the growth of demand for products.

Thus, the greatest opportunities for job expansion are in tho
fields where the unmet needs of the nation are so vast that servicir
these needs will demand manpower far in excess of the technologic
labor-saving gains in these particular fields. These vital underdevelope
areas of the life of the nation—housing, urban renewal, health, educatio
resource development—calling for an unusually high ratio of public
private outlays, are crucial to the war against poverty. Expansion
output in these fields would provide huge numbers of unskilled an
semi-skilled jobs which are insufficiently available in the convention
industries. Such an expansion in these areas would be an infinitely mo
practical approach to the uniquely high rate of unemployment an
poverty among young people and Negroes than assuming that thes
individuals can be so trained and educated that they will compete f
highly-skilled jobs. There would not be nearly enough of these skille
jobs to go around, in any case.

It is significant to note, in surveying this field, the historic lin
of division between Republican and Democratic economic philosophie
We have long associated the Republican economic philosophy wit
"watering the economic tree at the top"—the philosophy that help t
corporations for investment in producers' facilities, and to those person
high in the income structure who save much more for investment pu
poses than they consume in products and services, will be most bene
ficial to the economy at large. And we have come to associate th
Democratic economic philosophy with "watering the economic tree a
its roots"—the concept that direct help to consumers in the lower ha
of the income structure will be most beneficial to the economy at larg

Never was it clearer than during the past dozen years that th
chronically rising tide of idle manpower and plant, and the chronicall
low rate of economic growth, have resulted from emphasis upon th
first rather than the second of these two economic philosophies. No
can this proposition be refuted by the substantial length of the curren
economic recovery. In an important sense, this recovery has been s
long and is still going on, simply because we have not fully recovered
Idle manpower and plant are now extraordinarily higher than in 1953
even though a recession began near the middle of that year. Allowin
for the three business cycles through which we have passed since 1953

and for the fact that we are now near a cyclical peak, the chronic rise in unused resources has not been substantially interrupted. It is not surprising that most responsible analysts now expect a slowdown in an economic growth rate which has been too low even during the two most recent years, and that within a year or so unemployment will rise again, unless substantial corrective measures are undertaken.

Whatever the reasons may be, the basic economic policies followed by the Democratic Administration which took office in 1961 were, more than would have been expected, a continuation rather than a reversal of those policies pursued by the Eisenhower Administration—granted a large improvement in some welfare programs. Most important of these are the tax and monetary policies which have tended to redistribute income in the wrong direction, freeing more funds for expanding plant facilities already overbuilt in relation to the total demand for products.

Other illustrations of regressive policies are the tight rein upon Federal expenditures as a *quid pro quo* for the Kennedy-Johnson tax cuts; the inadequate expansion of social security, welfare, and minimum wage programs; the persistent attempt to repress the rate of wage rate gains, even though their lag behind advances in productivity has been the most important quantitative element in the consumption deficiency; and the failure to recognize that an immense program of housing construction and urban renewal projects—including about half a million new dwellings a year between now and 1975 to rehouse slum dwellers—could furnish perhaps half of the additional jobs needed during the next decade. Such a building program would make great inroads on poverty because the slums in which one-fifth of our people still live are both the roots and the offshoots of poverty. The rationalization that the basic continuation of the old conservative economic philosophy is something new or "pragmatic," and that the liberal approach is no longer relevant nor workable, simply will not stand scrutiny.

My specific proposals for needed changes in national policies are all based upon an *American Economic Performance Budget,* which I have developed over the years. This Performance Budget projects consistent and integrated estimations of quantitative aspects of our needs and resources, and portrays the related flows of incomes and outlays, both private and public, which would promote maximum employment and production. This budget takes full account of our traditional concepts of the appropriate divisions between private and public responsibilities, and of the high stress which should continue to be placed upon initiative in the private sector.

In line with this Performance Budget, any further tax reduction should be designed directly to help the poor and deprived. This could be accomplished by reducing or removing sales taxes on necessities, and by doubling the standard exemptions or credits in the personal income tax structure. Far more emphasis should be placed upon increased public outlays than upon further income tax reduction. The combination of these two approaches, relieving the tax burden on the poor and increasing public outlays, would, more than further income tax reductions, improve income distribution, reduce unemployment and poverty, be more responsive to the great priorities of our domestic needs, and contribute far more to the acceleration of economic growth.

In this connection, per capita and absolute Federal outlays to help meet the neglected priorities of our domestic public needs should be sizably increased immediately and enlarged enormously over the years. Per capita Federal outlays for housing and community development should rise from a negative figure of $1.56 in the original fiscal 1965 budget (when the government is expected to "make money" on these programs) to more than $15.50 by calendar 1970, and to about $16.50 by calendar 1975. In the aggregate, these Federal outlays should rise from a negative of $317 million to $3.3 billion, and then to $3.8 billion a year.

Federal outlays for education should increase on a per capita basis from $8.35 in the fiscal 1965 budget to more than $33 by calendar 1970, and to about $39 by calendar 1975. In the aggregate, they should be lifted from $1.7 billion yearly to $7 billion, and then to $9 billion.

Per capita Federal outlays for health and research should be lifted from $8.55 to close to $23, and then to more than $30. In the aggregate, they should be lifted from $1.7 billion to $4.8 billion a year, and then to $7 billion.

Per capita Federal outlays in the broad category of labor and manpower programs and other welfare services should be increased from $6.07 to about $9.50 by 1970, and increased slightly further by 1975. In the aggregate, they should be increased from $1.2 billion to $2 billion, and then to about $2.2 billion.

Per capita Federal outlays for public assistance should rise from $14.15 to more than $21, and then to more than $23. In the aggregate, the increase should be from $2.9 billion to $4.5 billion, and then to $5.4 billion.

Per capita Federal outlays for resource development should be lifted from $12.77 to about $15, and then to more than $15.50. In the aggregate, they should be lifted from $2.6 billion to $3.2 billion, and then to $3.6 billion.

These efforts, taken together, would within a decade, translate our potential abundance into actuality; neither quantitative nor qualitative shortages would exist in any of these vital areas. Allowing liberally also for defense, space exploration and international economic programs, the total Federal budget should be lifted from less than $98 billion dollars to $135 billion dollars, and then to $156 billion, over the same period of time. With optimum economic growth, these increases would result in a *smaller* Federal budget when measured as a percentage of total national production, and thus the non-Federal sector of the economy would become relatively larger. Similarly, the national debt would shrink to a much smaller percentage of total national production.

The Federal Reserve policy of tight money and rising interest rates, which represses economic growth, induces unemployment, and redistributes income along inequitable lines, should be replaced by a more rapid expansion of the money supply and much lower interest rates. This will require Congressional or Presidential intervention.

Within five years or so, the average benefits under the old-age insurance system, and in the form of public assistance to those not covered by this system, should be approximately doubled to close some of the gap between benefits and rises in living costs. This would require, in part, raising the amount of income subject to payroll taxes. However, the increases in Social Security payments should also be accomplished, in part, through Federal contributions financed by general income taxation, as the payroll taxes tend to be too regressive. Obviously, larger Federal contributions will be required for greater public assistance to those outside the Social Security system.

The minimum wage floor should be lifted to $2 an hour, and its coverage made broader by many millions of workers.

The whole farm program needs drastic revision, with the goal of income parity substituted for the concept of price parity, with help to low income rather than high income farmers, and with much more emphasis upon expanded consumption among the millions of Americans with inadequate diets, and among the hungry peoples of the underdeveloped nations.

The Economic Reports of the President, under the Employment Act of 1946, should be made the central vehicle for developing an integrated and consistent national economic policy, with quantitative goals for the reduction of poverty as a core feature. We have the productive potentials to reduce the number of persons living in poverty in the United States from more than thirty-four million now, to fewer than five million by 1970, and to fewer than three million by 1975.

Hyman P. Minsky
Tight Full Employment: Let's Heat Up the Economy

The single most important step toward ending poverty in America will be taken when tight full employment is achieved and sustained. Tight full employment exists when over a broad cross section of occupations, industries, and locations employers prefer to hire more workers, at the going wages and salaries, than they in fact do. In the specific context of the war against poverty tight full employment means two things: (1) employment opportunities for those now unemployed or underemployed (2) labor market conditions which tend to raise low wages relative to high wages.

Other anti-poverty measures, such as community facilities, enrichment of education, job training and relocation may be important as supplements; but unless tight full employment exists the anti-poverty campaign can only result in spreading poverty more equitably through the community. Without a realization that employment opportunities are vital to the success of the effort, the anti-poverty campaign can be characterized as a move to achieve fair shares of poverty for all. Tight full employment certainly is necessary, and it may also be sufficient, for the elimination of all except casebook poverty in the United States.

There are two kinds of poverty in the United States. One is due to unemployment and low incomes even though employed. The second, casebook poverty (which consists of those poor not now and not expected to be in the labor force), is due to the inadequacy of programs of transfer payments and income in kind. Indications are that unemployment and low incomes from jobs account for some 60 per cent of the families living in poverty. The unemployed and low income from employment poor will benefit directly from tight full employment. The elimination of casebook poverty requires a much more generous set of welfare laws than we now have. However, tight full employment will indirectly benefit these poor, for the employed and employable members of their family will be doing better, and the higher G.N.P. that will accompany tight full employment will make it easier for state and local governments to undertake adequate programs of transfer payment. Thus our primary concern here is with the largest part, but not all, of the poverty in the United States.

From a lecture presented in the spring of 1965 before a faculty seminar on poverty at the University of California, Los Angeles.

Hyman P. Minsky is Professor of Economics at Washington University in St. Louis.

Tight full employment will not only eliminate that poverty which is solely due to unemployment, but, by setting off market processes which tend to raise low wages faster than high wages, it will, in time, greatly diminish the poverty due to low incomes from jobs. In addition, by drawing additional workers into the labor force, tight full employment will increase the number of families with more than one worker. As a result, families now in or close to a "poverty line" will move well away from it. There may be a "critical minimum effort" that is needed to move families from poverty and deprivation to a state in which income, opportunities and horizons are ever improving. This critical effort may require that income move well above the poverty border. Multiple earners in one family is the way of achieving family incomes well above the poverty line.

The unemployment rate during 1964, 5.2 per cent, was the lowest annual rate achieved in the United States since 1957. The liberal and expansionary Kennedy and Johnson administrations have set as their interim target a 4 per cent unemployment rate. This target rate is a "slack" definition of full employment, which reflects an excessive fear of inflation. On the basis of our wartime experience and the experience of Western European countries (Sweden and Germany are worth noting) a working definition of tight full employment, allowing for voluntary labor mobility, technical dynamism, and seasonal factors, might be set at 2.5 per cent measured unemployment.

Given wages and prices, the volume of employment, and thus the unemployment rate, reflects what the economists call aggregate demand. If the war against poverty is a serious effort rather than a quite cruel example of political sloganeering, monetary and fiscal measures to make aggregate demand large enough, to achieve a target 2.5 per cent unemployment rate should be undertaken immediately. Current monetary and fiscal policy, which is being framed in the light of the Administration's evident satisfaction with the performance of the economy in 1964, is programmed for a $660 billion G.N.P. At this G.N.P., because of expected productivity and labor force increases, the unemployment rate is expected to remain pretty much where it was in 1964—that is, in the neighborhood of 5.2 per cent.

What level of aggregate demand would be needed in 1965 in order to achieve tight full employment? A rule of thumb is that for every 1 percentage point decline in the measured unemployment rate, there is roughly a 3 per cent increase in measured G.N.P. If we apply this rule to the difference between the expected 5.2 per cent unemployment rate and the tight full employment target unemployment rate of 2.5 per cent, we get a $53 billion gap between forecast and tight full employment G.N.P. Even if we modify this rule of thumb so that, when the unemployment rate gets below 4 per cent, the efficiency of a decline in employment decreases, the estimated tight full employment G.N.P. remains in the neighborhood of $700 billion.

It seems evident from the G.N.P. gap that expansionary mone tary and fiscal steps should be taken to raise this year's aggregate de mand to approximately $700 billions. This should lower unemploymen toward the reasonable 2.5 per cent target as well as increase the wel being of those already employed. Are there any barriers to such a use of monetary and fiscal policy, and if there are can we design a set o policy actions that will either get around or get over these barriers?

After the success that has been imputed to the 1964 tax cut, i can be assumed that the administration, if it were bold, could ge another $15 billion tax cut in 1965—which should expand demand to close to $700 billion. It is not an ideological opposition to fiscally manag ing the economy that prevents this. Rather it is a view that expanding aggregate demand would have other, undesirable effects that lead to the programming of a $660 billion G.N.P.

We do not live in a Pollyanna world where all good and desir able ends are attainable at no cost. In the hard interdependent world of economics, more of one very desirable objective almost always mean: less of another, almost equally desirable, objective. The addition of the elimination of poverty to the set of policy goals means a redefinition and a reconsideration of the importance placed upon such older, more conventional goals as full employment, economic growth, price stability and the international stability of the dollar.

Domestic price stability and the international stability of the dollar are two of the standard list of policy objectives which require modification, if not repudiation, in the light of the required higher priority for and tighter definition of full employment. However, these two barriers to tight full employment are quite different in nature. The domestic inflation barrier reflects a presumed structural relationship of the economy. The international monetary stability barrier reflects a policy commitment that can be abandoned whenever it is desired.

The half-hearted efforts toward achieving full employment under both Kennedy and Johnson (the 1964 tax cut *really* was more of a device to abort a feared recession) in part reflects a belief that there exists a stable inverse relationship between the unemployment rate and the rate of increase of wages and prices. The "interim" target unemploy ment rate of 4 per cent was set in the belief that at unemploymen rates higher than 4 per cent there is no real tendency for wages to rise, and that at rates lower than 4 per cent any stimulus to the economy will largely be absorbed by increasing the wages and incomes of the already employed rather than by adding job opportunities for those who are then unemployed.

We are now in a "policy box" that has been created by the repeated emphasis upon the inflationary potential of unemployment rates below 4 per cent. If labor and business both believe that the threat of inflation increases when unemployment rates decline, and that the threat becomes acute when a 4 per cent rate is approached, then, in a competitive push to protect their own interests, each decision unit will press for higher wages or prices as the unemployment rate decreases. That is, the forecast that inflation will be an imminent threat when the unemployment rate decreases toward 4 per cent is in the nature of a self-fulfilling prophecy: it helps set the framework so that which is forecast does in fact occur.

The existence of a stable relationship between unemployment rates and wage and price changes, that underlies the fear of tight full employment, is not a certainty. For one thing, all that has ever been observed has been a movement from slack to tight labor markets, and back again to slack. A long period—ten to fifteen years—of sustained tight labor markets has never been observed. The institutional arrangements designed to protect workers against some of the effects of labor market slack will no doubt be modified once labor market tightness is accepted as the normal state. Similarly, pricing policies designed to protect business against the effects of recessions can also be expected to wither away as the belief in the continued existence of prosperity spreads.

The movement to a tight labor market entails some inflationary pressures which are, from the point of view of the war against poverty, highly desirable. The heads of some 30 per cent of the families living in poverty are employed full time. Obviously the main path by which they can move out of poverty is by increased income from their job—which requires either changing jobs or higher wages. The evidence indicates that during periods of tight labor markets, low wages tend to rise more rapidly than high wages and that during periods of labor market slack high wages gain on low wages. Tight full employment will change relative wages in the right direction. However, given the existence of decentralized collective bargaining, the best we can expect is for wages to rise with productivity and prices to remain constant in the high wage industries. Therefore, in the low wage industries wages will rise more rapidly than productivity, and this will be accompanied by higher prices. A wage-price inflationary pressure which raises the relative wages of the present poor is hopefully inherent in our markets under tight full employment. Anyone committed to a successful war on poverty is also committed to the view that not all inflations are bad.

If labor market tightening does not change relative wages in favor of the low wage earners, then monetary and fiscal policy will have to be supplemented by an "income policy" designed to guide relative wages and prices in a direction consistent with policy objectives.

Increases in demand may not absorb the unemployed. Labor is not all alike; the labor force is heterogeneous and viscose. If increases in aggregate demand result in increases in the demand for highly trained labor, then all that will happen, in the first instance, is a bidding up of the wages and salaries of these classes of workers. As production techniques do not allow for the substitution of a 20 year old high school dropout for an electrical engineer in a research and development project, changes in relative wages *may not* increase the demand for the present poor. Thus any effective program of increasing aggregate demand to eliminate poverty must be designed so that it has an immediate impact upon the present poor. Potentially, the heterogeneity of the labor force is a real barrier to the generation of the right kind of tight labor markets.

The argument that a rise in aggregate demand will not increase employment, but that it will only increase wages and prices, is susceptible to experimental testing. All that is needed is to ease up on monetary conditions and cut taxes and see what happens. Although this is not the most efficient way to raise aggregate demand in order to eliminate poverty, appropriately designed spending programs are better, it is both quick and accepted. If too rapid an inflation results, the expansionary pressures can be eased. The only cost of such an experiment, if it fails, is a once and for all rise in the price level.

The need to protect the international stability of the dollar is the effective and operative barrier to monetary and fiscal expansion. First of all, the active use of monetary ease is ruled out by the need to keep both foreign and domestic "short term" balances in the New York money market. This banker role of the United States means that interest rates in New York must be high enough so that a "covered" move abroad of short term funds is not profitable. Therefore United States interest rates must be kept in contact with those in the more buoyant European economies. Secondly, the need to constrain the deficit in the balance of payments rules out too rapid a rise in United States G.N.P. A $700 billion rather than a $660 billion G.N.P. would mean from $1.5 to $2.0 billion more in imports. In addition, the move from slack to tight labor markets should result in a rise in the price of products made with low wage labor. Such a price increase will tend to increase imports and decrease exports. That is, a move to tight labor markets will increase the balance of payments deficit. A large deficit in the current situation can trigger a flight from the dollar.

To a considerable extent, ever since 1958, the needs of the dollar standard have acted as constraints upon expanding domestic income. Tight labor markets are not attainable because of the pecular bind that the dollar is in internationally. It is apparently quite appropriate

o allude to William Jennings Bryan and assert that, in part, the cross
hat the American poor bear is made of gold.

The elimination of the barrier to expanding aggregate demand,
lue to the international monetary system is simple: get rid of the gold
tandard. If for some subtle reasons, understood only to bankers, the
State Department and the Treasury, we cannot do this, then we can
uy economic breathing room by raising the price of gold. Of course
aising the price of gold subsidizes two vicious regimes—that of the So-
iet Union and South Africa—but at least it will enable us to get on with
he task of achieving a tight full employment economy and ending
poverty in America.

In our past—the first New Deal—we have the instruments to
ight poverty. W.P.A. and its associated N.Y.A. and C.C.C. took workers
s they were and generated jobs for them. The resurrection of W.P.A.
ind its allied projects should be a major weapon in the war on poverty.

W.P.A. was a labor intensive approach to unemployment and it
ailor-made its projects to fit the capabilities of the available labor.
W.P.A. must be contrasted with the standard public works programs,
avored by Trade Unions and their allied contractors as a solution to
inemployment problems. Programs of expanding standard public works
ire inefficient in the war against poverty, for it means providing jobs
or already affluent workers.

Work should be made available for all able and willing to work
it the national minimum wage. This is a wage support law, analogous
o the price supports for agricultural products, and it replaces the mini-
num wage law. Once work is available to all at the minimum wage, the
problems of "covered" and "uncovered" occupations are eliminated.

To qualify for employment at these terms, all that would be
required would be to register at the local U.S.E.S. Part time and seasonal work should be available at these terms: this will be a special
boon to low income farmers and farm workers.

National government agencies, as well as local and state agencies
would be eligible to obtain this labor. They would bid for labor by
submitting their projects, and a local "evaluation" board would deter-
nine priorities among projects.

This scheme generates "artificially" tight labor markets. It should
under present circumstances cost some $10 to $12.5 billion—and expand
G.N.P. by some $20 to $35 billion above the $660 forecast.

Once the tight labor markets have been created by having labor
demand accommodate to labor supply, standard monetary and fiscal
expansionary measures will generate excess demand for some particular
ypes of labor. This will signal where retraining and relocation efforts
ire needed.

Initially the wage support level should be fixed at the present minimum wage—which yields an income below the poverty line as now defined. Since tight labor markets imply that low wages rise relativ to high wages, as time goes by the wage support law should be raise from its present approximately 40 per cent to approximately 60 per cen of the median wage.

Such a rise in low wages relative to high wages will tend t force up the prices of the products that the low wage workers produce It becomes a matter of economic policy whether or not we want th price of these products increased. For example, hospital orderlies an attendants are low wage workers. It is desirable that their income should rise relative to those of high wage workers; but it does not follov that it is desirable that hospital prices be raised along with hospital costs Programs of wage supplement for particular classes of workers coul be part of the arsenal of weapons in a campaign against poverty tha uses tight labor markets as the principal weapon in the war.

To conclude, the way to end the biggest chunk of poverty is t generate jobs at adequate income for the people now living in poverty Although improvements in welfare and educational programs woul help, many of these programs bear their fruit only after a long delay and the fundamental problem is how to end poverty for the presen poor. The basic approach is straight forward—accept the poor as the are and tailor make jobs to fit their capabilities. After this is done programs to improve the capabilities of low income workers are in orde

National Academy of Sciences
Reduce the Flow of Unwanted Babies

It is now clear that the overwhelming majority of America couples approve and practice family planning. Until recently there wa little direct evidence to support this conclusion, but representative sam ple surveys—one in 1955 of white couples and one in 1960 of all couples— have provided statistical information on the prevalence of deliberat fertility control in the American population.

In 1960, about 95 per cent of couples surveyed favored the ide of family planning at least under some circumstances. Although Cath

From *The Growth of U. S. Population,* National Academy of Sciences-National Research Council, Publication 1279, 1965, pp. 9–13.

olic couples often specify that the rhythm method is the only acceptable means of birth control, about 90 per cent of them approved limiting family size and 80 per cent have either used or plan to use some sort of family planning.

In 1955, 91 per cent of white American couples who had experienced no difficulty in having children had used or expected to use contraception. In 1960, the number had grown to 96 per cent. The increase occurred among couples at all educational levels and of all major religions. No student of American fertility doubts that the proportion of couples using contraception has increased steadily for many years.

Encouraging as it is, the continuing increase in the practice of contraception should not obscure two significant facts: First, some 10 to 12 per cent of American couples in the childbearing years do *not* try to limit births to the number of children actually desired; and second, nearly 20 per cent of all couples with unimpaired fertility try to limit family size, but fail because of insufficient motivation or ineffectiveness of the method of contraception used. Moreover, the burden of excess fertility falls in overwhelming disproportion on the underprivileged, especially the uneducated.

In the United States, as in other countries, poverty, ignorance, and a high birth rate are closely related. In the whole population of the United States, the proportion of couples who have not used and do not expect to use contraception is presently about 14 per cent. Among white couples in which the wife had no more than a grade school education, the proportion is 28 per cent. Among non-white couples the proportion is 43 per cent. The highest proportion of couples who never employ contraception or who have children beyond the number they intend is found among non-whites who live in the rural South or who have a rural southern background. On the other hand, the 63 per cent of the non-whites in the United States who have backgrounds other than rural southern have a fertility little different from that of the white population.

The available evidence indicates that low-income families do not want more children than do families with higher incomes, but they have more because they do not have the information or the resources to plan their families effectively according to their own desires. About 17 per cent of white couples interviewed in 1960 reported that, before the last conception occurred, either the wife or the husband or both had not really wanted another child at any time in the future. Among the nonwhite couples, 31 per cent had unwanted children. Among couples in which the wife's education was grade school or less, unwanted children were born to 32 per cent of white couples and to 43 per cent of nonwhite couples. Further, in 1960 the last pregnancy was reported as unwanted by 25 per cent of the women married more than 10 years and by 45 per cent of those with more than three children.

Even when they try to limit family size, the underprivileged often do not succeed. Women interviewed in a national survey in 1960 reported that 11 per cent of all their pregnancies began when they were using contraceptives to postpone or avoid pregnancy. This is more than 20 per cent of all the pregnancies that occurred after the first attempts to practice family limitation.

In a surprisingly large number of couples, either the husband or the wife has had an operation to prevent further conceptions. In 1960, such operations were reported by 10 per cent of all couples in the childbearing years and by 19 per cent of those in which the wife was 35–39 years old. These operations were reported to be contraceptive in purpose by about 60 per cent of all the wives. It is likely that many of these couples might have preferred a less final family-planning solution if a contraceptive method that was completely effective, inexpensive, safe, and relatively easy to use had been available.

Failure to practice family planning effectively may lead couples to resort to illegal induced abortions. We have no reliable data on the number of illegal induced abortions in the United States, but estimates range from several hundred thousand a year to more than a million a year. It is also believed that a large proportion of such abortions involve married women who do not want additional children. Failure to use effective family-planning methods is probably one of the important reasons for resorting to illegal induced abortions despite the health and moral problems that such clandestine abortions involve.

Low-income families have more children than do others, although the difference is perhaps not as great as some people believe. For example, among married women 40–44 years old in 1960, the average number of children ever born was 3.4 in families with incomes of less than $2,000 and 3.0 in families with incomes between $2,000 and $4,000, as against the average of 2.6 for all the women in this age group. The average number of children born in the two low-income groups differed by less than 1.0 from the average for the higher-income families.

If all the families with incomes of less than $4,000 had borne on the average the same number of children as those with higher incomes, the total number of children born to all women 40–44 years old would have been reduced by 4 per cent and the average number of children born per woman would have been reduced from 2.6 to 2.5.

Even though the larger numbers of children in low-income families have relatively little effect on the average family size, on the total number of children born, or on the United States birth rate, it has a profound effect on the underprivileged family itself. It is further true that the higher birth rates in the low-income groups produced over 550,000 "extra" children by the time the wives were 40–44 years old. We know from other surveys that many low-income couples did not want to have these additional children simply because the additional children undoubtedly made it more difficult to provide a decent standard of living for the whole family. The problems imposed on families by excess fertility are not diminished by the realization that such excess fertility does not greatly affect the over-all fertility average.

In addition to the significant minority of couples having more children than they want, a much larger number have their children more quickly than they think desirable. In a study of more than 1,100 Detroit mothers having babies in 1961 (but no more than four children altogether), 45 per cent reported having at least one of their babies sooner than they preferred. For many mothers, the failure to space their children properly creates health problems and makes it difficult to give adequate care to each child.

Consider the implications of circumstances in which every couple would conceive only children they deliberately chose to have. For the majority of American couples with at least a high school education and enjoying a comfortable income, the result would be that the births they had would be spaced more in accordance with their desires. Couples would successfully terminate their family formation with the two, three, or four children that the vast majority prefer. Such a development in the less-educated sector of our population, which contributes disproportionately to excess fertility, would greatly diminish one of the conditions that perpetuates poverty in the midst of plenty in the United States.

In the opinion of many psychologists, deformation of character and personality in children, culminating, for example, in juvenile delinquency, often results from a feeling of having been rejected by their parents. Parental attitudes and behavior that produce this feeling of rejection are much more likely when children are born as a result of unintended pregnancies.

The likelihood of a successful education is known to be less for children born to parents who themselves are uneducated. The chance for a good education for children in such underprivileged homes is made even worse by excess fertility, which reduces the care and attention each child can receive.

It is evident from this discussion that basic principles concerning family planning can and should be presented early. High school and elementary school courses in general science and biology can emphasize the interrelations between population growth and resources. In addition, biology courses and courses on marriage and family can emphasize that reliable methods of birth control are available and desirable. They can emphasize that bearing too many children represents irresponsible parenthood. Such courses can also help students by identifying the health and social agencies that will gladly supply them with specific birth-control advice consonant with their religious principles.

A recent survey by the U.S. Bureau of the Census indicates that 16 per cent of first children born to white mothers are born within eight months of marriage, and 22 per cent within nine months of marriage. Another study indicates that the rate of premarital conception is highest among women who marry at a very early age. Since the husbands of these premaritally pregnant brides are also usually young, it is evident that many children conceived by teen-age brides are unwanted and will not receive good parental care. Other government statistics show that the mothers of approximately 41 per cent of the 245,000 babies born illegitimately in the United States every year are women 19 years of age or younger. Thus a large proportion of all illegitimate children are progeny of teen-age mothers. To reduce the number of such children born to teen-age mothers, high school education in family planning is essential.